Empowering Women in Russia

NEW ANTHROPOLOGIES OF EUROPE
Daphne Berdahl, Matti Bunzl, and Michael Herzfeld, editors

JULIE HEMMENT

Empowering Women in Russia

Activism, Aid, and NGOs

INDIANA UNIVERSITY PRESS
Bloomington and Indianapolis

This book is a publication of

Indiana University Press
601 North Morton Street
Bloomington, IN 47404-3797 USA

http://iupress.indiana.edu

Telephone orders 800-842-6796
Fax orders 812-855-7931
Orders by e-mail iuporder@indiana.edu

Library of Congress Cataloging-in-Publication Data

Hemment, Julie.
  Empowering women in Russia : activism, aid, and NGOs / Julie Hemment.
    p. cm. — (New anthropologies of Europe)
  Includes bibliographical references and index.
  ISBN-13: 978-0-253-34839-5 (cloth : alk. paper)
  ISBN-13: 978-0-253-21891-9 (pbk. : alk. paper)
  1. Women's rights—Russia (Federation) 2. Women—Russia (Federation)—Social conditions. 3. Russia (Federation)—Social conditions—1991- I. Title.
  HQ1236.5R8 H46 2007
  305.420947′09049—dc22

                                                                                          2006023720

2 3 4 5 6 13 12 11 10 09 08

For Valentina and Oktiabrina

And he went back to the fox. "Good-bye," he said. "Good-bye," said the fox. "Here is my secret. It's quite simple: One sees clearly only with the heart. Anything essential is invisible to the eyes."

Saint-Exupéry, The Little Prince

Contents

Preface
Tver', Russia, 17 May 1998

Valentina, Oktiabrina, Lena, and Lydia,[1] four members of the women's group *Zhenskii Svet* (Women's Light) sat in my rented apartment, armed with flip charts and marker pens. At my request, the women had formed pairs and sat on the small sofa beds at opposite ends of the tiny one-room apartment, debating eagerly. We had gathered together that day in order to undertake a process of group reflection. Our discussion was structured around three broad questions designed to assist the group in clarifying its goals and aims: where did we come from? (the group's history); where do we want to go? (the ideal); how to get there? (the action plan).

As the women spoke, interrupting each other in excitement, I struggled to jot down all that they said, anxious not to miss anything. The four made interesting pairs: Valentina, founder of the group and feminist historian, worked with Oktiabrina, a doctor committed to issues of women's health. She was a newcomer of whom we all had high hopes. She had only recently moved to the city from distant Siberia, propelled by a series of devastating economic losses that were all too typical of these post-Soviet times. She was now urgently seeking a niche for herself and looking for ways to solidify her activity. I watched as Oktiabrina listened intently to Valentina's detailed account of the group's history, frowning occasionally in consternation at some of the incidents she recalled. Lena, an English language teacher with an irrepressible sense of humor and sharp tongue, worked with Lydia, a sociologist and researcher, who had recently been laid off and was seeking ways to set up her own women's group. The two sat talking animatedly, and carefully making a list of the points they raised.

I had called the meeting now, with Valentina's blessing, because the group was at a crossroad. Until this point, their strong concern with independence had led them to avoid entering into collaborations with either the local administration or international donor agencies. But times were hard in the Russian provinces; these teachers, engineers, and doctors who were secure during the Soviet period now struggled to make ends meet as wages were withheld and prices skyrocketed. Some of the Zhenskii Svet women wanted to formalize their activities and locate sources of financial support; they were beginning to make tentative moves toward formal collaboration with external agents, and they had competing ideas of how to go about this. At a time of tumultuous social and political

---

1. With their permission, I used the actual names of Zhenskii Svet participants. To do otherwise would contradict the goals and motivations of our collaborative research process. With the exception of some foundation representatives, all other names are pseudonyms.

change, the group was unraveling and the women had begun to rethink their activism.

I conceptualized the seminar as a place where members of the group could clarify their personal goals and investment in it. Indeed, I wanted to clarify my own role and commitment; ten months into my ethnographic research, I felt I had something concrete to offer: insight into international donor priorities and acquaintance with both donor agency representatives and other Russian provincial groups. I began the day by asking the four women why they had agreed to come and what they wanted to achieve through the process. Valentina answered, "Because it feels as if we are picking up a dialogue and a tradition that began in the group earlier. Feminism is all about the unity of research and activism. A group cannot exist if it doesn't evaluate itself and define its purposes." Lena nodded, saying, "I agree that this is a new stage we are entering and that we need to unite. We have no clear idea of what, concretely, we want and we need to define that." Lydia's response was rather more analytic: "In the last four years I've come into contact with a mass of different and interesting ideas, I am interested in Western experience, interested in your (Julie's) evaluation of what the situation looks like here, and to what extent a third sector[2] is realizable here." Oktiabrina answered thus: "I'm also interested in some of these ideas, in feminism, in discussion of the role of women in society, because I'm not happy with the way things are today. Why did I come here today? Because I'm the kind of person who needs to act, and in order to act, I need to better understand."

By the end of that day, we had an enriched perspective of the history of the group and had reached a broad consensus: the women agreed it was time to formalize the activities of Zhenskii Svet in some way and to found a women's center. This meant embarking on a new strategy vis-à-vis local and global power-brokers, a "strategy of involvement," which entailed entering into limited forms of partnership with them. The women hoped this would enable them to establish a real "concrete, socially oriented project," as Oktiabrina put it, that would both sustain existing projects and enable Zhenskii Svet women to devise new ones. Valentina insisted, "and it must keep its original name—Zhenskii Svet. You see, our idea is linked to the two meanings of the word *svet:* globe/world, and light—Zhenskii Svet is above all a project of enlightenment" (*prosvetitel'nyi proekt*).

The chapters that follow provide the context for this snapshot and explain how we came to be sitting in my apartment that day. As the story unfolds, we learn about the concerns and issues that brought us into dialogue, the relation-

---

2. The model of the third sector is an export item brought to Russia by the foundations and agencies that promote the work of nongovernmental associations in post-socialist states. The term refers to a realm of informal groups—associations, clubs, or NGOs (nongovernmental organizations). It derives its name from its role in a triad, where the first is the state, the second is the private sector of businesses and enterprises, and the third is the realm of citizens' initiatives. As I discuss in chapter 2, the third sector is also a project of persuasion, one that has sought to transform purportedly dependent and politically passive Soviets into active citizens, savvy consumers, claimers of rights, and defenders of their interests.

ships that developed, and the ties that held us there. This book is in equal parts a story about the complicated trajectories of feminist activism in Russia and an account of the challenges of anthropological practice. In telling the story of Zhenskii Svet, I map my own attempt to achieve what some have called an engaged or public anthropology by working with activist women in a collaborative research project. I dedicate this book, with gratitude, to the two women who enabled, but cannot be held responsible for it—Valentina Uspenskaia and Oktiabrina Cheremovskaia.

Acknowledgments

I would like to begin by expressing my deep gratitude and affection for two people without whom this project could never have taken place—Valentina Uspenskaia and Oktiabrina Cheremovskaia. Thanks too to Lena Gauveling, Lydia Zalesskaia, Anya Borodina, Natalia Mamchenkova, Lydia Gadzhieva, and other participants of Zhenskii Svet for their friendship and generous willingness to welcome me into their lives and participate in this project. Countless people in Russia deserve my gratitude for the support and assistance they extended to me during this research. In Tver', I thank Nina Drozhdetskaia, Galina Tsarkova, Svetlana Konovalova, Tamara Kariakina, the faculty and staff of the Department of Sociology and Political Science at Tver' State University, and the many participants of associations and clubs who generously found time to share insights on their work. I am grateful to the activists I spent time with in Moscow, Pskov, St. Petersburg, and at numerous conferences and workshops, particularly to Larisa Fedorova, Liza Bozhkova, Tatiana Klimenkova, Elena Kochkina, Elena Ershova, Elena Potapova, Marina Pisklakova, Sasha Kareva, Natalia Vasil'eva, and Elena Iablochkina. Thanks also to Gabbi Fitchett-Akimova, Kristen Hansen, Mary McAuley, and Dianne Post for sharing their perspectives on their work with Russian NGOs with me. Finally, I am grateful to my "old" Muscovite friends with whom I have shared so much: Alyosha Danilin, Lena Danilina, Katya Genieva, Slava Shishov, Malvina Elenbogen and Marat, Andrei Kremenchugsky, Gosha Khan, Kiril Gopius, and Natasha. Their friendship, warmth, and insights got me interested in the first place, have sustained me over the years, and kept me coming back. No less importantly, their networks provided the infrastructure that made these frequent return trips possible (invitations, jobs, accommodation). For this, I am eternally grateful.

A number of institutions provided assistance through the different phases of this project. I am indebted to the Department of Anthropology at Cornell, the Cornell Graduate School, the Einaudi Center for International Studies, and the Cornell University Peace Studies Program, whose generous support made it possible for me to undertake research between 1997 and 1998 and to return to Russia at regular intervals. A predoctoral fellowship from the Mellon-Sawyer Democratic Detours seminar at Cornell provided me with a stimulating intellectual environment and financial support at a crucial stage of writing. At the University of Massachusetts, grants from the Provost's Office on Service Learning and the College of Social and Behavioral Sciences and the support of the European Field Studies Program in the Department of Anthropology enabled me to make return trips in 2004 and 2005; a fellowship from the Lilly Center for Teaching in 2003 granted me the most precious gift of all—release time to focus on writing.

I have benefited from generous feedback on this work from a number of friends and colleagues over the years. At Cornell, I was blessed with wonderful advisors; I'd like to express my gratitude to Davydd Greenwood, John Borneman, and Shelley Feldman, who provided guidance, direction, and critical insights from the beginning. I also thank Val Bunce, Aida Hozic, Matt Evangelista, Hector Schamis, Sidney Tarrow, and the members of my writers' group, especially Sara Friedman, Thamora Fishel, Susan Hangen, Smita Lahiri, Eric White, and Neriko Musha-Doerr. Other friends and colleagues from whom I have benefited greatly are David Ost, Cameron Ross, Peggy Watson, Hilary Pilkington, Nancy Ries, Bruce Grant, Nanette Funk, Julie De Sherbinin, James Richter, Janine Wedel, Joshua Roth, Beth Notar, Michelle Bigenho, and Barbara Yngvesson. Their support variously got me started, kept me on the right track, and encouraged me to keep going. A special and very warm thanks is due to Michele Rivkin-Fish, who has been a close and careful reader and a true friend throughout this project. At the University of Massachusetts, I have been blessed with wonderful colleagues who have been unwaveringly supportive through the latter phases of writing and through the grueling process of getting this work into print—thanks particularly to Ralph Faulkingham, Jackie Urla, Oriol Pi-Sunyer, Enoch Page, David Samuels, Betsy Krause, Art Keene, Krista Harper, Lynnette Leidy Sievert, Elizabeth Chilton, Michael Sugerman, Julie Graham, Arlene Avakian, and Mary Deane Sorcinelli. The graduate students of my Spring 2006 seminar on feminist anthropology are due special thanks for their thoughtful engagement with this work as it went to press: Larissa Hopkins, Deborah Keisch, Milena Marchesi, Graciela Monteagudo, and Julie Skogsbergh. I'm especially grateful to my reviewers, Hilary Pilkington, Ann Snitow, and Elena Gapova, whose critical insights enabled me to substantially improve the manuscript. I'd like to express my gratitude to Janet Rabinowitch at Indiana University Press and series editors Michael Herzfeld, Daphne Berdahl, and Matti Bunzl for their support. I'd also like to extend a special thanks to my editors, Rebecca Tolen and Miki Bird, and to my copyeditor, Candace McNulty, whose support and careful attention helped me bring this book to completion.

Finally, I would like to acknowledge the love and support of a number of friends and family through this long trajectory, particularly Drew Hemment, Pamela Hemment, Peter Hemment, Sondra Hausner, Cynthia Bond, Lisa Echevarria, Seth Johnson, Emma Krasinska, and Kate Thompson. Frank Hein had the dubious honor of being closest by during the various phases of this project. His love, support, and unfailing sweetness kept me fed, kept me sane, and kept me going; for this I will always be deeply grateful. Finally, my thanks go to our daughter Cleo, who appeared at a sensitive moment in this book's trajectory. She brought delight—and not a little sleep deprivation—to the writing process, and has reminded me of the power of a good story!

All of the photographs that appear in the book are my own, unless otherwise indicated. Portions of this book have appeared in print elsewhere; I am grateful to the publishers of these articles for granting permission for me to include these materials here. Parts of chapter 2 appeared in "The Riddle of the Third Sector: Civil Society, Western Aid and NGOs in Russia," *Anthropological Quarterly* 77 (2): 215–241. Parts of chapter 4 appeared in "Global Civil Society and the Local Costs of Belonging: Defining 'Violence Against Women' in Russia," *Signs: Journal of Women in Culture and Society* 29 (3): 815–840.

I have followed the Library of Congress system for transliteration of Russia words, except for given names in the text. In the hope of making for a smoother read for those who are not Russian specialists, I have chosen to use spellings that are common in U.S. usage and to dispense with punctuation indicating soft signs. All translations from the Russian are mine, unless otherwise indicated.

Empowering Women in Russia

Introduction: Gendered Interventions

"People sit on their grants and live—it's not a women's movement, it's the creation of jobs! If only they [the Americans] guessed what happened to their money." Looking at me, she added with a wink, "Don't tell them! They only support us because they think that where there are feminists, there are no Communists!"

Svetlana, women's activist and journalist

In late May 1998, I traveled to St. Petersburg to attend a conference with two of my women activist friends—Valentina, history professor and founder of the women's group *Zhenskii Svet* (Women's Light), and Natalia, one of the newer members of the group, an engineer in her early fifties who'd recently been laid off. As we sat on the bunks of the crowded overnight train, we discussed the possible scenarios. We were beginning our collaborative project to set up a crisis center in the provincial city Tver', and we hoped that we could make useful connections with other provincial groups.

The event was organized and funded by the American Association of University Women with the goal of forming a new women's information network. Women from all over the far-flung Russian Federation had been flown in to attend. However, despite the upbeat address delivered by the American convener, Elizabeth A. (a professor of women's studies), attempts at unity faltered. As was clear from their comments at the podium and from the discussion that erupted in the hall, the delegates were impatient both with the Americans who had brought them there and with each other. There was an atmosphere of confusion—while some were long-term activists, others had only recently set up women's groups and were new to the field of women's organizing. These administrators, state officials, and nongovernmental activists had little in common and were clearly at cross-purposes. And seven years after state socialism's "collapse," the mere presence of a foreigner did not excite; the message of women's unity that had once galvanized now seemed stale and out of sync with local realities.

All three of us were disappointed; I found solace by reverting to the role of ethnographer (a comfort denied my activist friends) and busied myself by jotting down some of the more pithy expressions of dissent. Of all the comments I captured that day, the comment by Svetlana stood out most starkly: the women's movement in Russia, she implied cynically, was a vehicle for creating jobs for elite women, not a grassroots movement committed to gender equity and universal sisterhood.

Since the demise of the Soviet Union, women's activism in Russia has undergone a number of phases. The first independent groups appeared in Russia in the late 1980s. They were part of a groundswell of civic initiatives and associational activity permitted by perestroika reforms, which became known as the societal movement (*obshchestvennoe dvizhenie*). As with other informal associations (*neformaly*), these first groups were mostly intelligentsia-led, loose groupings of colleagues and friends, discussion groups that organized around broad, transformational goals (Fish 1995). Inspired by the new, permissive climate of perestroika,[1] these were explicitly "political" in their orientation, insofar as they stood in opposition to the state socialist regime.[2] As state socialism unraveled and Russia opened to the rest of the world, Russian women activists were able to connect with foreign activists and groups for the first time. In the early 1990s there was a proliferation of horizontal exchanges and collaborations around women's issues between individual activists and groups in Western Europe and the U.S. In the mid-1990s, the pace and profile of these exchanges changed and intensified as they became institutionalized through the work of U.S.- and European-based foundations and agencies that were newly active in post-socialist states. Agencies such as the Ford Foundation and the Open Society Institute began to channel resources to women's groups as part of their broader commitment to assisting democratization and the transition to a market economy. This was due in part to international recognition of the transition's profoundly gendered effects: in the first democratic elections, women's political representation plummeted; early research suggested that women were economically marginalized by marketization. Indeed, indicators such as these urgently beckoned globally minded activists like Elizabeth A. But it had to do with broader shifts, too. What I call the "gendered interventions" of international foundations in Russia were enabled by shifts in global development agendas and the emergence of a new global apparatus for women's activism at the Cold War's end. Here, a concern with "gender"—meaning concern with inequities between men and women—was "mainstreamed" into agency activities. In Russia, foundations' goals were to contribute to the project of forging citizen activism by supporting women's participation in civic life. These organizations have supported diverse programs such as women's leadership training, the development of computing skills and electronic networking, business training, and health-related projects. These projects and campaigns have brought about significant changes in women's organizing, radically changing the look, purpose, and composition of women's groups.

As Svetlana's comment indicates, it has not all been smooth sailing. Russian women activists viewed these potential collaborations with a mix of intrigue and excitement; they were initially excited to make the acquaintance of foreigners and to enter into the "partnerships" that were promised; they were drawn by the promise of the "West" and what it symbolized to many Russian intellectuals at the time.[3] However, the reality of international collaboration has proven to be rather different than the promise.

Practitioners engaged in global interactions around gender (here I include activists and scholars as well as agency staff) are frequently convinced of the liberating effects of their work. In championing women's rights and women's issues in Russia, they see themselves as challenging the dominant narratives of transition. However, their interventions are nested within the complex logics they seek to resist. The mainstreaming of gender and its prioritization as a category of development was enabled by a certain set of conditions: the restructurings of the post–Cold War period and the global triumph of capitalism at the millennium (Comaroff and Comaroff 2001), processes influencing the entire range of interventions that donor agencies have undertaken into post-socialist states. Despite the best intentions of their practitioners, these gendered interventions were part of a messianic cultural project enacted in the aftermath of Communism's apparent demise. They were inextricably linked both to liberal triumphalism and to a neoliberal restructuring process. They were offered as part of a project to reeducate Russian citizens—to educate them out of collectivist framings and responses, away from focusing on the materialist bases of issues into embracing individualized solutions such as "self-help" and "voluntarism."

Within these projects, women's issues have been narrowly and selectively defined. For example, while there has been ample funding for projects that focus on computer networking, information technology, and self-help–oriented support groups, few grants support activists to combat the structural forms of dislocation women may be experiencing. To the consternation of many Russian women activists, this excludes things such as free day care and maternity leave rights, entitlements they came to take for granted under state socialism (Gapova 2004). The feminism that has achieved hegemony through gender mainstreaming is what Chandra Mohanty has called a "free-market feminism," a "neoliberal, consumerist (protocapitalist) feminism concerned with 'women's advancement' up the corporate and nation-state ladder" (Mohanty 2003:6). In Russia during the 1990s, "gender" became "a grant," as Oktiabrina, one of the Zhenskii Svet women, put it. And, like any grant cycle, it had to end. Since 2001, international funding for Russian women's projects has been drastically cut in response to shifting strategic priorities in the United States and Western Europe. In other words, Svetlana was right: foreign donors *did* support women's projects because they thought that where there was feminism there was no communism. I picked up a curious echo of her formulation in 2001, when Liza, a Moscow-based activist friend, told me about an encounter with an American agency representative in New York. In response to her pleas for extended funding, he replied, "You got your freedom, there are no more Communists, now get to work!"

This book traces the gendered interventions of international foundations in Russia from their inception in the early 1990s, through the boom years, until 2001 when support for women's projects waned. As Mary McAuley, director of the Moscow office of the Ford Foundation, put it, the 1990s were a "decade of experimentation" (2001); the immediate aftermath of the Soviet Union's collapse was a free-for-all. Russia was up for grabs, and the Russian state apparatus, unsure of its powers, permitted both Russian and foreign actors great latitude. Anthropologist Janine Wedel describes how, "as 'transition to democracy' came into vogue, carpetbaggers and consultants, foundations and freelancers rushed to explore, and sometimes to exploit, the new frontier" (Wedel 1998:4). In this environment, international interventions often were hastily designed, were at odds with local conditions, and had contradictory, unintended effects. A second task is to examine the implications of this situation for women activists and scholars alike. This book takes the paradox of gender mainstreaming as a starting point for exploring an alternative approach to gendered activism and international collaboration. Where does the critique of gender mainstreaming in neoliberal development leave local activists who are entangled in this troubling political economy? What are its implications for feminist activists like Elizabeth A., or people like me, a feminist anthropologist, seeking to achieve socially engaged research?

I undertook nineteen months of ethnographic fieldwork in Russia between 1995 and 2001. The majority of this time was spent in Tver', a provincial city of half a million located 170 kilometers outside Moscow, where the women's group Zhenskii Svet was based. I spent most of my time there immersed in the rhythms of daily life with group participants, many of whom became close friends. During the spring of 1998, I undertook a collaborative research project with members of the group wherein we strategized and theorized international aid. This collaboration enabled—and required—a different kind of intervention and involvement, one more intensely personal and less bureaucratic than those of large foundations. While it was also constrained, it was constrained in different ways, and remained based on an insistently local, non-institutional mission to create change. In tracing this collaboration, I argue for the necessity of linking critical anthropology with constructive political projects.

Perils and Pitfalls

These gendered interventions have had contradictory effects. On the one hand, international aid boosted the fortunes of women's activism. When Russian women activists first entered the international stage in the early 1990s, independent women's groups were few and far between. Since then, in large part due to global agency attention, they have proliferated. Russian women's groups work together as never before, "networking" and sharing information and a new language with each other. They take part in international events—such as UN-sponsored conferences and NGO forums—and are active in many of the main transnational feminist campaigns, such as the campaigns opposing violence against women and trafficking of women and girls. They have become savvy transnational operators, skillful publicists of their work in the national media, and a thorn in the side of the Russian government.

On the other hand, donor support has given rise to some uncomfortable ironies. Foundations funded women's groups to boost women's participation. However, despite their new international profile, the work of women's groups is little understood or appreciated at home; Russian women's groups do not have legitimacy among most Russian women. Most people are unaware of their activities, and many of those who are aware of them are suspicious of their goals. For complex historical reasons there is no commonly held perception of gender discrimination in Russia, and most people greet the notion of women organizing as women with suspicion. This is not because the issue is in some way new, or has never had political salience; on the contrary, the emancipation of women (*emansipatsii zhenshchin*) and the achievement of their freedom and equality (*ravenstvo*) was a prominent goal of Bolshevik-era social engineering (Aivazova 1998; Edmondson 1984; Khasbulatova 1994; Stites 1978). Women in the USSR received full civil rights and freedoms immediately after the October Revolution of 1917. However, in the seventy years of state socialism, some deeply unpopular policies were enacted in the name of this equality. Particularly unpopular were the legislative steps taken to ensure the "withering away" of the family—for example, the right to divorce, to abortion. These steps, introduced in the first family code of 1918, were unpopular among men and women of all classes, not only of the bourgeoisie.[4] As a result, by the 1980s there was a commonly held perception that socialism had emasculated men and *over-emancipated* women, and both men and women yearned for these policies to be reversed. Women's activism was discredited by its association with top-down, Party-mandated societal engagement.[5] Meanwhile, the term "gender," which was embraced in the 1990s as Russian women activists entered into dialogue with western feminism, is jarring to Russian ears. While it is a bona fide linguistic borrowing, the term stands out linguistically and conceptually because of the essentialist understandings so deeply embedded in Russian thinking.

The perestroika-era women's groups that were greeted with so much enthusiasm by European and American sponsors were not grassroots manifestations; they were anomalous in Russia, led by highly educated, progressive, socially oriented individuals. As I show in the chapters that follow, feminism and the concept of gender became useful to these women because it offered a rubric through which they could make sense of their lives at a time of great social dislocation and structural change. It was also a means of articulating a way forward; it offered a means to critique existing structures of power and social relations. Further, interest in feminism was expressive of a desire to reconnect with European thought and debates through literature and personal ties; to reestablish connections that the Bolshevik Revolution cut off and seventy years of state socialism constrained. Rather than a burgeoning social movement, feminism in Russia was a form of elite identification that expressed the yearnings and strivings of a certain class of people at a particular historical juncture. Collaboration with foundations has made these women's groups more rarified still. Like other internationally supported nongovernmental organizations, these groups are considered to be far from most people's concerns.

Russian women activists themselves are ambivalent about the ways international donor support has transformed their activities. Although women's groups work together as never before, this collaboration takes place on an increasingly uneven social field. A gulf has opened between those organizations that receive grants and those women's groups that remain out of the loop of international funding. While they prosper, some activists chafe at the new terms of engagement set by foreigners. Like NGO professionals everywhere, they find themselves preoccupied less with local issues than with pleasing donors and securing their own organizational sustainability (Regentova and Abubikirova 1995). Under these circumstances, women's groups are "like weathervanes," as one of my activist friends put it, spinning in the political winds of donor states.

Finally, as I have suggested, these projects to empower women are caught up in a complex and troubling political economy. Promoted under the auspices of the United States and Western European governmental project to assist Russia's transition to democracy and a market economy, they are hence part and parcel of the very economic restructuring processes that have undermined women's status in the post-socialist period. In Russia, the decade that has seen the promotion of women's rights has been a decade of intense economic dislocation. "Shock therapy," the economic policy that was endorsed and aggressively promoted by North American and Western European advisors and embraced by Russia's so-called "young reformers," called for radical restructuring.[6] State-run factories, enterprises, and bureaucracies were shut down and privatized, resulting in massive layoffs. During the decade touted as Russia's "transition to democracy," social indicators plummeted—rates of infection increased, male mortality rose dramatically, and a majority of the population found themselves to be impoverished. Early research indicated that women were especially hard hit by this economic restructuring. Guaranteed full employment and equality under state socialism, women as a group experienced democratization as demotion, a net loss rather than a gain (Gal and Kligman 2000; Posadskaya 1994; Watson 1993). They found it less easy to adapt to market conditions and have fared less well than men in the new private enterprises and businesses. Meanwhile, as the primary caregivers for children, the elderly, and the sick, women have been especially hard hit by cutbacks in state provisioning.

International women's empowerment projects are caught up in this logic. In Russia, women's rights and empowerment schemes were promoted at the same time that welfare systems were cut back. Indeed, feminist schemes have been promoted by the very same agencies that have overseen this dismantling. During the same period they were promoting civil society development and women's rights, international lending institutions such as the World Bank and foreign advisors put pressure on the new democratic government to follow policies of structural readjustment.[7] Further, international donor support encourages women's activists into a very different kind of work than that which they originally set out to undertake. Under the rubric of women's empowerment, women's NGOs are pushed into a gendered division of labor where they are made responsible for providing services formerly guaranteed by the socialist state. This presents a dilemma for Russian women activists and for those of us who work with them.

Where There Are Feminists There Are No Communists? Gender and Russia

To understand these gendered interventions, their reception and their complex, contradictory, and often unintended effects, it is necessary to examine them within a broader political geography, as Svetlana's ironic comment suggests. Her remark pushes us to think about two interrelated things: history and economics.

A brief foray into Russian and Soviet history reveals the ironies of the promotion of women's rights in Russia. Here I draw on recent Russian feminist scholarship, as well as the English-language historiography with which it is in dialogue.[8] In the late nineteenth century, Russian women were part of a global struggle for women's emancipation—the international movement for women's suffrage (Keck and Sikkink 1998:51–58). These *ravnopraviki* (equal rights activists), as they were called,[9] mostly educated bourgeois women, were in dialogue with first-wave feminists from the United States, England, and all over Europe. They attended the same conferences, read the same books, and studied together in schools in Zurich and Germany. The prerevolutionary Russian women's movement was smaller and less unified than many Western European ones, but still it was dynamic and diverse—suffragettes (*sufrazhistki*) sought political and legal equality; socialist women (*sotsialistiki*) fought for the idea of equal pay for women and women's membership in unions; radical feminists (*radikal'nye feministki*) fought for state support for maternity and for women's reproductive rights; Christian feminists (*khristiianskie feministki*) focused on charitable projects (Aivazova 1998:26).

Crucially for this story, women's organizing at this time was entangled and intertwined with socialist politics. Women were active in Marxist circles from the 1890s onward (Edmondson 1984:27). In fact, the main fault line running between these early feminist groups, and the main reason "the movement" was divided, resided in the question of the appropriateness of class struggle. While socialist-oriented women believed that women's emancipation could be guaranteed only by revolution, "bourgeois" feminists—as they were derided—placed emphasis on gaining political and economic rights. Interestingly, despite these dramatic differences in perspective, all of them perceived their struggle to be part of a general struggle for social "liberation"—liberation from Tsarist autocracy and against the patriarchal society that oppressed both men and women (Aivazova 1998:49).[10]

The "woman question" at the turn of the century became a political football. Political parties of all hues supported women's equality in order to bolster support for themselves. The Russian Social Democratic Labor Party, the nation's first Marxist political organization, included equal rights for women in its 1903 program, as did the conservative Constitutional Democrats, or Cadets (Uspenskaia 2000:144).

Ultimately, Russian women achieved suffrage and full political rights significantly earlier than their Western European and North American counterparts, as some contemporary Russian scholars take pains to emphasize. The attempt to bring about equality between men and women was one of the main planks of Bolshevik-era social engineering, and immediately after the 1917 revolution the Party implemented many of the measures that women activists had demanded. Through the 1920s, these rights were strengthened and expanded—women were guaranteed full employment, education, abortion rights, rights to a fault-free divorce (Goldman 1992). While these policies waxed and waned over the course of the next decades in response to the needs of the party-state, the principle held still: quota systems ensured women's political representation and access to professional qualifications and education. Crucially, the bourgeois division between public and private that relegated women to the domestic sphere was eradicated. However, this victory was vexed and the results were complex and contradictory. As Tatiana Klimenkova puts it, "Only after women had won these rights did the extent of their insufficiency become clear; in practice they had only received the possibility to act on a masculine field with masculine methods" (Klimenkova 1996:61).

The Soviet state appropriated the language of women's emancipation and equality for purposes of mobilizing women into full-time labor, while distancing itself from feminist causes. The "woman question," meanwhile, was pronounced resolved by Stalin in the early 1930s, and the Party's *zhenotdely* (women's departments), set up to ensure women's representation, were closed accordingly (Posadskaya 1994:8). There was no attempt to acknowledge or challenge the cultural bases for women's oppression. Gender equality was part and parcel of the project to create a gender-neutral *Homo sovieticus* (Soviet person). There was no real domestic relief; in this project, women's emancipation entailed the right to be "the same as" men, while no changes were expected in men's behavior. And as with social life in general during the Soviet period, elements of the old remained and interacted with the new; formal declarations of gender equality were undercut by "counter discourses" that asserted, even celebrated gender difference (Verdery 1996). As a result, a strong gender division of labor persisted throughout the Soviet period. Women were responsible for almost all domestic labor—childrearing, food preparation, care of the elderly and infirm. In the workplace women were clustered at lower levels of authority, and professions where they predominated, such as the medical profession and teaching, were "feminized"—downgraded in importance and poorly remunerated.

This history helps to explain Russian resistance to feminism and why the term "gender" is met with such confusion and hostility; it also helps to make sense of Svetlana's ironic attitude toward her American feminist colleagues. With the institutionalized, standardized approach of international feminists and their seeming unawareness of this history and of contemporary Russian conditions, the perceived irrelevance of feminism grew in many women's minds.

How did this history come to be forgotten? How did economics come to be so displaced? Fast forward to the tumultuous changes of 1989.

The Cold War Unravels: Democratization and NGOs

To explore this topic means returning to a watershed year—1989, the year the Berlin Wall fell, the year of "velvet revolutions" that swept the Eastern Bloc, taking pundits and scholars by surprise and captivating TV viewers all over the globe. Who can forget the media images of young men and women standing astride the wall that had divided Europe for decades, their exhilaration, and their champagne celebrations?

Scholars and commentators have analyzed 1989 in a number of ways. For some, the collapse of state socialism was celebrated as a triumph of liberal democracy—ordinary people rising up and throwing off the yoke of totalitarianism. Some even hailed it as the "end of history" (Fukuyama 1992)—the end of divisive ideology and the victory of capitalism.

To Russian activists in the provinces, 1989 meant a number of different things. Along with television viewers all over the world, Valentina and her friends celebrated the collapse of the Berlin Wall and the climate of democratic-oriented reform that accompanied it. It was a time of great optimism and unprecedented opportunity in Russia—to organize independently, to take part in the first democratic elections, to engage in debates about the path of reform and civic affairs. It was a time for travel, too—to forge connections and relationships across the former Iron Curtain and with scholars and activists in the formerly forbidden and, for some, much-idealized West (*zapad*).

The material dismantling of the wall was accompanied by a conceptual and symbolic dismantling—the unraveling of ideologies and certainties, reconfigurations of the conceptual map that had structured life in Europe, the United States, and much of the globe. The end of the Cold War marked the collapse of "a form of knowledge and a cognitive organization of the world" as well as the ostensible end to superpower rivalries (Verdery 1996:4). In the immediate aftermath of the collapse of Communism there was a great deal of idealism and optimism about the potential for global harmony that was broadly shared. Not only "cold warriors," but pundits, scholars, and activists of diverse ideological persuasion saw it as a time of opportunity. The United Nations envisaged an enhanced role for itself, and UN activity grew exponentially in the immediate post–Cold War period, inaugurating a new and productive global dialogue on progressive social issues. A new global apparatus for activism emerged amid the unraveling of the Cold War, sustained by UN conferences, new budgets for foundations and donor agencies. Between 1990 and 1998, the UN convened fourteen conferences on topics such as the environment, sustainable development, human rights, the status of women, and social development

(Riles 2001:187). Under the new mandate of "democratization," international agencies (like the UN) expanded into new regions, beyond the so-called developing or "third world," to the newly independent nations of the former "second world"—Eastern Europe and the former USSR. Despite the collapse of master narratives, this was a time for master solutions and the emergence of a new universalism, exemplified in the emerging sets of international standards and guidelines for national policies. In policy circles in the United States and Western Europe, one-size-fits-all concepts and strategies such as "civil society," "social capital," "human rights" were applied to a region that until recently had been off-limits. NGOs were the new agents of this project, proliferating in what some have described as a global "associational revolution" (Salamon and Anheier 1997).

This was accompanied by a serious reconfiguration, a paradigm shift. The end of the Cold War was succeeded by what feminist political philosopher Nancy Fraser calls the "post-socialist condition," a zeitgeist characterized by the absence or loss of a progressive vision of a just social order.[11] The collapse of the socialist alternative (the USSR and Eastern Bloc) left economic liberalism apparently victorious—the dual saviors of capitalism and democracy (now conflated) was a commonsense. This was the "global triumph of capitalism," its "Second Coming" (Comaroff and Comaroff 2001:291). The much-celebrated "New World Order" was an order dictated by the United States (unrivalled superpower) and characterized by the victory of capitalism. This new logic was manifest in the so-called Washington Consensus, the combined body of policies that guided international financial institutions in their dealings with Russia in the early post-socialist period, and in what came to be known as the "New Policy Agenda"—the new cluster of policy objectives that guided development interventions within and beyond the context of post-socialist states in the post–Cold War era.

Gender Mainstreaming and Civil Society

It was here that the gender projects I have described were situated. Building on their hard-won victories of the 1970s and 1980s when they had first brought a concern with women into development, women's movement activists skillfully used this new infrastructure to push their agenda both in policy circles and at the UN. Thanks to the efforts of some activists, the concept of "gender" was successfully integrated, or mainstreamed, into agency agendas (Buvinic 1996; World Bank 2000). In the immediate post–Cold War period, the notion of women's rights moved from its rather peripheral location on the map of donor agencies to center stage. Lending institutions like the World Bank were persuaded that improving women's status made good economic sense. Agencies began to promote feminist notions to address the global "gender gap": gender equity, women's rights, and the need for women's organizations. The status of women is now held to be an important indicator of development. International campaigns around women's rights gained momentum in the 1990s, culminating in the UN Fourth World Conference on Women in Beijing in 1995. This event marked the enlargement and democratization of participation in international campaigns; the parallel NGO forum permitted thousands of women to attend who were not government officials but the representatives of independent, grassroots associations. Indeed, Beijing marked the first entry of independent Russian women activists to the international stage (Sperling 2000). These combined forces created a new, international infrastructure for women's activism both within the Russian Federation and beyond.

In Russia and other post-socialist states, women's empowerment projects were promoted under the general auspices of the civil society promotion program. As I discuss in chapter 2, civil society emerged as a powerful concept in the context of post-socialist states. Classically defined as the sphere of public interaction between family and state, the concept of civil society reemerged in the 1980s, popularized by Central European intellectuals as a means of expressing opposition. It was used as a rallying cry, a banner under which the people of Eastern Europe and the USSR united to express resistance to socialist states (Garton-Ash 1990; Ost 1990). In the aftermath of the velvet revolutions, civil society offered an explanatory framework to make sense of the changes taking place in the region. It put a name to the forces that overturned totalitarianism. Civil society conjured up images of brave dissidents, popular movements, an apparently natural unfurling against the "unnatural" encroachments of the state. In the 1990s, the concept of civil society gained traction when it became a development project (Sampson 1996). The United States and Western European governments placed immense resources behind projects to support civil society development; they saw the promotion of civil society to be an effective means of promoting economic development and "good governance" (Richter 2004:2). Civil society became a cornerstone of democratization and the transition to a market economy, the projects that promised to bring economic development and prosperity to post-socialist states.

There has been a lot of water under the bridge since then. Talk of global harmony has given rise to darker discussions about globalization and the mechanisms of empire (Hardt and Negri 2000). In the light of the ever-widening gap that separates first world nations from the rest, the master solutions that were once so widely embraced (civil society, social capital, human rights) ring hollow. In Russia, market-oriented economic reform and privatization have resulted in extreme economic polarization; a vast gulf now separates the super-rich from the poor. Many commentators now view this new infrastructure for international activism as fatally compromised, inextricable from the neoliberal agenda that has achieved hegemony in the post–Cold War era. Some dismiss the civil society concept as a primarily rhetorical device for democracy's missionary work (Comaroff and Comaroff 2001; Hardt and Negri 2000; Mandel 2002), a device that simultaneously rationalizes structural adjustment policies and facilitates the cutting back of state social provisioning (Alvarez, Dagnino, and Escobar 1998; Foley and Edwards 1996). NGOs, which were planted as seeds for democracy within and beyond the region, have also failed to live up to expectations. In many cases they are vehicles for elite advancement rather than grassroots empowerment; some regard their new prominence as a sign of the cooptation and quiescence of social movements.

These same contradictions are apparent in projects carried out in the name of women's rights. As I show in the chapters to follow, transnational feminist campaigns against gendered violence, which became very prominent in the 1990s, have had troubling and contradictory effects. They have worked to deflect attention from other issues of social justice, notably the material forces that oppress women. International campaigns against the trafficking of women and girls (which became very prominent in development circles in the late '90s), although articulated in the name of women, express the security concerns of fortress Europe—criminalizing women without helping them, and eliding the fact that their exploitation is an immigration and labor issue (Berman 2003).[12] Clearly, in this environment, gender mainstreaming marks less the triumph of radical social movements than their demobilization and cooptation (Alvarez, Dagnino, and Escobar 1998b; Lang 1997; Paley 2001). It is crucial to emphasize that these projects have affected both women's movements in the West and those internationally active. As Ann Snitow, cofounder of one of the first feminist networks active in Eastern Europe and the former USSR, the Network of East-West Women (NEWW), puts it, U.S. feminisms became "unmoored" from the deeper structures that gave rise to them in the post–Cold War era. In this context, concepts like gender, participation, and civil society have been successful precisely because they are emptied of their radical content (Snitow 1999:35–42). The feminist conception of gender has been hitched to new, unsavory projects, displacing class and contributing to the "post-socialist condition" where it becomes increasingly difficult to speak of structural violence or economic issues (Farmer 2003; Fraser 1997; Gapova 2004).

The critique of gender mainstreaming and feminism's new prominence is of crucial importance, especially in the post-9/11 era when women's rights and gender are invoked by the U.S. and British governments to legitimize the bombing of "rogue" states, as when Laura Bush spoke of defending Afghan women's rights as a way to shore up support for the Bush administration's military campaign.

I find these critiques important and necessary. However, there are a number of dangers in ending the story here. First, these critiques potentially reinforce problematic conservative arguments, made not only in recipient but also in donor states—namely, that feminism is just a foreign import and has no relevance for women's lives. In Russia, this erases the many individuals who have gone against the tide to insist that women's rights matter, as well as the rich history of prerevolutionary Russian women's activism that contemporary Russian scholars now explore. Second, these critiques unintentionally shore up anti-Western xenophobic positions such as those laid out by President Vladimir Putin in recent years, in statements that cast suspicion toward NGOs that receive foreign funding. Finally, critiques such as these can obscure the potential for agency within the campaigns and obscure the dynamism and negotiation that takes place at all levels, but particularly at the level of the local. My purpose in this book is to offer a thick description of how one group of women's activists struggled within this compromised context to realize important changes for feminist goals, and to examine the complexities, contradictions, and constrained victories we were able to achieve.

What Is to Be Done? Moving beyond the Critique

The ironies of these times—what Comaroff and Comaroff have called "the Millennial Age" (2001)—have provided rich material for anthropologists. In their study of the dislocations of post-socialism, anthropologists have done what they do best; they have problematized and questioned, insisted on making uncomfortable juxtapositions, and held up a mirror to processes "at home." They have problematized some of the key concepts that undergirded the interventions of the 1990s—civil society, social capital, market economy, citizen's empowerment, women's rights—by showing where they come from (by examining the cultural baggage they carry with them), and by examining their embeddedness in complex relations of power and global forces (Gal and Kligman 2000; Hann and Dunn 1996). But where does this leave us? What are the implications for our practice? With an increasing number of scholars who seek ways to forge a more socially engaged anthropology in these times (De Soto 2000; Farmer 2003; Hyatt and Lyon Callo 2003; Lamphere 2004; Rivkin-Fish 2005; Sanday 2003), I argue for the necessity of linking critical anthropology with constructive political projects.[13] This terrain presents a dilemma to those who work in it—both Russian women activists, and people like me, who study them. The dilemma I suggest is particularly acute for those of us who work on topic of NGOs, where the boundaries between theoretical and applied are already fuzzy and where we may find ourselves drawn into "applied" forms of work.[14]

Thus, another task of this book is to trace my own involvement in these projects, to explore my own gendered intervention, if you will. It tells of my attempt to move beyond the critique of international aid, by attempting to forge a more democratic, dialogic research process.

As I undertook ethnographic research among women's groups, attending American- and European-led seminars and foundation-sponsored conferences, I became aware that even women at the forefront of projects for social renewal expressed frustration and disappointment at the way projects were conceived and implemented. In the aftermath of communism's collapse, Russia was conceptualized by many as a blank slate (Bridger, Kay, and Pinnick 1996). American or Western European advisors and experts frequently had very little base or background in Russia and were reluctant to consult their Soviet peers (Bruno 1997; Rivkin-Fish 2004; Sampson 1996; Wedel 1998). Despite the language of partnership adopted by donor agencies, and despite the best intentions of agency staff, their gendered interventions have proven to be largely unidirectional. International foundations and agencies are guided by agendas set in Geneva or New York, often pushing issues that have little local salience. Projects that focused on gender were often blind to local knowledge and disregarded other issues, issues that the majority of Russian women activists considered most pressing: unemployment, alcoholism, the chronic shortage of housing, military service. Indeed, caught up in their own constructions, some agency representatives I came across seemed to reject these materially based concerns as a form of false consciousness. In my research on feminist campaigns against violence against women, I found that many North American or Western European feminists dismissed discussions of economic factors as a rationalization for male-perpetrated violence. The standard response was the assertion that economics is not the true issue, for "rich men also beat their wives." While of course this is an accurate and important fact, in the post-Soviet context, it appears extraordinarily disconnected from local concerns and shows little awareness of the extent of economic dislocation in Russia and its devastating effects on the lives of women and their families. As an ethnographer, I took this disconnect seriously as valuable data. As a feminist committed to achieving a more socially responsive, engaged anthropology, I determined to do better. At the same time as I wanted to investigate this topic, I did not want to reproduce these patterns through my own research. What alternatives were there? What insights could anthropology bring to this context, and what methods could I locate to facilitate a more dialogic engagement?

Tver' and Zhenskii Svet

My approach to forging an alternative kind of gendered intervention involved using and adapting participatory action research (PAR) in my work with the provincial feminist group Zhenskii Svet. PAR is a social change methodology that has its roots in popular struggles in the global South to make research a more egalitarian and collaborative effort. Variously described as a method, a style, or a philosophy (Fals-Borda and Rahman 1991:16), participatory action research emerged as a direct challenge both to the logic of conventional social science and top-down development initiatives (Freire 1970). In casting research as a collaborative endeavor between outsider researcher and members of a community group, it seemed ideally suited to the ideologically laden social field of post-socialist Russia. As Dudwick and De Soto remind us, this is a "radically unequal power context, in which the Western ethnographer becomes the symbolic bearer of Western authority and Cold War victory" (Dudwick and De Soto 2000:6). Participatory methodologies offered a means of achieving the collaborative research that so many scholars have written about (Lamphere 2004; Mertz 2002)—an approach that is particularly appropriate in the context of unstable or unraveling states (Mertz 2002:369). Although I was wary of the way participatory approaches and methodologies had been appropriated by groups I did not sympathize with and skeptical of evangelical accounts that posit PAR as the answer, I saw promise in this approach.[15] PAR offered a way to conceptualize my role, as well as a way to achieve a more dialogic, democratic research encounter.

Zhenskii Svet is a small, university-based women's group, dedicated to women's education and consciousness-raising. It was founded in the provincial city of Tver' in 1991, long before the arrival of Western foundations, in the first wave of independent organizing in Russia. I first made contact with the group in 1995 when undertaking preliminary research, and I was drawn by its interesting profile. As Valentina, its founder, explained to me, it was both explicitly feminist and explicitly informal. Both facts made it unusual, even anomalous. Like most provincial groups, Zhenskii Svet existed on the periphery of grants and funding. Unlike most other groups, however, it retained a commitment to its informal, diffuse status. The group was not registered with the local authorities and it had no bank account, no office space, no telephone, yet it was very active and had accomplished a great deal. In addition to its feminist educational work, the group had run a number of socially oriented projects for women over the years—free health consultations, free computing courses for unemployed women. Valentina was well connected within Russian feminist circles and knew many of the main players; she had refused to enter the more formalized interactions that characterized the 1990s women's movement because she was concerned by the changes she saw occurring, processes that contributed to what she called the "profanation" of feminism (reducing "gender" to a "grant," in Oktiabrina's terms). However, by 1997, when I returned, the group was at a crossroads. Times were hard in the Russian provinces; these teachers, engineers, and doctors who were secure during the Soviet period now struggled to make ends meet as wages were withheld and prices skyrocketed. Some of the Zhenskii Svet women wanted to formalize their activities and locate sources of financial support; they were beginning to make tentative moves toward formal collaboration with external agents and they had competing ideas of how to go about this. At a time of tumultuous social and political change the group was unraveling, and the women had begun to rethink their activism.

The Zhenskii Svet women embraced a participatory, collaborative style in their organizing. They held critical views about international aid, recognizing both the potential pitfalls and the benefits to be gained through collaboration with international agencies and foreign feminists. They thus welcomed my idea of exploring alternative forms of collaborative research. Our collaborative research process became a discursive space where we posed questions about the terms and models offered by foundations and agencies. Together, we strategized international aid, ultimately deciding to work with international agencies to undertake a number of more formalized projects, including the founding of a women's crisis center in the city. In telling the story of our collaboration, I show how the women of Zhenskii Svet worked to hold on to their projects while engaging these global discourses and resources, and how they struggled to make gender matter.

Our collaborative work and this mode of engagement pushed me to reevaluate some of my earlier conclusions about international funding. It propelled me into new intimacies and new proximities, new relationships and involvement that forced me to view the world of aid differently. Initially conceptualizing my project as a straightforward critique of democratization and international aid, I came to see it differently—as a site of agency and creative compromise, where the global and local come together in dynamic improvisation.

In Russia, however unlikely and misunderstood by the majority of the population, feminism has taken root, in exciting, encouraging, and often unexpected ways. To women such as Valentina and her colleagues, gender is not merely "a grant." Unlike the activists profiled in some critical accounts (Riles 2001), the women activists I worked with in my research were deeply concerned by the changes brought about by the presence of international agencies. Although they did not speak of "globalization" or use the language of anticapitalism (a discursive impossibility in the post-Soviet period), they were cognizant of the dangers and pitfalls and struggled to root their work, in order that it made local sense.

In Russia and other formerly socialist contexts, feminist expression has always been about a complex interplay of global and local, a form of borrowing from an often idealized "West" (Gal and Kligman 2000:9). In the late 1980s, a time of political and social turbulence, the concept of gender came to make sense to a small, highly educated group of women because it offered a rubric through which they could rethink their lives. It offered them a way of understanding and critiquing structuring forces and a way to articulate their desire for reform and for new social relations. Like many of the ideas that percolated at this time associated with the societal movement, feminism was a means of expressing resistance to state socialism. In the early 1990s, as the effects of market-oriented economics were felt, "gender" became a rubric through which women could make sense of their own losses, choices, and options. In their puzzling about the correct role of the nongovernmental sphere, the Zhenskii Svet women posed questions about accountability and responsibility in the post-socialist era. Who should be responsible for child care, for the elderly, the sick, and the needy? In many ways, Zhenskii Svet and other groups like it functioned as a kind of workshop, a discussion forum where women could process the privatizations that were taking place—the retrenchment of the state and the related cutbacks in social provisioning that hit women particularly hard. Involvement in societal organizations became an endeavor that could enable them to articulate a new role and place for themselves. It was particularly compelling to these highly educated, professional women who worked in education or medicine and who were accustomed to having a particular role or input into society.

As international agencies arrived and attached material resources to this nongovernmental activity, the meaning of women's involvement in societal organizations shifted. The presence of grants and funding opened up new opportunities at the same time that it imposed new constraints. In post-socialist Russia (as in other "developing country" or "democratizing" contexts), it is impossible to separate out the category "gender" from the resources now attached to it. In the new marketplace of NGOs, gender and gender-based organizing have ironically become a specialized system of knowledge and a new basis for professional expertise. However, it would be a mistake to dismiss them and regard them merely as locally compromised. Embracing this framing enables groups to undertake new work and new projects.

Writing Collaboration

This book is as much about relationships as it is about the politics of intervention. Relationships, informal practices, and mutual assistance have been prominent themes of recent anthropological scholarship of post-socialism. Studies have examined the centrality of informal networks during the Soviet period, and the unexpected ways these have been reanimated and transformed by the processes of transition (Ledeneva 1998; Rivkin-Fish 2005; Sampson 1996; Wedel 1998). This theme peeps through the chapters that follow. However, I am interested in relationships in other ways, too: centrally, in the relationships between the researcher and those conventionally described as research subjects—in this case, the relationships between myself and the participants of Zhenskii Svet. Throughout the book, I explore the rhythms and contours of the relationships that made our collaboration possible, using a metaphor suggested to me by Valentina, drawn from an unlikely source.

Due to this orientation, the tone and voice of this book differs from what social science conventionally delivers. As I tell the story of our collaboration, I use the first person and include information about myself. This reflexivity is tied to the feminist concern to rethink fieldwork relationships (Berdahl 2000b; Enslin 1994; Silverman 2000; Stacey 1988); it is also tied to my analytic concern and commitment to explore the ways the researcher is implicated and complicit with the broader political economic processes in motion. Anthropology is necessarily reflexive. Unlike scholars of other disciplines, anthropologists cannot pretend to stand comfortably outside the processes we analyze. Through the reflexive endeavor of ethnography, our own involvement and implication in daily life becomes apparent; the fiction of objectivity is harder to maintain, which means we have to think all the more carefully about our work and its implications (Abu-Lughod 1991; Behar 1996; Clifford 1988; Clifford and Marcus 1986). The proximity and intimacy of our relationships with our "informants"—in many cases, people who have become our close friends—often means anthropologists undertake interventions on behalf of people they care deeply about and feel indebted to, if not responsible for. The interventions ethnographers undertake may be conceptualized in different ways: as forms of reciprocity, advocacy, or activism. However, this dimension of ethnographic work often remains on the periphery of anthropological texts; commentary is often relegated to footnotes and the reader is forced to read between the lines to piece this activity and these relationships together.[16] Doing participatory, engaged, or collaborative research forces us to reconfigure our priorities (Enslin 1994:558). In my case, the relationships forged through collaborative research have greatly influenced how I write. I have chosen to present myself in relation to my friends, to make my own involvement clear and include my own role in my account. PAR is a method and philosophy that doesn't serve as a defense one can hide behind; rather, it is an approach that forces us to steadfastly confront the self that observes.[17]

With Julie Mertz, I agree that within the dramatic and often violent context of unraveling states, where ethnographers find themselves "side-by-side with their subjects, digging down to examine the very constitution of selves, agency and society as it occurs from minute to minute in action and interaction . . . reflexivity [is not] a flourish, but a brass-tacks methodological necessity" (Mertz 2002:359). Here, the challenge of gaze ("when one person looks into another's eyes" (Mertz 2002: 355)), the question of where to draw the line between action and observation is especially acute. One of the objections leveled at Western feminist scholars during the 1990s rush to document post-socialist women's lives was that they left themselves out of their accounts. Anthropologist Hermine De Soto's East German colleague Carola B characterized communication she had with Western feminist researchers in the early 1990s as a "one-way street." The scholars she met neither disclosed anything about themselves, nor aimed to learn anything from the East German women they encountered (De Soto 2000:86). My Russian activist friends see this approach as problematic, too. It is important to them that I communicate the mutuality of the learning (or "self-education" process) that I document. I highlight and detail the stages of our collaboration to draw attention to this theme. My use of the first person and reflexivity is tied to my analytic concern. I scrutinize myself as part of my scrutiny of the research process, the process of acquiring knowledge and imagining, creating, and implementing a project.

To the extent possible, I have striven to make the book itself collaborative; I have dragged drafts of this manuscript back and forth during my trips to Russia in order to share my analysis with members of the group (2001, 2004, 2005). Valentina, who knows English well, has provided detailed feedback, at times, urging me to reconsider my formulations. The book combines my analysis with their critical commentaries, quoting from some of the public presentations we have made on our work. However, it remains to be added that for all these attempts, this is my own "partial account" of our collaborative research process.

1 Muddying the Waters: Participatory Action Research in Tver'

> "You're not from around here," the fox said. "What are you looking for?" . . .
>   "No," said the little prince, "I'm looking for friends. What does tamed mean?"
>   "It's something that's been too often neglected. It means 'to create ties' . . . "
>   " 'To create ties'?"
>   "That's right," the fox said. "For me you're only a little boy just like a hundred thousand other little boys. And I have no need of you. And you have no need of me, either. For you I'm only a fox like a hundred thousand other foxes. But if you tame me, we'll need each other. You'll be the only boy in the world for me, I'll be the only fox in the world for you . . . "
>
> Antoine de Saint-Exupéry, *The Little Prince*

What do foxes, little boys, and taming have to do with the topic of feminism in Russia? That was precisely my thought when Valentina, founder of Zhenskii Svet (Women's Light) quoted from *The Little Prince* during a talk we gave about our work to the Cornell University PAR Network in 1999.[1] I had asked her to present with me on our collaborative research project when I learned she would be in the United States six months after my return from the field, and she had responded with enthusiasm and jokes about our feminist *tok shou* (talk show). We told the story of our collaboration in the form of a dialogue, working from a series of questions we had drawn up: how did we, the British, U.S.-based anthropologist and the Russian activist and scholar, meet and come to undertake a collaborative project? Why did members of Valentina's group agree to work with me, a "Western" outsider? Inevitably, in addressing these questions, we emphasized different things—I spoke of my theoretical and methodological preoccupations with power in the anthropological exchange, and how I hoped to achieve a more democratic form of engagement. She spoke of how she came to found the women's group Zhenskii Svet, her goals and aspirations in organizing and her interest in collaborating with Western feminists. The quotation was elicited by a final question from the audience: how did we feel now that the project had ended? How were we mourning the loss of the relationships? Valentina paused, and with a glint in her eye that quite disarmed me said that it reminded her of Saint-Exupéry's *The Little Prince:* "You remember? That you are responsible for those whom you have domesticated, or something like that." Everyone laughed; it was a wonderful performative moment and a great way to

Valentina and author present to the Cornell University Participatory Action Research Network, February 1999.

close, but I was thrown. I had only dim recollections of the book and couldn't quite remember the context she was referring to. Domesticate? What did she mean?

This chapter is about power and politics, the power dynamics inherent in social research and the politics of ethnographic engagement. It tells the story of my own attempt to achieve a more democratic form of research through participatory action research methodology and how this brought me into contact with Valentina and Zhenskii Svet. In the first half of the chapter I consider the particular ethical challenges of conducting research in post-Soviet Russia and explain why power emerged as such a pressing concern. I introduce participatory action research (PAR), a social change methodology I embraced as a means to achieve a more dialogic form of feminist research practice. In the second half of the chapter, I introduce my partners—Valentina and Zhenskii Svet. I arrived in the group at a particularly critical juncture in its development. Originally committed to working on a voluntary basis, members of the group had begun to question this as they became steadily more impoverished. My presence as a foreign outsider stimulated discussions about the future of the group and the potential for collaboration with international donor agencies. The chapter ends as we began to contemplate a collaborative research process, laying the ground for the story that unfolds through subsequent chapters.

I recall our joint presentation and Valentina's quotation from *The Little Prince* for a number of reasons. First, it recalls her playfulness and the tone and spirit of our engagement. Second, it evokes the edginess of our collaborative work. Although this was of course a public discussion of power, it was very safe. It took place on my territory and was attended by scholars who were interested in the issue and sympathetic to my concerns. Valentina's presence as community partner was unusual and slightly daring, but her agreement to participate already marked her compliance. In quoting from *The Little Prince* and throwing me off guard, she shook things up. Her comment signaled her awareness of the complex relations of power that were circling between us and brought the contradictions of the event to the fore. It also pointed to the intimacy between us that was borne of the collaborative work we undertook and the responsibilities this entailed. As I look back on the event and her comment, I like to think about it from different angles: what *did* she mean? Who domesticated or tamed whom, and with what consequences?

On the Unraveling of the Cold War and New Possibilities for Feminist Collaboration

The unraveling of state socialism in the Soviet Union facilitated new kinds of interactions between state-socialist East and capitalist West; borders became porous, and it was newly possible to forge personal and institutional relationships across the first–second world divide. Soviet citizens traveled out (as exchange students, on scientific "joint ventures," later as tourists) and curious Westerners (scholars, activists, tourists, then investors) were allowed in. I was one of the early beneficiaries of this new traffic. I traveled to the Soviet Union in 1989 on a private invitation to stay with Russian friends I'd recently met in England; I returned in 1990 to live for a year in Moscow, studying Russian as I taught English. Back home in the United Kingdom, my knowledge of Russian language enabled me to pick up a series of research assistantships, and these jobs enabled me to keep returning to what was now post-Soviet Russia. Through these trips I saw the problematic side of the participation offered through democratization.

Beginning in the early 1990s, the United States, British, German, and other Western European governments sent funds to Russia and other newly independent states of the former Soviet Union to assist in the democratic transition, as I have explained. But the process, like other development encounters, was deeply fraught. Despite the rhetorical persistence of terms like "partnership" and "collaboration," democratization was conceptualized as a one-way street. The North American and Western European advisors and experts who brought "know-how" to Russia (such as accounting, management, organizational technologies and skills) and who directed this flow of aid frequently had very little base or background in the culture, history, or politics of the region and were reluctant to consult their Soviet peers (Bruno 1997; Sampson 1996; Wedel 1998). In the immediate post–Cold War period, these interventions were driven by a missionary zeal that was blind to local knowledge. Indeed, here local knowledge was specifically discounted as a Communist legacy. As anthropologist Janine Wedel describes in her influential critique of aid during these years, according to the post–Cold War vision of development, the "second world" (post-socialist states of Eastern Europe and the NIS) was constituted as "misdeveloped" rather than "underdeveloped." Hence, aid to post-Communist countries "was about exorcising the legacies of communism" (Wedel 1998:21). Russia was presented as a blank slate, and the experience, values, and qualifications of Soviet people were specifically discounted. As a result, many of the Russian people who were initially most enthusiastic and Western-oriented grew steadily more disenchanted about the potential for these so-called East-West exchanges to offer arenas for dialogue, mutual learning, and respect.[2]

What was true of these mainstream development initiatives was also true of the first feminist exchanges, despite the best intentions of their participants. As state socialism unraveled, Western feminists were able to achieve direct dialogue with Soviet and East European women for the first time, free of Party minders. They met not only with the representatives of official women's organizations, but with dissidents, writers, and researchers, women who were at the forefront of projects for social change. The dismantling of the Berlin Wall and collapse of the regimes in 1989 paved the way for more sustained relationships and collaborations. Western feminist scholars and activists rushed to join in solidarity with Russian and East European women. A mass of horizontal relationships formed under the rubric of sister city schemes and academic exchanges. These macro shifts created the conditions for new intimacies and relationships to form—as Russian and American or British people were invited into each other's homes on private invitations. However, euphoria and optimism about the potential for collaboration was swiftly supplanted by disillusion and disappointment on both sides. As the old borders came down, new ones took their place: socioeconomic barriers of class, new distinctions, and a clash of ideas.

Motivated by sincere concern at the changes afoot, Western feminists cast dire predictions about the forms of exclusion that would accompany the transition to a market economy. They urged women to organize in response to their increasing political marginalization and issued warnings about embracing traditional femininity and gender roles. In so doing, they positioned themselves as experts, big sisters. This had the discursive effect of reinforcing post-socialist women's "backwardness" (Kurti 1997), suggesting that they had moved from Soviet gender equality to a place of "uncivilized" gender relations. Women from the former East bloc felt patronized by these commentaries and disagreed with many feminist analyses.[3] As Nanette Funk, a North American feminist philosopher who was at the forefront of these early exchanges, describes, "Friendships that survived years of the Cold War and the divided Germany disintegrated rapidly once the Wall came down in November 1989" (Funk and Mueller 1993). Western feminists were pushed to reevaluate their assumptions and rethink the terms of East-West exchange.

These early exchanges between Western feminists and East European women were my point of departure. Why didn't feminist insights make sense to post-socialist women? How *did* they view the changes taking place? As an anthropologist, I took the clashes seriously, as valuable moments for reflection on competing forms of knowledge. As a feminist committed to activism, I wanted to do better. That is, I shared the feminist concern about the gendered processes underway and wanted to hold on to my commitment to social change.

Thus, method was very much on my mind as I embarked on this research project. In such an ideologically laden social field as post-socialist Russia, the former superpower now cast as loser to the triumphant liberal-democratic capitalist West, how should one conduct research? In a context so newly sensitive to Western intervention, when part of my project was to examine Western intervention itself—how could I go about this in a way that was both sensitive to the people I was working with, and self-aware in a way that accepted and did not write out my own role and agenda? How to do it critically, challenging and not reinforcing the dominant narratives of transition? How could I learn from these early feminist exchanges and avoid reproducing those mistakes?

Was it possible to undertake research that was not only of interest to the academic community in the United States and Western Europe, but which was of use and of service to the people I was working with?

Culture and Power

Although the post-socialist context was a new terrain for up-close anthropological work,[4] the pitfalls and problematics of power in the fieldwork encounter were not new. Since the late '60s, when the "classic" paradigm (Rosaldo 1989) crumbled under the weight of Marxist, post-colonial, and feminist critiques, scholars have been preoccupied with the issue of power in social research. The comfortable image of anthropology as champion of non-Western people was overturned when the traditional "objects" of anthropological inquiry began to speak back. Post-colonial, subaltern, and feminist scholars drew attention to anthropology's historical complicity with colonialism and showed how anthropological representations of non-Western people had contributed to cultural exoticism and shored up notions of the civilized West (Abu-Lughod 1991; Asad 1973; Harrison 1991). In drawing attention to power in the ethnographic encounter, these critiques challenged both anthropologists' right to represent the "other" and their right to "be there" in the first place.

Women's/feminist studies encountered similar challenges when critiques by women of color and women from developing countries (the so-called third world) forced Western feminists to confront some painful truths. Although conducted in the name of women, feminism was a predominantly white, middle-class, first-world project (hooks 1981, Moraga and Anzaldua 1983). These critical accounts forced feminists to acknowledge that, although intended to empower, feminist textual production could actually silence marginalized groups; scholarly accounts could inadvertently re-colonize less privileged groups by portraying them as passive, oppressed, and homogeneous (Mohanty 1991; Spivak 1988).

These critiques were a profound challenge to the identity of both disciplines and rocked them to their very foundation; in their different ways, both women's studies and anthropology have considered themselves to be counter-hegemonic projects that work in the interests of oppressed groups.[5] Having the mirror held up to them in this unflattering way was traumatizing and left scholars with a real dilemma (known as the "crisis of ethnographic authority" or the "crisis of representation"). How to do research and write scholarly accounts without reproducing these forms of marginalization?

Anthropology's concern with reflexivity emerges out of these political shifts and the theoretical debates that ensued. Since the 1980s, anthropology has been increasingly preoccupied with power in the ethnographic encounter (as researcher meets informant), and later, at the moment of representation as we write our texts. How are we positioned as we undertake our research and writing? Whom do we silence, whom do we privilege? What are the implications of our presence and what are the effects of our analyses (Abu-Lughod 1991; Clifford and Marcus 1986)? In response to these questions, some critical anthropologists have advocated new, collaborative relations of research. While some have explored collaboration at the level of representation—working with informants at the level of writing or recording, or by producing experimental texts (Behar 1993; Crapanzano 1980; Shostak 1983), others have placed emphasis on ethnographic practice and the possibilities for activist engagement (Enslin 1994). Feminist scholars, particularly those contemplating crosscultural or transnational forms of research, have adopted various metaphors to express this latter goal—"conversation" (Haraway 1991), "speaking with" (Alcoff 1994), and "coalition" (Grewal and Kaplan 1994).[6]

Committed to the potential of ethnography and its power to yield insights into what Trondman and Willis call "lived-out-ness," the "nitty-gritty" of life (2000:12), at the same time that it keeps the global in view, I sought a means to achieve collaborative relations of research. In support of this, I turned to participatory action research (PAR). PAR is a method or a "philosophy" (Fals-Borda and Rahman 1991) that emerged outside anthropology and women's studies, and that is centrally concerned with social justice and power. It was devised by practitioners and scholars working in fields traditionally seen as "applied"—education, development studies, human service studies—as a direct challenge to the top-down and appropriating practices of traditional social science research and development interventions. Indeed, this approach turns conventional social science research methodology on its head by recasting research as a collaborative endeavor between outside researcher and community group. It does not just study problems, but works to devise solutions; it is a social change methodology.

As I read, I came to understand the diversity of participatory approaches. Some practitioners, rooted in Marxist theory and the adult critical literacy work of Paolo Freire, aim to achieve radical social change, while others are more closely associated with liberal values and organizational change interventions (Whyte and Whyte 1991).[7] And this is not restricted to the academy. Although little known by scholars of anthropology or women's studies, PAR is a perspective that has percolated far and wide. Freirian-inspired methods have been widely used by progressive social movements from rural Appalachia to Latin America. Participatory methodologies have also been used within institutionalized development projects, to forge alternatives to top-down patterns of intervention (Chambers 1997; Fernandes and Tandon 1981). In recent years, participation has also been "mainstreamed" into the agendas of international development agencies, with all the contradictions this process entails. Indeed, the World Bank now asserts participation as a core value and advocates the use of participatory methodologies in its programs. While this may look encouraging, some have argued that it is just paying lip service to these new values and that in fact it continues its old practices of top-down economic development (Cook and Kothari 2000; Jordan 2003).

PAR was certainly not unproblematic. By the 1990s, "participation," like "gender," was another empty signifier, embraced by a majority of international NGOs and donor agencies yet devoid of any radical content. I was wary of the ways that participatory methodologies have been co-opted, wary too of the evangelical tone of some of the literature that rather simplistically posits community "participation" as the answer to the ethical dilemmas of research (who is the "community"? Who gets to participate? How can research be truly collaborative from the start?) However, it seemed to me, as it has to others, that the costs of not engaging outweighed the risks (Farmer 2003; Hyatt and Lyon-Callo 2003; Scheper-Hughes 1995).

PAR offered a way to move forward. It seemed to be uniquely compatible with the goals of critical ethnography; committed to local knowledge, it involves different stakeholders in a group research process, yielding rich ethnographic knowledge about lives and sense-making processes. It is deeply concerned with power, designed to uncover the structural causes of problems through collective discussion and interaction. It is reflexive, insofar as it forces one to confront the self that observes. While it cannot resolve inequities between and among social groups, nor the global inequities that cast some people as "researchers" and others as members of "community groups," it acknowledges the power-laden research relationship as a given and accepts the ethical responsibilities that go with it. What is more, beyond the abstractions of much anthropological and feminist literature I had explored, PAR offered distinct tools to facilitate the desired collaboration. I saw in PAR a means by which I could think about collaboration "beyond writing," at the level of fieldwork practice, to paraphrase feminist anthropologist Elizabeth Enslin (1994). The PAR literature contained specific models, sample questions, case studies, and tools I could draw on and adapt. And as the diversity of participatory approaches I discovered attests, it was not rigid but quite elastic. I was particularly inspired by the work of some anthropologists and feminist researchers who have turned to PAR to achieve a more socially responsible, activist-oriented form of scholarship.[8] Action research appeared to offer a means of facilitating the kinds of contingent, situated coalitions that feminist scholarship has sought and discussed (1994).

My goal in short was not to "do PAR," or to embrace it wholesale; I was not a practitioner seeking a site for an intervention, but an ethnographer seeking to undertake a more dialogic kind of research practice. As I set out for the field, my idea of PAR was that it could be a discursive space wherein anthropologist and informants could discuss, identify, and work out ways to resolve local problems. In the end, talking about PAR gave me a framework through which to conceptualize my project. It helped me to locate a fieldsite and a women's group to work with; it enabled me to negotiate my role and the terms of our relationship; and it became a means of initiating a productive "conversations" (Gibson-Graham 1994:220) with group participants.

Finding a Group: Preliminary Research in 1995

Despite the fact that new women's groups were few and far between and largely unknown to most Russian people, I experienced no difficulty in tracking them down. These groups were made easily accessible to interested foreigners by the burgeoning (mostly English-language) literature that documented and celebrated their activity.[9] However, it was less easy to find one receptive to my ideas and goals of collaboration and combining research with activism. By the mid-1990s, the better-known Russian women's groups formed a well-trodden path for foreign feminist researchers. During a visit to the Moscow Center for Gender Studies in 1995, I had flicked through a huge and well-thumbed visitors' book. Replete with messages of goodwill in several European languages, it read like a *Who's Who* of international feminist activism and scholarship. By 1995, women activists regarded this traffic in mixed ways. The original euphoria of the first East-West collaborations had given way to a perceptible weariness among some Russian women activists, particularly those in Moscow, which was often the first and only port of call for foreign visitors. I had run into other foreign researchers who lamented the difficulty of gaining access to activists, all of whom were too busy, or too weary, to grant more than a brief audience. It was hard to imagine locating myself there.

I sought to expand my connections with nongovernmental organizations (NGOs) by searching the Internet. Via the Network of East-West Women (NEWW), a Washington-based feminist NGO that was founded in 1991 by a group of Eastern European and U.S.-based scholars and activists to support the nascent women's movement in post-socialist states, I made contact with a number of Russian women's groups. My search coincided with the launching of the NEWW On-Line project, a new electronic communications network that connected grassroots women's organizations, NGOs, and individuals in the formerly socialist states of the Eastern Bloc and the United States.[10] Sitting at my computer in Ithaca, New York, I received introductory announcements from

Tver' State University. Photograph courtesy of Frank Hein.

women's groups all over Eastern Europe and the former USSR, explaining their aims, role, and agendas.

One of these was Zhenskii Svet, a small women's group based in the provincial city Tver'. The online announcement described the group as an educational and consciousness-raising group and listed an impressive range of projects and events: a women's oral history project, an annual women's week, and a crisis center for women victims of sexual and domestic violence. As a former women's crisis center volunteer and counselor, I had a particular interest in the new crisis centers that were beginning to be founded in the post-socialist states. Finally, the group identified itself as *feminist,* which set it apart from the vast majority of Russian women's groups I had come across, most of which took great pains to explain that they were not feminist. As I have explained, feminism was a dirty word in Russia; it carried diverse, contradictory, and mostly negative connotations.[11] I was intrigued to find out how and why this group differed and what its members understood by feminism.

Valentina and Zhenskii Svet

I traveled to Tver' in the summer of 1995 to meet with the members of Zhenskii Svet and was captivated by the charms of the city and my host. This was Valentina, the founder of Zhenskii Svet and a professor in the Sociology and Political Science Department of Tver' State University. She is a small, slight, energetic woman in her mid-forties. She met me at the station and we took a bus to the center of the town. I was struck by the contrast between this provincial town and Moscow. Although a sizable city, it felt small, and I found its sleepy pace charming after the oppressive bustle of Moscow. At the same time I was struck by the impoverishment and air of neglect. Barring a few glitzy stores and banks, there was little evidence of the new wealth of the bubble years in Tver'. The dilapidated Soviet-era infrastructure and housing continued to crumble, with no prospects of repair. From the station, Valentina took me to her home, a three-room apartment where she lived with her husband (a computer scientist) and two sons (one a teenager, one in his early twenties). The apartment had lofty ceilings and was located in a nineteenth-century style building on the main pedestrian street. Like most non-privatized apartments in the city, it was awaiting state-sponsored *remont* (renovation); the paint was peeling and the water pipes were corroding. Indeed, like many old apartments in the city, it was *bez udobstv* (without conveniences): it was not hooked up for hot water and had no bathtub or shower. However, despite this, her home was warm and full of energy. The living room was crammed with material evidence of her commitments and connections, both locally and abroad. Her bookshelves, which reached from the floor to the high ceiling, were packed with books in Russian, English, and German on women's history, gender studies, sociology, and philosophy. Interspersed between them were souvenirs from her recent foreign travel (postcards of different European cities, photographs of herself with friends). University colleagues and activists routinely dropped by; the phone was always ringing. I came to learn that her apartment served as the unofficial headquarters of Zhenskii Svet, which did not have premises of its own.

As we spoke that first day I was excited to discover that we shared similar interests and tastes. Valentina is a scholar with a deep and long-standing interest in women's issues and feminism. I was excited to learn that she was an admirer of Alexandra Kollontai, the Bolshevik feminist who did so much to advance women's issues in the face of the opposition of her comrades during the early Soviet period. Intellectual affines, we had read some of the same books in Russian women's studies and enjoyed the same feminist authors; we particularly discussed the problematic terrain of Russian women's studies.[12] Her narratives about her own activism were of a different genre from those I was hearing from women's movement activists in Moscow, and I was transfixed by the freshness, vitality, and optimism of her accounts. In Moscow the buzz and optimism of the perestroika years had faded, and my acquaintances had no time for the kitchen conversations that had captivated me during my first trips to Russia in the early 1990s. There, people were engaged in the practical but dull business of making a living in the new market conditions. Here, partly due to the lack of market-based opportunities, the spirit still remained. As she spoke about Zhenskii Svet, Valentina painted a brave new world for me, where local women (teachers, scholars, doctors, lawyers) came together and undertook women-oriented community projects on a voluntary basis. She told me that over the

Ulitsa Trekhsviatskaia, the central pedestrian street in Tver'.

years the women in the group had achieved a great deal with very little. She explained to me that there was no crisis center, although the idea of founding one had a history in the group. Some of the contemporary projects were computer courses for unemployed women and seminars on women's health, which were all offered to local women for free. "All we have done, we have done on the basis of enthusiasm!" Valentina told me, proudly. This was a place of no money, but lots of soul.

Our collaboration began with a conversation about method and the potential for transnational feminist solidarity. Her eyes lit up as I described my goals, nodding eagerly. She told me that much of what I was saying characterized her early attempts in founding the group.

She had first become interested in feminism and women's issues as a graduate student when she explored nineteenth- and early twentieth-century European history. Between the lines of the official Soviet canon, she read of women's suffrage movements that united women from Russia, Western Europe, and the United States. This was something of a forbidden topic. Feminism and women's suffrage movements had been written out of the official Soviet narrative of Russian history, discredited as Western bourgeois deviations. Meanwhile, the "woman question" had been pronounced resolved in the 1930s by Stalin. At some personal risk—penalties were attached to those who undertook work that was considered ideologically unsound—and against considerable odds, she had been able persuade her advisor, an elderly, *intelligent* historian, to allow her to write her dissertation on the topic, circumventing the inevitable problems with the university authorities by naming it "a critical review of the Western women's movement." With the support of her advisor, she traveled from Tver' to Moscow (a three-hour train journey) to consult a closed department (*spetskhran*) of one of the Moscow libraries, where she was able to gain access to feminist texts. The Party exerted tight control over foreign literature, and works deemed ideologically unsound were not permitted to circulate. However, they were kept in libraries, accessible to Party elites and to those with special permission. As a professor in the late '80s, she took advantage of the more liberal intellectual environment of the perestroika era to introduce new courses in sociology and political science devoted to women's issues and feminism ("Women and Politics," "The History and Sociology of Feminism"). Though viewed with some skepticism by her colleagues, particularly the more conservative faculty, who regarded this strand of Western thought as suspiciously cosmopolitan, her courses met an enthusiastic reception from students.[13] She was a very popular teacher, as became clear to me through my subsequent work in her department. In contradistinction to Soviet pedagogical norms, she embraced a loose, nonhierarchical style, encouraging students to take responsibility for their own learning. She emphasized critical thinking and encouraged her students to follow the leads that interested them. This, and her gentle, respectful personal style, set her apart from some of her more conservative and hierarchically minded colleagues.

In 1989 she set up an informal *kruzhok* (discussion circle) on women's history for her students, where she brought this literature to their attention. She was always keen to bring about a unity of theory and practice, and she was eager to bring these insights outside the academy—hence, she began to turn her attention to women's consciousness-raising. Contra the official line that women's equality had been achieved, Valentina was only too aware that gender stereotypes persisted. She wanted women to be aware of the social stereotypes and myths of femininity that constrained them. Making the most of Gorbachev's resurrection of the woman question in the mid-1980s (the women's councils, *zhensovety*, closed down by Stalin in the 1930s were reestablished at this time), she traveled to colleges in the *oblast'* and to some factories in Tver' to run seminars on the dialectics of women's emancipation for women teachers, students, and factory workers. In 1991 she made a shift to community-based organizing by setting up her own independent feminist women's group, Zhenskii Svet. In Zhenskii Svet her diverse projects came together: she led discussions on women's history and contemporary women's activism, encouraging participants both to learn about a forbidden past and to realize their own capacity for social activism. She explained that she saw the group as an "ideological center" for local women activists, laughingly admitting that most people did not really agree with the need for such a thing. She acknowledged (mischievously quoting Lenin) that the group was "*strashno daleko ot naroda!*" (terribly far from the people, that is, elite and intellectual), but added, "*pust' budet malen'kaia, no eta tozhe vazhnaia*" (even though it's small, it's also important).

From there, things had snowballed. Her feminist activism brought her into contact with Western feminists, something that had formerly been impossible and which in the late '80s and early '90s was still somewhat risky. One anecdote she later told me communicates the spirit of these times. In 1990 an official delegation of Social Democrats and women's movement activists from Bonn and Tver's sister city Osnabruck came to the city. After reading in the local paper that one of the German delegates was to give a lecture on women's position in Germany, Valentina showed up at the appointed venue and introduced herself to the person in charge of the event as a local university teacher who was interested in the women's movement. He told her that there would be no lecture, but that the foreign delegates would shortly be arriving to listen to a jazz concert. This was typical. Even in the late Soviet period, foreign delegates were carefully shepherded on tours that had this Potemkin village characteristic. They were invited to attend formal events with special guest lists and carefully shielded from gaining exposure to everyday life. Disappointed, Valentina decided to stick around to listen to the concert. She was rewarded by much more—the man she had spoken to, who had taken an interest in her, brought one of the women delegates over to meet her. The German woman, Renate, was a leading figure in the Osnabruck women's movement, and she was delighted by this lapse in stiff Soviet etiquette. She told Valentina that in the three days they had been in Russia, they had only attended formal, official functions, and that any questions about the status of Soviet women met with stony denial and the response "there are no women's issues in the Soviet Union." She was fascinated by Valentina's counter-narratives about the position of women in the Soviet Union and her women's group and invited her to join them for dinner after the concert.

Recalling this incident, Valentina told me that she recognized her transgression as soon as she entered the dining room. This was clearly a gathering of *vlast'* (the authorities), local elites, and dignitaries; she felt *chuzhoi* (foreign), out of place. After sitting a while with Renate and not eating anything, she slipped out, to be interrogated by a woman from the administration. When it became clear that she was not on the official guest list, she was scolded, a humiliating experience that reduced her to tears. However, this serendipitous meeting ultimately led to her first invitations to travel to the West. After much ado, she was sent an official invitation to visit women's groups in Osnabruck.[14] In 1991 she went to Germany for the first time, where she learned about the German women's movement, and seeing how "developed" it was, returned with new ideas for her own group. In 1992 Zhenskii Svet received its first foreign visitors when some of the women she had met made a return visit to Tver'. In what was at the time a transgressive and remarkable move, they came unofficially, on personal invitations that were issued by Valentina to visit Zhenskii Svet. They stayed with Valentina and her colleagues in private homes, rather than in hotels with official guides. Her activity also brought her into dialogue with like-minded Russian women in other cities who began to identify as feminist and to set up women's groups at the same time. Like her, these women were mostly located in institutes and research establishments and had come into contact with feminist texts and ideas as she had done. In 1991 she attended the first independent women's forum in Dubna, which marked the first attempt to unify the disparate women's groups into a Russian women's movement.[15]

I was captivated by her account and excited by this pioneering tale. I understood that Zhenskii Svet was a radical and transgressive project. Although independent organizations were legalized in the late 1980s and societal (*obshchestvennyi*) groups mushroomed during this period as I have explained, it was very rare to organize as women. For complex reasons, some of which I have already outlined, gender-based organizing did not make sense to most Russian people. Indeed, many were hostile to the notion. Dissidents who campaigned actively for "human rights" were derisive of feminism and women's organizing (Chuikina 1996; Gessen 1997). Valentina told me that over the years she had experienced a fairly consistent low-level harassment. In the early days, she had been summoned to meetings with representatives of the local women's councils or the city administration and admonished for her inappropriately familiar attitude toward visiting foreign dignitaries. In 1994, a rather menacing article appeared in one of the local papers penned by a male journalist, describing Zhenskii Svet (Women's Light) as a *chuzhoi svet* (foreign light) in the city, which sought to corrupt "pure Russian women" with its alien and inappropriate ideas and philosophy.

Further, I recognized that Zhenskii Svet was rare *among* women's groups, too. From my reading of the emergent Russian women's studies literature and from my preliminary research, I was aware of other feminist-oriented groups, mostly in Moscow and St. Petersburg. However, few of these had an outreach dimension. They were loose clusters of friends and acquaintances and were not open to women outside these circles. Valentina's aspiration to reach out, to connect with women of different walks of life, and to undertake community-based activism set Zhenskii Svet apart. Although university based, it was not restricted to academic circles and was open to the public. Diverse women had attended over the years, teachers, engineers, doctors as well as academics. The majority of them did not consider themselves feminist; indeed, as I would learn, many of them shrugged feminism off as "academic" and irrelevant to them. They were drawn by Valentina's considerable charisma and by her personal authority, her *lichnost'* (personality). Indeed, in the city, she had a small but fiercely loyal following. She showed me other magazine and newspaper articles about her and her group that praised her work. These were mostly written by women who either were former students or had passed through Zhenskii Svet. One article she showed me, titled "*Feministka*" (feminist), disrupted stereotypes about feminists as man-hating, hostile, barely human anomalies by portraying her as scholar, wife, and mother. The message was underscored by the accompanying photograph, which portrayed her as a rather glamorous young woman, combing her hair while one of her young sons sat next to her.

As we sat talking, I realized that Valentina was the perfect partner for the project I wished to conduct. First, from our different locations we shared similar ideas about research and activism and were both committed to bridging the gap between theory and practice. She used her university base (her own privileged location) in order to undertake community-based projects. In addition to the theoretically informed activism that occurred under the auspices of Zhenskii Svet, she had set up an evening school in gender studies that was free and open to the public, taught by herself and a few colleagues. Against hierarchical models of learning, her vision was that Zhenskii Svet would be a "roundtable of equals," where members brought their own themes to discussion, and where leadership was rotating. Second, she was specifically interested in forging a different, participatory form of collaboration with Western feminists. She had long been in dialogue with Western women (first through feminist texts, then through women's movement conferences and seminars and visiting scholars). Her dream now was for groups from the East and West to collaborate, to unite, for exchanges to take place that were solid and real. She was critical of the institutionalized feminist collaborations that were taking place and held back from them. By the mid-1990s, Russian women's groups were beginning to formalize and unify, in part in response to forthcoming elections,[16] in part because they were becoming more integrated into global feminist movements and campaigns. In preparation for the UN Fourth World Conference on Women in Beijing in 1995, women's groups were encouraged (and funded) to formalize and form networks in order to increase their profile. The Beijing conference was a pivotal moment for Russian women's organizations. It marked the entry of Russian women activists onto the international stage, and their participation was enabled by international donor organizations. Indeed, Valentina participated in this Moscow-led drive in 1994 by founding *ANZhI* (the Association of Independent Women's Initiatives), a societal organization in which she and fellow activists united with two other local women's groups. However, she had steadfastly refused to register Zhenskii Svet with the local authorities, preferring that her group remained a local club, an informal space. Although she understood the need to create temporary unions, Valentina expressed caution about this unifying process; she was concerned about the new hierarchies and atmosphere of competition between groups that this created. She explained to me that she had always seen her *obshchestvennaia* (voluntary) work as a way of resisting formalization. It was a way of avoiding being owned or compromised by belonging in a structure. As she said about herself, "*Ia kak koshka, sama po sebe*" (I'm independent like a cat). Unity, she would argue, only makes sense around specific issues. Her commitment to working informally and keeping critical distance on the world of grants and funding into which women's organizations had been ushered was compelling to me and seemed compatible with my own orientation. It is important to note, however, that it had very different origins. While my critical stance on the processes in motion derived from the critical paradigm—power/knowledge and critique of Western capital—hers was different. When I shared my analysis with her in July 2004, Valentina insisted that her reluctance to engage with grants and funding was less due to a critique of Western aid than to what she called "psychological discomfort." In a comment that speaks volumes about Soviet cultural logics of money, morality, and labor, she told me that she didn't see her activism as "work," and hence it made no sense to her that it should be remunerated. Smilingly, she called her approach "anachronistic," out of step with the times, but added that she would do it that way again.[17]

But these are contemporary insights. By the end of that first two-day visit in 1995, we had an agreement: she invited me to return to Tver' to do my dissertation research based with Zhenskii Svet. She suggested a number of possible roles for me (as a lecturer, consultant) in the university and in the women's group. As she recalled during our talk at Cornell that day, "Maybe I didn't know so much about your research [methodology] then, but remember, we began to dream about the possibility for Western feminists to come not only to organize round tables, or to tell something about fundraising, but to *participate* in our activity. Without money. You have no money, I have no money, but we have skills. We are very resourceful people. We decided, what can we do together? To find a possibility to come to us, and work with us, live with us, eat with us!"

Back in Tver', 1997

"The only things you learn are the things you tame," said the fox. "People haven't time to learn anything. They buy things ready-made in stores. But since there are no stores where you can buy friends, people no longer have friends. If you want a friend, tame me!"
"What do I have to do?" asked the little prince.
"You have to be very patient," the fox answered. "First you'll sit down a little way away from me, over there, in the grass. I'll watch you out of the corner of my eye, and you won't say anything. Language is the source of misunderstandings. But day by day, you'll be able to sit a little closer . . . "

Antoine de Saint-Exupéry, *The Little Prince*

True to my promise, I returned to Tver' in 1997 to undertake my dissertation research. True to her promise, Valentina welcomed me to Zhenskii Svet and set me up with a job, teaching cultural anthropology at the university to a group of her students. Our discussions of participatory methods and the scope for crosscultural collaboration had succeeded in bringing us into dialogue and facilitated a relationship with this group, but what next?

Despite my familiarity with Russia, I experienced cultural shock as intense as any fledgling anthropologist. Although the women participants were broadly welcoming to me and seemed to appreciate my desire to achieve collaborative (*sovmestnye*) projects, it was far from clear how this would take place, or what exactly I could do. Before I could be participatory, I had a lot of learning to do.

I was thrown off by what I learned about Zhenskii Svet. I found that some of the activities I had read and heard about were plans and did not exist as actual projects. There was still no crisis center, although one of the members told me she was interested in setting one up. In the early 1990s Valentina and some other Zhenskii Svet women had begun working with German activists from sister city Osnabruck to set up a crisis center in Tver', but the plan had fallen through. Further, the very qualities that had drawn me to the group now appeared daunting. It was more amorphous and complex than I had understood; projects tended to be run by individuals, rather than by the group, and there was no real coordination between them (Natalia's computer classes for unemployed women; Oktiabrina's seminars on women's health). Some of the work I had learned about overlapped with other initiatives Valentina had set up, such as the Evening School in Gender Studies, another community project that offered classes that were free and open to the public. Zhenskii Svet, the "roundtable of equals," defied my notions of what a group should be. It had no premises, no telephone, and it met erratically. There was no clear division of labor in the group, and I soon realized that key conversations and decisions took place and were made outside of group meetings. While I embraced this intellectually, I found it methodologically challenging. How could I introduce a democratic, group-oriented project in this environment? Could my method allow for this? Clearly this called for a shift of stance.

The fox offers advice that is instructive to ethnographers, particularly those who seek participatory engagement. Learning requires taming—a letting go and a willingness to be led. Indeed, I let go of my desire to be participatory for a bit, and retreated into the more familiar stance of participant observation. Under Valentina's watchful eye, I immersed myself in the rhythms and rituals of the group and its participants, attending group meetings, visiting with them at home. Sure enough, day by day I was able to sit a little closer.

The Zhenskii Svet I came to know through my research was a loose affiliation of women that met once every week or two weeks, depending upon people's schedules and obligations. The women met at six o'clock after work in the municipal library, in a poky little room from which the fierce caretaker chased them at 8:00 PM when the library closed. It was a fragile and imperfect arrangement, since group members were not able to leave materials in the room between group meetings. During the period I spent in Tver', groups of between eight and fifteen women showed up to talk about their concerns and the problems facing them, learn about the activities of women in other cities and other countries, and devise strategies for change. Occasionally, when Valentina had a specific agenda in mind—a lecture to deliver, some important information to impart, or if she had invited a guest speaker—meetings attracted larger numbers, and up to thirty women crammed into the small space.[18] The meetings were lively and dynamic, generating enthusiasm and warmth that spilled over. At the end of each meeting, the women clustered outside on the streets, continuing conversations, making plans to get together in twos and threes to discuss various projects and local events further.

As I have explained, one unusual aspect was the group's openness to newcomers.[19] Meetings were public, and though the nucleus was made up of Valentina's friends and ex-students, new and unaffiliated women showed up quite regularly, having heard of the group through newspaper articles, radio interviews,

Tver' municipal library. Photograph courtesy of Frank Hein.

or the grapevine. The group comprised women of different ages and motivation, though they were almost exclusively of the intelligentsia. First, there were Valentina's students and ex-students, young women mentees, who had become captivated by her energy and were eager to spend more time with her. Young women such as these tended to participate in the group for relatively short periods of time but to stay in contact with Valentina through their subsequent career moves. However, some of them stuck around for significantly longer, attracted to the group because they regarded feminism itself as a career strategy. Smart, ambitious, and pragmatic, these young women attended the group in order to make contacts with Moscow-based and international networks, perceiving it as a possible way out of their constrained provincial circumstances. Many of the young women I got to know in the city through my teaching at the university, and through Zhenskii Svet, spoke with concern about their futures. Newly trained in social work, sociology, psychology, they were all too aware that few employment opportunities awaited them in the provinces. Some considered leaving the city, either for Moscow or to go abroad. For many Russian women, marriage to a foreign national offers the only realistic chance to leave for the West, and several women of my acquaintance (including two members of the group) told me that they had applied to the U.S.-Russian dating agency that was situated a few blocks from the library where Zhenskii Svet met.[20] Feminism and involvement in women's activism provided a much more desirable alternative.[21] With Valentina's support and encouragement, several of the young women I got to know in my fieldwork used the information they gathered in the course of women's group meetings in order to make applications to foreign universities.[22]

The majority of group members, however, were adult women aged mostly 30 to 55 who, because of their stage of life and family responsibilities, did not realistically contemplate leaving the city (though they may have fantasized about it). Most were highly educated professionals, teachers, engineers, doctors, journalists, who either remained clustered in poorly paid or unpaid state employment or had been squeezed out of their jobs and were seeking new opportunities. Whether married, divorced or single, employed or unemployed, many of the women in the group felt that women suffered disproportionately in the new democratic Russia and that their position had worsened in the last years. While it was clear that both men and women were adversely affected by reforms (lost their jobs or did not receive their salaries), many of them felt that it was left to women to pick up the pieces. Forced to scrimp, save, and draw on all their Soviet-era reserves of inventiveness and frugality, these highly educated women spoke with alarm of how their own and friends' husbands were unable to adapt, and of how they thus found themselves the mainstay of their families' survival and maintenance. The group offered women such as these companionship and support as they struggled to find solutions to their problems. It also offered a forum for discussion and debate, and as such was very welcome to women struggling to stay intellectually alive through the dull struggle of survival.

As I got to know group participants, I became more attuned to their life circumstances and came to understand the impact of market reform on individual women's lives. As I have explained, most of the Zhenskii Svet women worked in the crumbling and poorly provisioned state sector (in hospitals, schools, universities). They had little choice; in the provinces the private sector was underdeveloped and there was scant foreign investment. By 1997, state sector salaries had diminished to ludicrous levels.[23] What is more, during the period I was in the city, salaries were regularly withheld. The genteel veneer of the city, its air of ease and general comfort and the good humor of my acquaintances, meant that their economic insecurity was easy to miss. I met new people in neutral places, in the course of group meetings at the local library, at city events, or at mutual friends' homes. Often it was only when my acquaintances invited me home that I realized the full extent of the hardships facing them. In common with people all over the Russian Federation and former USSR, they mostly lived in cramped apartments, often without hot water or telephones, often sharing living space with extended family members (in-laws, elderly parents, aunts). Some lived in rooms in communal apartments and shared a kitchen and bathroom with neighbors. As I got to know them better, I learned that many of my friends had experienced some form of hardship that constrained them—alcoholic neighbors, unemployed spouses, loss of savings, even temporary homelessness.

Through my observations, I came to understand Zhenskii Svet as a kind of study group where a specific kind of consciousness-raising took place. It was a space where women came to reevaluate their identities and pasts and to figure out a way forward in the midst of Russia's bumpy and uncertain transition. It was a site where new subjectivities were formed, a new kind of consciousness was generated, and where action plans were synthesized.

Few embraced the identity of "feminist." Although I never heard group members voice any antagonism toward feminism, perhaps out of respect for Valentina, some shied away from it on the grounds that it was "academic," and therefore not relevant or comprehensible to them. Valentina was never evangelistic in her goals and did not seek to convert group participants; however, it was clear that belonging in the group had brought about subtle shifts in identification. In Zhenskii Svet, "gender" became a lens, a framework through which women could make sense of and revision their past choices and move forward. Several of the women in the group adopted what they called a "gender approach" (*gendernyi podkhod*) in their commentaries on the processes around them. Lydia, with whom I worked closely in the first months of my research, was an unemployed woman in her mid-fifties. She had lost her job at the Federal Employment Agency when its funding was cut. Women were the first to be let go. She understood this to be a *gender* problem, and spoke of this as her first experience of sexual discrimination. She had come to the group shortly afterward and was engrossed in finding ways to set up a support network for women who had fallen into similar circumstances.

Oktiabrina, with whom I ultimately worked to set up the crisis center, was a doctor in her mid-thirties. She was a relative newcomer to the group, having recently moved to Tver' from Siberia when her husband lost his job. They lost their life savings in the move when their bank collapsed, taking the proceeds of the sale of their apartment with it, and she now found herself uneasily dependent on her in-laws. Uprooted and struggling to find her feet in a new city, she had come to the group for support as much as out of interest. "Gender" offered a way for her to review and narrate her past choices and present dilemmas, and to talk about a way forward. She had benefited greatly from the Zhenskii Svet "corridor"; when I met her she was offering free health seminars to local women and looking for ways to do something more permanent. She dreamed of being able to bring about a unity between what she called her hobby (issues of women's health, the women's movement) and her career, to make a living by doing what she enjoyed best.

Shifting Gears: From Western Outsider to "Tamed" Partner and Friend

In preparing for research, I had imagined that the hardest part would be finding a group to take me on. Instead, this had worked out fairly easily. As I have explained, talking about collaboration and participatory engagement provided a framework for me to negotiate access. I found the shift to participation much trickier. I was welcomed to Zhenskii Svet by its founder on the basis of shared values in order to explore possible collaboration, but there was no already agreed upon project or clearly articulated need that the group felt poised to address. Indeed, as I got to know participants, I realized they had different, sometimes contradictory ideas of what Zhenskii Svet should look like and what it should undertake. The shift to a more participatory form of engagement happened slowly, as we got to know each other, and when it did happen it was summoned forth by Valentina and members of the group. Although the first months of research felt like a retreat from participatory engagement, it is clear to me now that it contained the seeds of our action project. Participant observation was a necessary precondition for the collaboration to take place; it was the basis of my familiarity with the group and facilitated my understanding of their problems, needs, and interests. Our collaborative research was dialogically negotiated—rather than a static method that I brought in, it emerged organically, in interaction with members of the group.

The first six months of my stay in the city was a period of adjustment during which I lived, worked, and ate with members of the group, as Valentina had put it.[24] Despite the new openness and the traffic back and forth between Russia and "the West" (zapad), few of the women had traveled outside the former Eastern Bloc and had experienced only limited encounters with visiting foreigners. My foreignness was initially a marker of difference that had to be overcome, and I found the women curious about me, but hesitant. I interpreted this as part Soviet legacy, part fear that as a woman from the affluent and much mythologized "West," I would be judgmental and critical of them.[25] Other aspects of my subject position (age and gender) allowed for moments of identification. I was able to achieve an easy intimacy with some of the younger women, while some of the older women (including Valentina) took me on as a kind of younger sister, or mentee. As we spent time together, they got to know my struggles and sensemaking as I got to know theirs. As a single, childless woman of thirty, I was something of an anomaly. I found my new friends caught between envy (that I was independent and free to travel) and pity (that I was "alone" and had no family). They saw me sweat over my lesson preparation, recognized that I was struggling to apply for grants to support myself, and helped me find clients to tutor English. And since I was "alone" in Russia and in their city, they felt responsible for me. As they got to know me better, my Western-ness became a kind of a resource that was appropriated in different, often playful ways. My friends derived subversive pleasure in publicly embracing me as a member of Zhenskii Svet—when we traveled to visit women's groups in other cities, or during local official events. To do so was an implicit challenge to Soviet-era constructions of Western-ness and foreignness. We all enjoyed these transgressions and joked about how I was becoming Russified, or about moments when I was attributed Soviet identity—as when my university wages were withheld alongside theirs. This latter incident caused great hilarity, and my friends joke about it to this day. The sums in question were so paltry that they were of little more than symbolic value (in this case, my earnings for teaching one class over eight weeks were about $30). The humor lay in the fact that the absurdity of "our system"—the much-derided, dysfunctional, and crumbling Soviet/post-Soviet state—could also be inflicted upon visiting foreigners.

Over time, a sense of shared purpose grew. My friends introduced me to other local associations and groups and to friends who were engaged in other forms of societal work they thought I would be interested in. I attended local meetings and seminars with them. At the same time, I traveled to other cities—bringing back information and brochures. Sometimes I was an envoy, carrying letters in time-honored Soviet style and passing greetings to friends in other cities. Other times I made connections of my own, returning with stories about other crisis centers, other women's projects, other forms of activism. My Western-ness enabled me easy access where it was difficult for most of my provincial colleagues to tread; I visited the offices of international foundations and agencies (the Ford Foundation, the American Bar Association, and the International Research and Exchanges Board (IREX) and became acquainted with their representatives. We discussed these findings during Zhenskii Svet meetings, which were transformed for me. No longer the observer, I joined them in their discussions and plans. Gradually, a new "partial but shared, externally related identity" (Gibson-Graham 1994:218) formed around a set of shared preoccupations about the scope and possibilities of the nongovernmental sphere. This became the basis for a collaborative research project.

The Research Question

My research questions had long been established: I was an ethnographer interested in the cultural process associated with transition, studying the development encounter from the perspective of Russian women's groups. However, my commitment to participatory methods and collaboration required something more. Participant observation has many virtues—it allows research to be open-ended and allows the researcher to be guided by local knowledge and concerns.[26] However, for all the virtues of the method, there is something macabre in the relativist stance of a participant observer. As I used to joke with my Russian activist friends, *everything* is interesting to an anthropologist, be it standing in lines for food, visiting the new night clubs of the nouveau riche, or exploring the contours of poverty. Whether systems collapse or thrive—it is all good anthropological data. Indeed, in the marketplace of publishing, bad news often sells best. My commitment to collaborative research required that an additional research question be generated in conjunction with group members, or that existing questions be reformulated—and that these new questions would be of significance to them.[27]

The main topic of our discussions was the changing possibilities of the nongovernmental field. While engaging Valentina's commitment to the *gendernyi podkhod,* the women in the group were also aware that "gender" and women's activism had become marketable; they knew that resources were now attached to this activity and that some women had begun to make a career out of it. They saw how some local actors were beginning to use this to their own advantage. Since the women's movement had become "fashionable," members of the local elite (women in the city administration who were former Party or state officials) had begun to found women's organizations. For example, in the spring of 1998, a group of local powerbrokers led by the president's representative to the *oblast'* founded the Women's Assembly, a new umbrella organization that aimed to unite and support disparate local women's groups. At the same time, other local societal groups had begun to win grants from international agencies. The Zhenskii Svet women were ambivalent about this. They expressed sharp disapproval for people who they considered engaged in *obshchestvennaia rabota* (societal work) for gain, and for what they regarded as appropriations of the women's movement (they regarded some of these initiatives, including the founding of the Women's Assembly, as a bid for political capital by political elites). They were proud of their voluntarism and attached to their independence, yet at the same time they had begun to consider the costs of this purist approach. Some were looking for ways to make their women's activism more concrete in order that they could do more for local women, but equally crucially, in order that they could sustain themselves. Zhenskii Svet had always been as much an emotional and psychological survival strategy for group members as an attempt to enlighten and improve the lives of other women. Now, in 1997, the crunch was becoming more acute.

Zhenskii Svet was at a crossroads. Oktiabrina, Lydia, and other group participants were beginning to rethink their activism and its purpose. In the absence of wages and a functioning social safety net, they could no longer afford voluntarism. Valentina was also reevaluating. She sensed that she was on the cusp of something and was unsure how to proceed. At the same time that she was committed to maintaining the informal, loose identity of Zhenskii Svet and did not want to see this compromised, she recognized the need to move to a different kind of engagement. The buzz of questions within the group became urgent. Should the informal *group* become a more structured and permanent *organization*? Should it seek the support of foundations and agencies, of the local administration, or retain its commitment to the "outside"? Should it maintain its educational and consciousness-raising orientation, or was it time to become more formally political?

In spring 1998 we began a series of seminars. The first phase of our collaboration was a seminar discussion, a sense-making project about the future of Zhenskii Svet and the possibilities of Western aid and support to women's groups. Out of these discussions, participants devised a series of action projects: a Center for Gender Studies and Women's History, a publishing house, and a project to set up a women's crisis center, in which I was centrally engaged. The next chapters tell the story of this shift to specific projects and institutionalization in more detail; they map the implications of what Valentina called a *strategiia vovlecheniia* (strategy of involvement), a tactical decision to collaborate with the local authorities and international donor agencies on specific projects. At the same time, they flesh out the context within which we were working —democratization and civil society aid, its local manifestations, changes and the new opportunities and constraints of women's organizing and women's activism.

Participation, Ties, and Taming

But I will let the next chapters tell that tale. This is a chapter about responsibility, ties, and the politics of ethnographic research, and I want to return to the questions I set out with: the status of our collaboration and the nature of the relationship between Valentina—a dynamic, charismatic, impoverished academic, embracing feminism in a hostile provincial environment—and me, a British, U.S.-based feminist anthropologist interested in forging a more collaborative and democratic form of research. Who was taming whom? And what was the responsibility that was forged between us?

Valentina and I met at a time of seismic geopolitical shifts—the unraveling of state socialism, the end of the Cold War, and the bumpy road that was referred to as Russia's "transition." Our relationship was made possible by these political and economic changes; only a few years earlier it would have been quite impossible to do conventional ethnographic research in Russia, let alone participatory research with an independent community group. We were drawn to each other for a number of reasons. As is common between anthropologist and key informant, there was a strong personal chemistry between us, and we were able to identify with each other. Although at very different stages of life, we were both in a liminal space. I was a graduate student embarking on dissertation fieldwork; she was caught between the possibilities of the shifting nongovernmental field (social entrepreneurialism, career feminism). She sensed that she was on the cusp of something and was unsure how to proceed. We shared a similar narrative; we both identified as feminist and were concerned by the transformations in women's activism brought about by Western aid. Valentina drew me in and invited me to her group. Although she was first mentor, guiding and coaching me into usefulness in my work at the university and within local groups, ultimately we embarked on a learning process that was mutual.

The first ten months of research, which I experienced as something of a failure, a retreat from PAR, were a necessary precondition for a participatory process. The ties that were forged between us during this period enabled the participatory project to take place. During this time I got to know Valentina and other group participants and was integrated into their familial and social networks. Indeed, some of the women used kinship terminology to express their relationship to me (I was "adopted," I was a "sister"). The intimacy and sense of trust between us permitted PAR. As I will go on to show, the women who participated in our eventual seminars were the women I was closest to. They came to the meetings and engaged in the process out of a sense of responsibility to me and to the dialogue we had begun. Our PAR process emerged organically, in interaction with members of the group. It required that I move and change, too. I undertook it as a tamed member of Zhenskii Svet, not as a straightforward Western outsider.

My Western outsider status was crucial at all stages of the project, but it did not remain static. To Valentina it initially represented the internationalism that she held dear. Embracing me as a Western feminist colleague was a means by which she demonstrated her disdain for the boundaries and codes of the Soviet era and her commitment to a new, post–Cold War, democratic future. One of her explicit goals in founding her feminist-oriented women's group was to challenge the Soviet parochialism and suspicion toward the West that was the legacy of decades of anti-Western and anticapitalist ideology. As she put it during our presentation at Cornell, "From the beginning, we were very involved in relations with our Western friends; it was a form of resistance to this tendency to nationalism and militarism, which I don't like. The projects of our group were maybe to break this prejudice, or stereotypes concerned with Western people and Western things."

To the other group participants, my Western-ness was initially a marker of difference that intrigued; it became an item of play. As our research project took shape and became an investigation of the political economy of grants and funding, the significance of my Western outsider status shifted once again. It became a useful resource that she and other members of the group were not shy to deploy. As I show in subsequent chapters, Valentina was well aware of the power of my Western-ness and used it strategically. As our collaborative project got underway, she sent me to knock on office doors, to meet with local power-brokers (the head of the municipal social services, the president's representative to the *oblast'*, the mayor), and to lobby for support for our crisis center project.

When we broached the question of my role during the presentation at Cornell she brought the house down by calling it "the post-Soviet exploitation of Western intellectual resources!" In order to unpack that statement and understand how this project of intimate exploitation played out, we need to move on with the tale.

2 Querying Democratization: Civil Society, International Aid, and the Riddle of the Third Sector

Nineteen ninety-seven was a peculiar year to be in Russia. It was the height of the short-lived boom period, and the year before the bubble burst in the devastating economic crisis of August 1998 that caused foreign investors to flee in droves. Since the early 1990s foreign capital had flooded into Russia, the new frontier of capitalist expansion. Most got no further than Moscow. During 1997, many Russian acquaintances informed me that 80 percent of Russia's wealth resided there. Some of this new wealth derived from the provinces—this was a time of expropriations and privatizations by Russia's nascent oligarchs, and foreign investors, too (Wedel 1998). Moscow was a quite different city than the drab, gray mausoleum I had become used to and gotten fond of in the early '90s. It was pronounced to be the world's third most expensive city, the main streets were crammed with exclusive shops, cafes and bars, and newly constructed glitzy malls—establishments that most citizens could only look upon as museums and that I could not afford to frequent. Fast food chains such as Sbarro and Baskin-Robbins set up on street corners next to their better-publicized competitors McDonalds and Pizza Hut. The wide streets, which used to be nearly empty except for buses, trams, and a few Zhiguli, were now jammed with expensive traffic, the new cars of the new elites. The expatriate community had expanded and diversified massively during this period. The new capitalist Russia offered an exciting opportunity for young Western professionals to make their careers (and sometimes a killing) as journalists, venture capitalists, consultants, and aid workers. In response to this, many people from the provinces had begun to refer to Moscow as "the West."

These changes were slower to take effect in the provinces, but by 1997 they were taking hold. In Tver' there were new markers of what my Moscow friends called "civilization"—an Ecco shoe store, an Yves Saint Laurent cosmetics store —and the food stores were well stocked with cookies and candies from Germany, frozen seafood, lobster and shrimp, luxury teas and coffees, and chips, snacks, and candies from the United States. In fact, one had to work fairly hard at times to locate domestic food products, a fact that caused many people some consternation.[1] There were bars and clubs, a casino, and a strip joint, all of which pointed to the existence of well-heeled mafias. The new influx of international capital and its uneven distribution in the city made for some strange and bemusing juxtapositions of which its citizens were only too aware. One beautiful summer day towards the end of my research, I was invited to join a friend and her cousin, who was visiting from Moscow, on a walking tour of the city. Alla, a music teacher in a local music academy, took us to some of her favorite places. We walked along the pedestrian main street, down to the Volga, and through the city park. We rode the carousel eating ice cream and took a one-hour boat trip on the Volga, rolling our eyes at the loud disco music pumping from the speakers. Then her cousin, Irina, led us to her favorite street, whose Bolshevik-era name summed up so many of the new ironies and contradictions of the city. On *Ulitsa Ravenstva* (Equality Street), the opulent palaces of the so-called "new Russians," with their tall iron gates and fences, their tinted glass and huge garages, boldly towered over their crumbling wooden *izbushki* (peasant-style log houses) neighbors. We laughed and photographed ourselves standing, arms linked, by the street sign. My favorite icon to these Russian capitalist times, however, was located a short distance away, on the potholed road that ran from the railway station to the city center. A huge and imposing construction of steel and tinted glass, it was the abandoned shell of the Tver' Universal Bank. It had crashed in the early '90s, taking the savings of thousands of local people, including those of my friend Oktiabrina, down with it.

In 1997, Tver', like other provincial places, was a "city of contrasts," as my friends ironically used to say. This was a stock phrase of Soviet textbooks, used to describe London, New York, and other imperial cities, to allude to the contradictions of capitalism. Although "privileged" by its proximity to Moscow, resources were drained from it. And the negative effects of free-market-oriented economic restructuring were beginning to be felt. Under the tutelage of IMF advisors, Russia's new democratic governments had eroded Soviet-era social guarantees—universal, free health care, full employment, state-subsidized day care—and failed to install new structures in its place. Without any serious articulation, purposeful discussion, or acknowledgement, the state socialist social contract had been dissolved.[2] Russian people struggled to deal with the new post-socialist phenomena of unemployment, withheld wages and hyperinflation in the absence of a functioning social safety net.

The women of Zhenskii Svet urgently debated the question of social responsibility—in the light of the collapse of state support, who should be responsible for guaranteeing citizen's welfare, for taking care of the old, the young, and the infirm? Should societal groups step in? Or was it the role of the state? It was here that international development agencies stepped up to offer a solution. In keeping with the neoliberal vision that was hegemonic at Cold War's end, their diagnosis for Russia was to cut back the state and place responsibility upon the individual or private actors. Working in concert with international lending institutions, agencies such as the Ford Foundation, the MacArthur Foundation, and USAID foresaw a restructuring that would enhance the role of non-state actors. According to this formulation, citizens groups and associations of civil society (or NGOs, as they are known in development terminology) would play an increasingly active role, fulfilling the responsibilities of the crumbling state sector. In the mid-1990s, international donor agencies began to bring these

models and resources to the provinces, moving away from Moscow and Petersburg where they were originally based. Representatives of foundations such as
the British Charities Aid Foundation, Eurasia, and the Open Society Institute
visited Tver' and other provincial cities, seeking to collaborate with community
groups as part of their mandate to strengthen civil society. Through seminars
and training sessions they offered both material resources—grants and books—
and "know-how" to these fledgling NGOs—management, accounting, fundraising skills and technologies of organizational development, and models that
taught the value of this activity.

This chapter focuses on one such model, the third sector. This term is used
widely in the Russian-language promotional literature international foundations use to advertise their activity, and in the instructional materials they produce. Although incomprehensible to most Russian people, it has become a crucial signifier for those involved in the community-based activism I explored in
my research. The following is an excerpt from one of these promotional brochures, "Charity for Dummies." Published in Russian by the British Charities
Aid Foundation (CAF) and authored by Olga Alekseeva, the information officer
in the Moscow office of CAF,[3] it was widely distributed among nongovernmental organizations in Russia. I first came across it in the library of Lydia, one of
the Zhenskii Svet women. An enthusiastic participant in local groups and associations, Lydia had accumulated a wide variety of third-sector support materials; Alekseeva's text had fallen into her hands when she attended a CAF seminar
in Tver'.

> This book seems too emotional for a textbook. It appears too dry and practical for
> journalism. Let me tell you a secret—I have done this on purpose, so that you, my
> readers, could not only gain an intellectual understanding of the third sector, but
> in order that you could feel in your heart the people who live and work in it.
>
> The third sector is not a spy novel. The third sector—truly, truly—isn't the
> name of a secret military organization in Zimbabwe; it's not even part of a football
> field.
>
> It's you and I. That's what this book is about. About us. Surprised? Let's think
> about it some more. When you are sold a color television and it breaks down
> within a week, and the technician shrugs his shoulders—who will help you defend
> your consumer rights? That's right, the consumer defense organization. . . . When
> your only son is sent to serve in the army in a hot spot, to whom can you run for
> assistance? To the Soldiers' Mothers committee. There, you will find mothers and
> fathers who, just like you, don't want to wait for acts of kindness from the military
> committee. When your child falls seriously ill, who is the first to offer help? The
> society of parents with disabled children. It's all the third sector—noncommercial
> organizations, formed by people to resolve their problems, or just in order to be
> together. (Alekseeva 1996. *Tretii Sektor, blagotvoritel'nost' dlia chainikov*. London:
> Charities Aid Foundation)[4]

The term third sector that this text teaches and celebrates refers to a realm
of informal groups—associations, clubs, or NGOs. It derives its name from its
role in a triad, where the first is the state, the second is the private sector of

businesses and enterprises, and the third is the realm of citizens' initiatives.[5] Beyond this, as Alekseeva's text suggests, the third sector is a project of persuasion, one that has sought to transform purportedly dependent and politically passive Soviets into active citizens, savvy consumers, claimers of rights, and defenders of their interests. The third sector represented a riddle to the Russian activists I worked with in my research; although many found the idea captivating, they were troubled by the way it had transformed their work. For this reason, the third sector offers a good site from which to rethink the forms and logic of political activism encouraged by international development agencies in the post–Cold War period.

In this chapter I examine the project to build a third sector in Russia, grappling with the riddle that it represents. In so doing, I move beyond the local conditions of the Zhenskii Svet women's lives to consider the broader political geography within which they were situated. In many ways, this is an account that belongs to the preliminary phase of our engagement, the pre-collaborative moment when I was newly making sense of the nongovernmental scene in Tver'. In the first half of the chapter, I examine the discursive prominence of the third sector by accounting for its rise and tracing its origins. I show how it is linked to the concept of civil society, which has been a key term of democratization. Starting in the 1980s as a rallying cry of East European oppositionists, it took on a quite different meaning in the '90s, when it became central to a new, neo-liberal vision of development that encourages nongovernmental groups to take on the functions of the state. In the second half of the chapter, I consider the significance of these shifts by investigating the third sector ethnographically. Here, I present what I learned about the third sector and its contradictions as I accompanied members of Zhenskii Svet to local meetings of societal organizations. The chapter presents our mutual sense-making and theorizing, and also traces the halting steps of our collaboration; the subplot is the collaborative project that failed and never got off the ground.

The third sector that has been created by international donor agencies bears little resemblance to the civil society that was desired by Russian actors. Neither does it deliver what it promises: rather than allowing a grassroots to flourish, the third sector provides a structural and symbolic framework for the reproduction of former elites of the Soviet regime. It facilitates the gendered distribution of power and resources and contributes to the formation of hierarchies, jealousies, and competition between groups. Many local Russian actors who work in this terrain are well aware of these problems, though they may frame them a little differently. Yet many remain committed to the idea, and still desire forms of East/West engagement and connection. I show that despite its shortcomings, the idea of the third sector remains compelling to local actors. Third sector has become an important part of the imaginary repertoire of Russian activists; it is a site of contestation and sense-making (between money and morality, state and society) and it has shaped peoples' ideas of what is possible, permissible, and desirable. In this way, it offers a rich site for an investigation of the "construction and contestation of new cultural landscapes" and the "emergence of new asymmetrical power relations" in transforming post-socialist states (Berdahl 2000a:1).

From Civil Society to the Third Sector

The dusty term, drawn from antiquated political theory, belonging to long, obscure, and justly forgotten debates, re-emerged, suddenly endowed with a new and powerful capacity to stir enthusiasm and inspire action. (Gellner 1994:5)

The promotion of the third sector in Russia has to do with the popularity of the concept of civil society, which has been a crucial ideological signifier of democratization. The meaning of civil society has shifted considerably in the course of the past two decades, in response to social and political change in the region. Here I explore these shifts in order to provide a framework through which we can understand the plight of the people who "live and work" in the third sector, in Alekseeva's terms.

Classically defined as the sphere of public interaction between family and state, in former socialist states civil society came to mean that which was not determined by the Communist Party. It reemerged in the 1980s, as Gellner so memorably described, popularized by Central European intellectuals as a means of expressing resistance to socialist states.[6] As Vaclav Havel, one of the leading Czech dissidents, put it, "The various political shifts and upheavals within the communist world all have one thing in common: the undying urge to create a genuine civil society" (cited in Wedel 1998:85). The concept of civil society was central to the project of "anti-politics," an oppositional stance that opposed the socialist state by addressing the individual.[7] As expressed by Adam Michnik, a leading force in the Polish Solidarity trade union movement, "Such a program should give directives to the people on how to behave, not to the powers on how to reform themselves. Nothing instructs the authorities better than pressure from below" (cited in Garton-Ash 1990). Though commonly, especially retrospectively, read as a desire to *join* the capitalist West, this civil society was an imagined "third way" between communism and capitalism. As David Ost describes it, these East European advocates saw civil society as a sphere of expansive civic participation, a "permanently open democracy," in which civic activity is "based neither in the state nor in the marketplace, but in the vibrant political public sphere itself" (1990:30–31). Confidence in civil society was expressive of a longing for a moral and just society, governed by values that transcended dirty politics, where the individual was able to exercise his conscience and "live in truth." In this way, it invoked a new Europe, unfettered by ideological borders, boundaries, and constraints (Ost 1990).

But my interest here is in the way the concept of civil society functioned as a signifier. Civil society was the stuff of conversations, bartered back and forth, which ultimately legitimated the intellectual, entrepreneurial, philanthropic, and educational transactions of transition. Although they represented only limited circles, these Central European oppositionists and their ideas had a disproportionate effect. Indeed, they were often key consultants after the velvet revolutions and found easy dialogue with North American and Western European scholars and policymakers (Wedel 1998). In response to their debates, scholars in the West of left and right became newly persuaded by the concept of civil society. Conservative subscribers to the "totalitarian" school took this as confirmation of their worldview, which saw citizens inevitably resisting an oppressive state, and interest in the concept of civil society on the right took off in the 1980s (Foley and Edwards 1998). Meanwhile, Western leftists interpreted dissident and oppositional activity to be manifestations of a newly energized left opposition within state socialist society; it appeared to be compatible with new left visions of participatory democracy (Habermas 1989; Ost 1990).

The democratic revolutions of 1989 appeared to confirm this, and the concept of civil society came into a new vogue. Civil society now signified the triumph of capitalism and the collapse of the socialist alternative. In scholarly circles the concept became something of a catchall. As Seligman puts it, "It has been picked up in the West, used (and often misused) by writers on both the political right and the left to legitimize their own social programs and has entered academic discourse with a vengeance that is somewhat disquieting" (1998:79). This is evidenced by the "neo-Tocquevillian" swing among social scientists in the post–Cold War period.[8] One example of this is Robert Putnam's influential work on social capital (Putnam 1993; 1995). According to Putnam, "Social capital refers to the features of organization such as networks, norms and social trust that facilitate coordination and cooperation for mutual benefit" (Putnam 1995:67). He regards social capital as a vital ingredient for a healthy and successful democracy. Informal associations and groups play a crucial role in his analysis by generating social capital, which will then percolate to the broader society, recreating the polity. Although addressing a perceived crisis of civic life in the United States, and other advanced industrial societies, Putnam's work is an explicit call to action worldwide. Posing the suspiciously Russian-sounding question, "what is to be done?" (Putnam 1995:75),[9] his work was an invitation to scholars to investigate the apparently universal phenomenon of social capital across other cultural contexts.[10]

Indeed, it proved to be widely influential. This was not just an arcane debate; in the nineties, the concept of civil society (and its companion concept, social capital) became central to a new vision of development that was "driven by beliefs organized around the twin poles of neoliberal economics and liberal democratic theory" (Hulme and Edwards 1997:4). In the context of a broad discussion of the global development industry, Hulme and Edwards provide a helpful sketch of paradigm shifts over the last thirty years. While in the 1970s the dominant paradigm was the "myth of the state," assuming that the state could provide for the needs of citizens, in the '80s this was supplanted by the "myth of the market," which held "that the private sector can provide for the consumption needs of all consumers" (Hulme and Edwards 1997:4). The seismic shifts of the post–Cold War era we have explored gave rise to a new formulation, "the myth of the market plus civil society" (1997:4).[11] In the mid-1990s, the World

Bank shifted its priorities to emphasize the importance of both civil society and social capital.[12] It was this new formulation that created the conditions for the global NGO boom, or "associational revolution" (Salamon and Anheier 1997).

Thus it was that in former socialist states, civil society became a project, something to be implemented (Sampson 2001). Civil society was "central to western aid programs in Eastern Europe, linked intimately to privatization aid" (Hann and Dunn 1996:9). According to Janine Wedel, the U.S. Congress devoted $36 million to support "democratic institution building" in Poland and other ex-Communist states between 1990 and 1991. By 1995, the United States had obligated $164 million to promote political party development, independent media, governance, and recipient NGOs (Wedel 1998:85). Meanwhile the EU and private foundations also channeled funds to support NGOs and civil society.[13] In Russia, civil society promotion found material expression in the project to build a third sector of NGOs. As I have explained, during the 1990s donor agencies channeled a great deal of support to associations and groups and encouraged them to believe in the importance of their work. As one American political scientist put it (writing in *Surviving Together,* an English-language journal that documents and maps post-socialist NGO activity), "The new metaphor is society as a three-legged stool—market sector, public sector and civil sector." All three have to be in balance, and the third sector "should be an equal player with the market and government" (Rifkin 1997:8).

Aid to women's group formed a proportionally small yet ideologically significant portion of this aid. This is testimony to the important role women played in this sphere.[14] However, it also points to some of the gendered realignments of the post-socialist period that international donor agencies have contributed to. Against discussions of post-socialist transition that posit civil society as an open and neutral space, feminist scholars of Eastern Europe and the USSR such as Barbara Einhorn (1993), Susan Gal (1997), Hilary Pilkington (1992), and Peggy Watson (1997) have pointed to the ways in which the liberal democratic ideal of civil society rests on a gendered division between public and private that relegates women to the private sphere. From this perspective, programs that focus on supporting women's participation in civil society are problematic insofar as they reinforce this gender division, contributing to the political marginalization of women as a group.

Donor support has led to the proliferation of NGOs in Russia; according to one recent account, there were over 450,000 civic groups registered in January 2001 (Henderson 2003:6). In many ways this funding looks like a success story. My argument here is that this new version of civil society is quite different from what activists desired and what donor agencies promised. In the 1980s, civil society indexed the hopes and ideals for a post–Cold War era: boundarylessness, joining Europe. The civil society that dissidents yearned for was a realm of citizen empowerment, of discussion and debate. The third sector is a far cry from this vision. First, it looks very different. It is an institutional sphere that has very concrete referents that can be counted, mapped and encouraged—NGOs (Sampson 1996).[15] Its participants are less often politicos engaged in critical debate, than people intent on developing their careers.[16] Despite the folksy, grass-rootsy flavor of much of its promotional literature and talk of empowerment, charity, and voluntarism, the actually existing third sector is a professionalized realm of NGOs, inaccessible to most local groups. Second, it undertakes a very specific kind of work. Dissidents had used the concept of civil society to express their opposition to the socialist state. The anti-state piece was crucial then. Now that the Party was over (as the irresistible pun went), and capitalism had ostensibly triumphed, civil society became hitched to a new anti-state project—the neoliberal project to cut back the state. This second anti-state project entailed distinct and violent policy shifts, an abrupt end to the socialist social contract, which for all its flaws had provided citizens with a safety net from cradle to grave. Under state socialism, employment, education, healthcare, and day care had been constituted as rights. This new formulation changed all that.

According to the new vision of development, NGOs have two distinct roles: (re)education and service provision. Reflecting the shifts in post–Cold War development agendas I have described, donors and policymakers imagined the NGO to be a "magic bullet" (Fisher 1997:442). They conceptualized NGOs as training grounds that would instill liberal democratic values (social capital and habits of cooperation, trust, and participation) and prepare citizens for public life. Thus, in Russia, as in other post-socialist states, NGOs were sown as seeds for democracy; they were central to the exorcism of communism.[17] As exemplified in Alekseeva's text, much of the work that takes place in the third sector is persuasive; there is a great deal of emphasis on new language, on the media and educational projects that seek to explain and convince, almost to "convert" Russian people into its message of responsible citizenship.

In placing the emphasis on individuals, this model elides the importance of broader social and political conditions in structuring associational life. Indeed, it obscures some major structural reconfigurations. In Russia, the third sector takes on more than its global proponents and local participants have bargained for. In the third sector, NGOs (most of them women's groups) are encouraged to become service providers. In the 1980s, civil society signified the independence and autonomy of civic organizations from the state, yet here NGOs, the ostensibly nonstate actors, are reconfigured as "partners" of the state, stepping in to take on the responsibilities it divests itself of.

Critical scholarship of neoliberalism notes similar tendencies worldwide. In the United States, as in Russia during the 1990s, civil society discourses served to legitimize the restructuring of relations between citizen and state and to redefine the "public sphere." And they were implicated in a similar project of persuasion, too. Drawing on ethnographic work in U.S.-based nonprofits, anthropologist Susan Hyatt describes the restructuring of citizenship that took place as the welfare state was dismantled. She shows how civil society discourses worked to create a new kind of political subject who is perfectly suited to neoliberal governance—the volunteer. Unlike her predecessor, the political subject Hyatt calls the citizen, the volunteer does not expect social benefits from the state. Instead, she is "empowered" to take responsibility for herself and provide service to others (Hyatt 2001a). This transformation is achieved via a series of technologies—individualizing strategies such as "self-help"—that work on the individual and encourage her to behave in a certain way (Cruikshank 1999; Hyatt 2001a). This Foucauldian scholarship suggests that neoliberalism gives rise not to the state's retrenchment, but to its subtle extension. Civil society and the relations and institutions it fosters are not separate from the state, but instead are intimately entangled (Hyatt 2001a:204). This entanglement is manifest both in the new forms of political subjectivity (the "neoliberal citizen") and in the new institutions that the neoliberal project brings into being—agencies that are both public and private and that may receive substantial state subsidies (Hyatt 2001a:207).

The civil society concept is clearly compromised. However, despite this new critical turn in scholarship, donor agencies remain and development discourses continue to percolate in former socialist contexts. Civil society and the third sector remain crucial signifiers that activists have to engage, since collaboration with donor agencies means taking on the models and concepts they promote. I push the critique of NGOs further to pose a series of questions about this process of engagement: What sense do women activists make of injunctions to engage in charitable or voluntary activity in the context of massive societal upheaval, the collapse of social safety nets and former certainties? How do they navigate these circulating and clashing values and discourses in their work? What does the third sector look like on the ground and what scope for citizen empowerment does it afford its participants? Attention to the "gaps, slippages and difference between ideas that purport to be the same" (Gal and Kligman 2000) in this project—such as civil society, voluntarism—can tell us a great deal.

Despite what I regarded as its actual effects (rationalizing privatization and reduced state support), I found that the idea of the third sector continued to appeal to many of my informants. The kind of women most commonly drawn to informal associational activity in the 1990s were teachers, doctors, engineers, highly educated women who were not of the party-state but who had considerable cultural capital in the old regime. Invested in the kitchen discussions and debates of the perestroika period, these people had great hopes for political reform but found themselves devalued and shut out from the new sources of economic and symbolic capital in the new, democratic Russia. Voluntary or societal work offered them a way to recoup. The model of the third sector appealed to them because it affirmed this informal activity; according to the model of the third sector, community groups, associations, and clubs are integral to the workings of a healthy society. The individualizing logic did not repel; indeed, I found that the emphasis on individual rights, responsibilities, and self-help strategies within third-sector literature resonated with the women activists I spoke to. While they objected deeply to the specific policies the neoliberal formula entails—the slashing of social safety nets and the removal of former entitlements—they embraced the individualizing logic, since it represented a move away from Soviet discourses that were thoroughly discredited.[18] What is more, in comparison with the other two spheres—business and politics—the third sector was regarded as a righteous location. Here we see an interesting constellation, where Soviet cultural logics of money and morality combine to articulate a gendered form of allegiance to the third sector. The market and formal politics were regarded as dirty, but also as masculine domains. In contrast, in these constructions the nongovernmental (or nonprofit) sphere was seen to be decent, moral, and in this way peculiarly feminine.

Engaging the Riddle of the Third Sector in Tver'

Lydia was a participant in Zhenskii Svet and a former university teacher in her fifties. When I met her she was formally unemployed. She had quit her teaching job when her department had been unable to pay her salary and had moved to the Federal Employment Service to work as a sociological analyst. Two years before I met her, she had lost this job when initially generous state funding was cut back. Forced to make layoffs, her boss began to exert pressure on some members of the staff to leave: to leave, as it were, of their own volition (in order to avoid paying unemployment benefits). Although both men and women staffed the office, he targeted the women in the group. Lydia experienced this as a profound shock, a profound "crisis," as did her female colleagues, who went through the same process. She told me that it was the first time she and her co-workers had had to face the idea of unemployment. She was shocked at the callous disregard of her rights. She was upset about how her boss, a former *military officer,* she emphasized, had "pressed" her to leave. Agitated by the memory, she told me that the pressure was so intense that one woman had been "on the verge of a heart attack." Lydia's account evoked the profoundly destabilizing social dislocation she and her colleagues had experienced at this time. Unemployment was distressing to her not merely on account of the financial burden it placed but because it was an attack on her dignity, on her very identity, her sense of self. It also cast a blow to her worldview. She was shaken by the fact that a person of education and high social standing (an officer) had behaved in this way. Thanks to her husband's modest but steady income, she had been able to manage by taking on a variety of informal jobs. However, she retained a sense of bitter disappointment.

Like many unemployed (or formally employed but unpaid) women with higher education, Lydia began to participate in meetings of several local associations, including Zhenskii Svet. Lydia sought me out as soon as I joined the group; she knew I was interested in the new Russian crisis centers and told me that she was interested in setting one up. This plan came out of her own experience of gender discrimination in the workplace and her own success in dealing with it. She told me that a group of her co-workers had come together to challenge their unfair dismissal and won some satisfaction. They called themselves *Sovremenitsa* (contemporary woman); although they had since scattered and found jobs in different places, she told me that they still met occasionally. She planned to register the group as a societal organization and wanted to concretize their activities by setting up a center that would provide support and advice to unemployed women. I was moved and compelled by her story and impressed by her resilience and determination. Keen to collaborate, I eagerly hitched myself to her.

Her interest in associational activity and women's activism had begun when she had attended a seminar on women's leadership in Tver' in 1996, run by an American woman, a professor of women's studies and representative of the American Association of University Women. Since then Lydia had become an enthusiastic participant of all things pertaining to societal organizations. In addition to Zhenskii Svet, she attended diverse local seminars and meetings—the founding meetings of new local associations, and NGO seminars that were organized locally or by the visiting representatives of donor agencies. Her interest extended beyond the work of societal groups to the biographies of individuals engaged in them. She followed the philanthropic and entrepreneurial activities of influential women in the town in the local papers, marveling at the good luck stories and commiserating with the bad. More than any of the other women in the group, Lydia was interested in the new technologies and models of the third sector; she was an avid consumer of the literature foundations distributed. I took her to be a kind of ethnographer and theorist of the third sector and wanted to learn from her accounts. She was less tightly integrated into the relationships within the group and gravitated toward me, the outsider. I ultimately came to realize that I was an important interlocutor for her, that my interest in her greatly stimulated her telling.

She told me that she had first learned about the third sector when a representative of the British Charities Aid Foundation came to the city and gave a seminar in the municipal library. "We didn't know what it was," she recalled, "it's a new sector of life." Explaining its relationship to prior forms of organization, she told me, referring to the seminar,

> Everyone thought that the term *obshchestvennaia rabota* (societal work) was no longer meaningful, because in former times it signified primarily Party, *Komsomol*, or union work. And there was a strong element of obligation associated with it, it barely differed from state work, and in general it was too formalized. That's why I don't like to use this term. It has a lot of baggage . . . that's why I have reformulated it for myself. I'm dividing up a new sphere of activity for myself. It's very interesting for me, very meaningful, and I see myself as a new professional in this area. I see it to be quite a responsibility. It's practically a new profession.

Here, Lydia refers to the deep mistrust of collective action that is the legacy of the Soviet period. As she suggests, the notion of *obshchestvennaia rabota* is compromised by its Soviet association. During the Soviet period, the term signified enforced, Party-mandated activity. Each person was required to undertake extracurricular activities on behalf of the *Komsomol* (Communist youth organization) or the Party. An individual's performance in this area influenced the distribution of perks and privileges, affecting professional advancement.

This has resulted in a deep mistrust of both formal and informal politics and collective engagement in the post-socialist period. For Lydia, the third sector provides a new way to reclaim or to rehabilitate voluntary social work.

In the course of our acquaintance, Lydia and I met frequently—in her tiny apartment or in the university library—to discuss local nongovernmental developments and the third sector. She was a wonderful source of local information and I was fascinated by her enthusiastic involvement in this world. What always struck me in her accounts was the intense sense-making process that she underwent and was still undergoing at the time of our conversations. Indeed, for Lydia, the third sector seemed to represent all that was good about civilized human nature. On one occasion, she astonished me by saying that "Chekhov was a man of the third sector." Later, in the course of an interview, I asked her to explain what she meant:

> It's a matter of character, that determines where a person chooses to put his energies—in business, bureaucracy, the state, or the third sector. What does it depend on? On old culture. There were probably people of this type even in Soviet times. Not to call it third sector, we never had such a sphere, but these were exactly the type of people who today would be people of the third sector because of their character. They are socially oriented, unselfish, accomplished. . . . We can take Chekhov as a particularly indicative person in this light. . . . I think it is possible to say that people by their very makeup can be in one way or the other material for the third sector.

She continued,

> I told you, I have a very interesting friend who works at the university. She is in charge of students' practice teaching sessions in schools. The phrase "third sector" never passed her lips; she's not interested in it as I am, because she's too busy. But by her very makeup and activity, by her selflessness, by the amount she puts into her work—nobody pays her money for it, she does it totally altruistically—she is for me a kind of ideal.

Here Lydia appropriates what she considers to be the best aspects of Russian culture and society in the name of the third sector. For Lydia, as for Olga Alekseeva, the author of the "For Dummies" text she had shown me, the third sector was a place where the best social instincts can meet and work together to make a difference, a site of moral and enlightened citizens' activity. However, unlike Olga Alekseeva, who appears to be addressing the public in general, Lydia's narrative expresses a great deal about her opinion of the correct role of a certain strata of society, the intelligentsia.[19] For Lydia, the best social instincts are located in the best of society. Hers is not a vision of regular folks (the "grassroots" in NGO-speak) pulling together. Rather, hers is a vision of an enlightened few acting as example and inspiration for others to follow, of an elite acting in the name of the people (narod).[20] Thus, the moralizing dimension of third sector discourse was appealing to her. Lydia's narrative and reclaiming of the category "intelligentsia" illustrates the negotiations between past and present that characterize post-socialist society (Burawoy and Verdery 1999; Grant 1999). Unlike Alekseeva, she does not emphasize the newness of the third sector. Rather, she uses "third sector" to reaffirm a set of values, an orientation that is widely perceived to be anachronistic. What is more, her interpretation of the third sector enables her to neutralize the fearful uncertainty of the present. In invoking Chekhov she summons up a timeless vision of Russian culture, according to which people like her have a secure role.

Lydia's imaginative engagement of the third sector helped her make sense of the changes she had been through and articulate a dignified way forward. She was not run down by *byt* (everyday life), or the drudgery of making money. Through engaging the third sector and debating it, she affirmed her own status as someone concerned with the big questions of social reform, with Russia's path of development, and as someone whose opinion mattered. But beyond this, the third sector was a very active project for her. Lydia really *lived* the third sector; it performed a kind of structuring role around which she had built a new life and routine. In addition to attending seminars and trainings through which she hoped she would gain tools and knowledge that would assist her in launching her own organization, she was engaged in an almost daily round of visits to friends and acquaintances, wherein she discussed the third sector and its manifestations and told them about the group she wanted to set up. Ultimately, Lydia was able to convert the moral capital she had generated into a more material form of power: on the basis of her third-sector portfolio, her formal qualifications, and her employment history, she was ultimately appointed director of a newly founded, government-funded Center for Women and Families in 1999. Her appropriation of the third sector assisted her in a kind of networking that eventually landed her a job.

In the fall of 1998, I joined Lydia in this project to make sense of the third sector. She introduced me to people engaged in societal work she thought I would be interested in; we began to attend the local meetings of societal groups, swapping our impressions. Lydia introduced me to the actually existing third sector—the new apparatus and technologies that were beginning to emerge in Tver' and to transform the *obshchestvennoe dvizhenie* (societal movement). And we shared materials: she shared her library with me, introducing me to key texts in the third sector; later on when I learned I had won a grant for my research I was able to pay her to collect newspaper articles on societal organizations and the third sector for me.[21] In return, I brought materials from trips to Moscow and other cities, switching her on to some of the resources offered through Moscow-based NGOs. She was excited to have me join her in her project. She associated me, a British woman, with the third sector despite my protestations that I understood it no better than she. After recounting her latest thoughts and updating me about the activities of other local organizations that we both knew, she would quiz me, asking questions such as "Is that how the third sector *should* be? Is this the *real* place of the third sector?" Although I could not provide satisfactory answers to these questions, I was compelled by her quest. Perhaps this was the collaborative project I yearned for?

The Humanitarian Institute

One day in December 1997 we attended a seminar together at the Humanitarian Institute, a third-sector support unit I had learned about not long after arriving in the city. The institute was registered as a societal (*obshchestvennaia*) organization, but it had received support from the city administration. It was situated in spacious, well-located offices in the center of town—the former offices of the *gorkom* (the city committee of the Communist Party), as I later learned. The Humanitarian Institute was one of the first (and few) recipients of international civil society funding in Tver'. Since the mid-1990s it had received several large grants from foundations such as TACIS (the EU program of Technical Assistance to the CIS) and Eurasia. Its raison d'être was to strengthen the local noncommercial sector, both by running trainings and seminars for members of local NGOs and by lobbying the local administration for support. Depending on the terms of the grant it was working under, seminars could be one- or two-day events or could be ongoing over a series of weeks.

I was aware that the Humanitarian Institute was contentious in the city, in large part due to the identity of its directors, a husband and wife team who commanded significant clout locally. Katya had been an active *komsomolka* (member of the Young Communist League); her husband Pavel was the former director of the Marxist-Leninist Institute, the municipal ideological center of the Communist Party, which was responsible for the dissemination of Party propaganda and the preparation of Party cadres. In 1992 what was once "Marxist-Leninist" became "Humanitarian," and the institute was swiftly privatized, to undertake a variety of new civil-society-friendly projects, including the dissemination of third-sector material. Research confirms that this move is typical of many noncommercial endeavors. Just as they have made easy transitions into business, those who thrived under the old state socialist regimes have proven to be adept at mastering the symbolic order of NGOs and projects (Sampson 1996). This trend has been compounded by the policy of many foundations, which have specifically sought to send members of the local and regional administrative elites abroad on training schemes. Katya is a graduate of the Johns Hopkins Third Sector Enablement Training program, where she spent several months, coming home with a diploma and a host of useful acquaintances with other NGO professionals, which in turn facilitated the networking back home that won the support of Moscow-based foundations.

As I rattled my way to the Humanitarian Institute on the trolleybus that day, I realized I had been there before: the building also housed the local newspaper where Lida, one of the Zhenskii Svet women, worked as a journalist. I had visited her there on a number of occasions to interview her about her work and her experience. Of Armenian descent, Svetlana and her husband had arrived in

Tver' as refugees, fleeing conflict in Azerbaijan some years previously. Both journalists, they had been fortunate and were able to find staff positions on local newspapers. They were poorly remunerated, but they were able to make a living and had a foothold in the city. As I entered the building on the first floor, I was struck by the contrast between the institute and the impoverished conditions in which my friend worked upstairs. The institute looked every inch the NGO: it had obviously been recently refurbished and had undergone what was known as *evroremont* (European-style renovation), and it was furnished with office chairs and a large meeting table. It was strikingly well equipped for its provincial circumstances and had several computers, printers, and a Xerox machine (all of which were conspicuously lacking in Lida's workplace).

Lydia introduced me to Katya, who met me graciously and introduced me to the facilitator of the seminar, Viktor, a NGO consultant from the provincial city of Vladimir. She explained that he was a graduate of the same Johns Hopkins program as she, that they used the same Johns Hopkins methodology (*metodika*) in their workshops. Viktor told me that he was a historian and worked at the museum in Vladimir; he continued to do this alongside his consulting work for the third sector.

This seminar, designed for the representatives of nongovernmental organizations, was one of a series offered under the auspices of a European grant. In addition to myself, there were six others present—all representatives of local societal groups and all women. As we sat down around the large conference table and the session began, I relaxed as I recognized the participatory format we were invited into. It was familiar to me from my participation in workshops in graduate school and in nonprofits. One by one, we introduced ourselves—me, the anthropologist conducting research on women's groups and civil society development; Marina, the director of a booklovers' club; a young woman representing an organization called "Sobriety," an organization that worked against alcoholism; Lena, who represented a club for the protection of homeless animals; Natalia, who explained she ran human rights seminars; Iulia, who worked at a children's day care; and Lydia, who introduced herself as a representative of her nascent women's group *Sovremenitsa* (Contemporary Woman).

The theme of the seminar was partnership (*partnerstvo*) in the third sector; partnership between spheres—that is, how societal organizations can work with each other, and find other partners in the media, businesses, the state legislature, and other organs of power. Viktor's facilitation style was gentle and respectful; he used the first person (*ia*) in his accounts, drew frequent examples from his own work in the museum in Vladimir, and coaxed the women participants into sharing their own experiences and ideas. We began by brainstorming about the qualities and behaviors ideally suited to holding negotiations. Together, with Viktor gently guiding us, we generated two lists, which he wrote in marker pen on a flipchart. Under the heading "Always Yes," we listed: delicacy, punctuality, flexibility, listen attentively. Under the heading "Never" we listed: be late, behave badly, make assumptions about someone on the basis of their nationality/family problems/place of residence. After we had reflected on these for a while, Katya gave us a model to consider—the pyramid. This, it appeared, was a key aspect of their methodology. The process proceeded in typical Western workshop fashion, with Katya interpreting the pyramid for us. "The pyramid can help us choose our partners," she said. "If we want to work with the city Duma (legislature) for example, we need to understand how it works, how it makes decisions."

After snacking on biscuits and drinking tea, we ended the session with a game. Viktor broke us into pairs, and asked us to address questions such as—how to select a partner, what can they offer us? what can we offer them? We then fed our ideas back to Viktor, to be written up in marker pen on the flipchart. Until this point, the women had been compliant, polite and respectful, good students. A couple of the women were old hands at the institute and had attended many seminars; they were keen to show their mastery of the terminologies and had been swift to give examples as requested. But here, things began to unravel. While participants had no difficulty in drawing up extensive wish lists (money, computers, office space), they were stuck when it came to the reciprocal relation. "They don't need us," my partner Vera muttered to me crossly. Viktor shook his head gently at this negativity, and wrote up the world "image" (*imidzh*) in red letters. "Politicians need to build an image for themselves," he told us, "to look good in the eyes of the community. You can offer them the opportunity to provide you with support."[22]

On my way home that day, I mused on the experience. I felt I better understood the appeal of the third sector after this. According to the model, the three sectors exist in a kind of harmony. The third sector, the space of citizens' initiatives, is able to count on support, and on *recognition,* from the other two (government and business). According to this logic, the third sector is a repository of human resources, a rich mine of skills, expertise, and energy, and therefore it is within the state's interests to call on it. Third sector thus offers a very dignifying formulation to its participants. The stance of an actor of the third sector is no longer that of a supplicant, accepting benefits from a paternal socialist state, but of a professional, negotiating for a contract on equal terms. According to the model of the third sector, community groups, associations, and clubs are integral to the workings of a healthy society. However, how realistic was it? The contradictions of the institute were obvious and plain.

The third sector message was undercut by the fact that its representatives, those who had gained access to the third sector and its resources, were members of the former elite, the former party-state. Viktor and especially Katya had won grants on the basis of already existing connections. The case of the Humanitarian Institute illustrates both the fluidity and dynamism of elite realignment and the continued importance of informal networks in the post-Soviet era. Contrary to their intention of creating new civil spaces, international foundations have reanimated old elites. Here, the *nomenklatura*[23]—a kind of Communist Party–approved management class—are able to draw upon cultural capital and *blat* connections generated under the old system (Ledeneva 1998; Rivkin-Fish 2005; Wedel 1998).[24] These informal connections—themselves a product of the Soviet shortage economy—are not eradicated, but transformed by the on-set of market relations (Ledeneva 1998; Rivkin-Fish 2005). From my participation in the seminar, I could see that there was considerable social distance between the trainers and the participants. Despite the participatory methods, Viktor's gentle facilitation style and the message of empowerment, there was a very definite division of labor in the third sector offered here—between the U.S.-trained experts, who put out the message, and the impoverished community groups (mostly made up of women) who were its consumers.

Finally, the message itself was problematic. As is true for other development technologies, the third sector is more than a simple technical model—a road map for civil society, a methodology to assist organizational development. The third sector is also a project of persuasion, a distinctly moralizing project that seeks to transform purportedly dependent and political passive Soviets into active citizens, savvy consumers, claimers of rights, and defenders of their interests. The notions of self-help and empowerment that it posits can be seen as "techniques of governance" that are both voluntary and coercive (Cruikshank 1999). Like other techniques, it has powerful subject effects, reshaping peoples' ideas and notions of what is possible, permissible, and desirable. In placing the emphasis on individuals, this model elides the importance of broader social and political conditions in structuring associational life. In Russia, there is no benign state agent waiting to collaborate with nongovernmental groups. At the local and federal level, the state is reluctant and suspicious of NGOs and reluctant to heed them. Although the conception of "partnership," or "social partnership" (*sotsial'noe partnerstvo*), did gain popularity in the late '90s and was embraced at the level of local governments, it was often used as a means to appropriate the "nonstate" sphere and to pass resources to insiders (Salmenniemi 2005). The state has become even less benign since 2003, when President Vladimir Putin began to signal his hostility to NGOs, particularly to those that receive foreign funding. Meanwhile, few of Russia's new business elite engage in philanthropic activities. Indeed, a few of those who have done so have been subject to harassment from state officials.[25] The problem with the third-sector formulation offered to activists in the 1990s was that in Russia there is no place to prepare people to go. People are talked into taking responsibility for themselves as individuals in the absence of structures that are assumed to exist; they are citizens in waiting.

Local Interpretations of the Humanitarian Institute

My account of the Humanitarian Institute confirms the consensus portrait of the new third sector that has been brought into being by Western-identified foundations. Rather than a naturally unfurling organic entity, the civil society of the third sector in Russia is a costly project, installed by Western design. Moreover, it is very different from the civil society that activists desired and donor agencies promised. It is a constrained place, shot through with new hierarchies and dependencies. While it claims to nurture the local and the grassroots, it enables a small circle of elites to flourish, many of whom were agents of the old party-state (Abramson 1999; Kalb 2002; Mandel 2002; Richter 1999; Sampson 1996). What is more, the third sector that is promoted and supported by foundations introduces a market logic and sensibility to nongovernmental activity. Activists have been forced to adopt an entrepreneurial idiom in order to survive in the world of grants and funding, where NGOs compete against each other for scarce resources. Meanwhile, most community groups are outside the loop and can only dream of involvement, or look on jealously.

In a study that assesses the impact of international assistance on the Russian women's movement, James Richter points to the fact that many of the larger foundations operating in Russia (such as Eurasia and Ford) prefer to create "resource centers" or clearinghouses, rather than funding lots of small projects. Secondly, control over grant funds is frequently placed in the hands of one person within the organization (Henderson 2003; Ishkanian 2003; Richter 1999; Sampson 1996). This concentration of material and intellectual resources provides an ideal opportunity for empire building, which is disillusioning to those outside the distribution networks.

Through my interactions with international agency representatives, I knew that the donor community was becoming aware of this situation. By 1997 there was a creeping sense that foundations had reinforced some of the very tendencies that they had sought to overcome. Political scientist Sarah Henderson, who worked as a consultant for the Ford Foundation while conducting her own research, mentions a 1994 Ford Foundation internal report on aid to the Russian women's movement that acknowledges the new hierarchies and rifts set in motion by the influx of grants and funding (Henderson 2003:137).[26] I was aware that other agencies were consulting Russian NGO activists to solicit their advice; indeed, I had witnessed this in Tver'. Some adjustments were made in response. For example, the Ford Foundation broadened its scope by supporting women's organizations in different regions of the Russian Federation that had different, less feminist and Western-oriented profiles. However, agency representatives were constrained by the conditions of their own work from doing much about it. For example, although Ford Foundation staff recognized the dangers of placing too much control in one pair of hands, the Foundation had only three program officers and could not administer multiple small grants. Agency representatives told me that it was more efficient to "trust" one individual or one central organization than to administer multiple small grants.[27]

However we choose to make sense of it, the strategy of working with small circles of trusted individuals certainly undermined the message foundations were selling. In Tver', the Humanitarian Institute, like other NGO support centers or clearinghouses I came across in my research, was contentious in the city and regarded with jealousy by members of other community groups. Rather than stimulating trust and social capital, it sowed distrust. I had picked up mixed messages about the institute prior to going there. Many of my acquaintances had known Katya for years as a *Komsomol* activist and in her subsequent guises. At the same time that they told me she was "*molodets*" (a smart woman) and conceded that she was doing some good work, they were skeptical of the utility of her project for other organizations. Some of my informants told me they were disenchanted with the Humanitarian Institute because it contradicted its own claims. Although it advertised itself as a regional resource center for the noncommercial sector, it was not truly open. Irina, the director of a small women's group, told me that she was always put off when she called, either by being told to call back or to make an appointment. This offended her because it contravened local norms of polite behavior, and because it contradicted the center's own claims to openness. Indeed, from talking to Katya and her staff, I learned that training sessions and seminars were available only to members of officially registered organizations, sometimes only on a competitive basis. This precluded the participation of interested persons or groups that had not yet formalized, or did not wish to do so, by registering with the state. Crucially, there was a perception that information intended for local groups was actually withheld from them. In the course of my fieldwork, I heard numerous accounts of Katya's unwillingness to distribute her resources, and one story that circulated was that one of her frequent attendees had consulted with someone to ask, "*Is it possible* to apply for a grant without Katya Viktorovna?" Contra Putnam's assumption that social capital is widely accessible, the social capital that was generated by the institute and its activities was perceived to be concentrated in her hands.

These skeptics were highly dubious about the new science of the third sector regarding it as a new and self-serving ideology. As one of my informants said of Katya, "Although (she) speaks about charity, what she's really doing is taking care of herself. It's a new way to build a career and create a job for herself." This skeptical take on third-sector activity parallels intelligentsia constructions of the Soviet division of labor, whereby capable specialists were forced to work under the didactic instruction of bureaucrats and party workers who make up and enforce unnecessary rules. Informants who were not aligned with the third sector had a stock of tales to recount about its absurd manifestations, and in the course of my research I heard numerous ironic commentaries about the newly minted skills and technologies of the third sector, the glossy certificates that are issued to participants of training programs and workshops, and those who are captivated by them and relate to them without irony. These were groups that would announce, proclaim, and use third sector terminologies with abandon, in ways that defied comprehension, advertising themselves and the services they purported to provide, and taking up considerable space in the local papers.

What to make of the Humanitarian Institute and this contention? On one level, this example illustrates the complex ways in which the third sector reinforces old networks and hierarchies and enables the reproduction of old dependencies (Bruno 1997; Mandel 2002; Sampson 2001; Wedel 1998). It reproduces what Verdery has called "socialist paternalism" (1996:24), where old elites prosper and regular folks are kept busy guessing at the logic of their power. As anthropologist Daphne Berdahl puts it, "The interplay between above and below, between the known and the unknown, between the state and its citizens was crucial in sustaining the socialist system in East Germany" (Berdahl 1999:46). But my point is neither to denounce the institute, nor to imply as my informants did that it signaled no change. From participant observation—attending seminars, speaking with other participants—I can assert that the center largely did what it was supposed to do, disseminating third-sector literature and running seminars to the extent that granting agencies required. From conversations with agency staff, I learned that in privileging groups with which it had a formal relationship, the institute was only obeying donor agency requirements.[28] However, this logic was not clear to local activists. Contention about the Humanitarian Institute attests to local awareness of the contradiction between the third sector ideal and its social reality. They knew that unless a group was already well resourced and connected and had a material base from which to launch community initiatives and grant applications, it was unlikely to succeed. Rather than condemn the message, however, local activists condemned the messenger. Their third-sector critique was highly personalized, focusing on Katya and the symbolic and material resources she had been able to accrue.

Lydia was torn in her assessment. Although she acknowledged that Katya was a quite different type of person from herself—in terms of both her temperament and her Communist Party background—she admired her for what she had been able to achieve. She told me that she had been to a number of Katya's seminars and got a lot from them. "Nothing spiritual" (*nichego dushevnogo*), she explained, but she had received valuable pragmatic advice, for example information about setting up an NGO, management, and fundraising. In her opinion the institute was really a business center, despite being registered as a noncommercial organization. Indeed, she told me that Katya herself acknowledged this and had once said, "Societal organizations are also a kind of business" (*obshestvennye organizatsii—eto tozhe biznes*).

While Lydia generally disapproved of this formulation—she was quite clear that the third sector was more than business—she wanted in. More than most of the women in the group, Lydia wanted to see Zhenskii Svet formalize and have more to do with the third sector. She was eager to get her own women's project, a crisis center to combat economic violence and sexual discrimination in the workplace, off the ground and was beginning to look around for support. She showed me a copy of another how-to book widely circulated by international agencies, "How to Set up and Manage a Women's Crisis Center," and wanted me to find out about grants and possibilities for funding. Since I had never met the other women in her group—despite my repeated requests, it had never worked out; Lydia explained to me that the women were too busy—I was a little hesitant. It had become clear to me by then that like many societal organizations, this group met rarely. In this case, a group had formed when women came together in solidarity over the specific circumstances of their job loss. Once a support group that provided significant psychological and practical assistance to each other, it now had little life. I wasn't sure I was appropriately positioned to work with them on a project such as this. However, I was eager to work with her and agreed to do it.

Valentina's Views

As I pondered my way during those early months, Valentina was an important interlocutor for me. She had a critical perspective on the third sector. Unlike many of the women activists I spoke with who asserted that civil society was the same thing as third sector, she saw them to be quite different and distinctive. Civil society had been a key term for her at the outset of her activity; like many of the pioneering activists of the late 1980s and early 1990s she had used the term to explain and articulate her activity. One day in 1999, during one of my return trips to the city, as we sat reminiscing about the early days and the changes Zhenskii Svet had gone through, Valentina pulled out the founding document she had written in 1991 to show me. It stated that the purpose of Zhenskii Svet is to "contribute to the development of civil society." As she read from the document, she smiled—"Nobody knew that term at the time," implying its current fashionable status.

Like Lydia, she had come across the concept of the third sector when local organizations like the Humanitarian Institute began winning grants and then running training programs in its name. Although she was also interested in watching it percolate, the model or idea of the third sector did not resonate with her as it did with Lydia. I attributed this in part to scholarly skepticism about the new NGO methodologies and about the swiftly minted diplomas and credentials that were distributed to traveling Russians on democracy-promoting programs, which I think she and many other women I spoke with regarded as little more than prestigious souvenirs. When I shared my analysis with her in July 2004, she had the following commentary to add: at this time (1997) she did not see her activism as "work" or as professional activity that should be remunerated. Rather, she explained that she regarded this as activity that should take place after the workday was finished—her preferred terms were "voluntarism," "enthusiasm," or *liubitel'stvo* (amateur activity). She told me that she had experienced a certain "psychological discomfort" with the term "third sector," because it seemed "commercial" and "technical"; it suggested a sphere that she did not feel ready to participate in. Expressed from the vantage point of her professional feminist activism in 2004, this commentary spoke powerfully of the rapidity of change—and how cultural logics of money, morality, and labor were transformed rapidly through the NGO sector. What was puzzling in 1997 made perfect sense in 2004. What captivated me most at the time was her powerful critique of the effects of international funding: she felt that the bureaucratization that took place in the third sector, and which third sector represented, excluded or marginalized the people who were doing valuable community work.

Between us, "third sector" became shorthand for the troubling changes occurring in Russian non-governmental activity. However, it became clear to me that our critiques had different roots. My critique stemmed from my position-ality as a U.S.-based anthropologist, concerned with culture and power. As an anthropologist, I looked at the inappropriateness of technologies, the clashes with local conditions and realities; I was critical of the lack of regard for local knowledge that so often accompanied the importing of Western models (Hann and Dunn 1996). I focused on the political economy of the third sector and the contradictions of the third-sector model, where talk of charity and voluntarism worked hand in glove with the violence of neoliberal capitalism. And I was pre-occupied by a central paradox: in Russia, in the aftermath of socialism's col-lapse, it had become almost impossible to talk about material rights and justice for fear of being branded Communist. Valentina's critique was different, emerg-ing from her positionality as a highly educated member of the *intelligentsiia* who had been opposed to the Soviet regime and was committed to democratic projects for social renewal. She was interested in the use and applicability of Western concepts and remained deeply convinced of the potential for good in the East-West encounter. Although critical of the processes she saw unfolding, she was not unreflexively critical of grant-making bodies or their representa-tives. Like most of the women activists I encountered in my research, she in-sisted that she would much rather trust a U.S. or European partner organization than "our authorities!" (*nasha vlast'!*). And unlike some of the critical recipients of democratization aid whose accounts I had read, she did not speak in terms of colonization or neocolonialism.[29] Indeed, she shuddered at the anticapitalist language adopted by the elderly representatives of the Communist party, who gathered regularly under the statue of Lenin downtown and who held the only anti-IMF placards I ever saw in the city. She was angry at the frequent condem-nation of U.S. financiers in the press, such as the newspaper article that was published in one of the local papers while I was in the city denouncing billion-aire philanthropist George Soros. Through his Open Society Institute, Soros was one of the most active donors in post-socialist states. He funded higher educa-tion through the 1990s, supporting universities and institutes and providing small grants to individual academics.[30] Valentina insisted that Soros's money kept Tver' State University afloat and pointed to the hypocrisy of the author of the article, a university professor who, it later emerged, had himself accepted one of these individual grants. She saw in these critiques shards of the old pa-rochial, reactionary anti-Western ideology that she loathed. Valentina's cri-tique of the third sector was not of aid per se, but of what she viewed as its unintended effects. Specifically, she was concerned about the ways the third-sector model and aid more broadly interacted with and reinforced previously existing structures and mentalities.

As I have explained, Valentina founded Zhenskii Svet out of a desire to challenge Soviet-era formality and bureaucratism. Her feminism was an "anti-political" kind of a formulation; Zhenskii Svet was a project of enlightenment, to encourage self-realization (*samorealizatsiia*) and to free the individual from the psychological bonds of state socialism (where their basic material needs had been met in return for political passivity). She insisted that the third sector stifled this spirit by unintentionally reproducing or reinforcing Soviet-era tendencies and elements of the Soviet state. She told me she was concerned about the effects of the third sector, pointing to the fact that foundations compound the reflex of passivity that she called "the socialist syndrome"—that is, of waiting to be given rather than going out and doing. In her view, foundations step into the slot vacated by the Soviet state, occupying the same structural position and affecting people's psychology. I asked her to explain what she meant. As she put it, "Under socialism, we went to the government and asked for and received funds. Now we go to foundations. It's the same process, the same psychology. Capitalism or socialism—what's the difference?" She sighed. "We used to live from Party congress to Party congress, but now we live from grant deadline to grant deadline!" In sum, Valentina saw that the "third sector" acted as a brake on women's community initiatives—encouraging them to look instead for solutions outside themselves. For her, the third sector came to symbolize the formation of a class of professionals who become guardians of a new type of knowledge, where the information flow and the consciousness-raising process she regarded as essential stopped, and failed to reach people.

As an example, she pointed to Marina, one of the young women who had briefly attended Zhenskii Svet and whom she had mentored. Marina and I had met at the Humanitarian Institute seminar, and I had been impressed by her description of her activities (human rights work). Valentina shook her head sadly when I told her about this; she was familiar with Marina's ideas, but told me that they remained a plan. She told me that Marina "refuses to do anything until she has won a grant. I've told her—you have to start, put time, energy in, otherwise you have no experience and won't win a grant. But she refuses. I suggested she take part in (our) seminars on women's leadership, but she didn't show up. I suggested she take over Anya's [free] legal consultancy work while she's away. She said, we can't, we can't do anything until we have some money."

Valentina's comments about the stifling effects of the third sector proved to be prophetic. Around this time, Lydia and I had begun to work on a UNIFEM grant application to provide resources for her nascent "crisis center." Violence against women was emerging as a central plank of donor priorities, and agencies were eager to encourage women's groups to undertake this work. Lydia's project to provide support for unemployed women appeared to fit their rubric. I picked up the forms and we threw ourselves into the endeavor of grant writing. Since the forms required English language applications and I was a native speaker, I took on the bulk of writing, glad to be able to apply the skills I had learned in graduate school productively. However, after several days of running back and forth and badgering our friends for data of existing plans and projects, I realized my mistake. I had produced a long, impressive-looking document about which I began to feel very uneasy. There was a gulf between the product (the grant application) and our actual conditions; although Lydia had a plan, a conception, her group was elusive and amorphous. Further, I was not integrated into it and would be leaving the city in six months. Seduced by the third sector, we had reproduced the troubling tendencies it encouraged.

The third sector offers a good site from which to rethink the forms and logic of political activism encouraged by international development agencies in the post–Cold War period. Donor support has led to the proliferation of NGOs in Russia, groups that undertake diverse activities. However, this version of civil society is very different from what activists hoped for and agencies promised. Rather than being a realm of debate and discussion, the third sector is an institutionalized sphere, peopled by professionals and elites, beyond the reach of most local groups. Further, it has troubling effects. The third sector actively ushers women's groups into an unsatisfying division of labor, whereby they are made responsible for the reproduction of society, rather than questioning its development. In curious ways, at the same time as they reeducate and stimulate new values (self-help, self-reliance, participation), foundations reinforce aspects of the old system, as a number of insiders, including Valentina, have pointed out (Abubikina and Regentova 1995; Pitsunova 1998). However, moving beyond some of the polarized discussions that tend to regard NGOs as either "good" (liberatory social movements, evidence of "globalization from below") or "bad" (elite and fatally compromised by their complicity with neoliberal restructuring), I have shown that the good and bad are intertwined and interdependent. It is important to add that without foreign assistance, nongovernmental groups and the people they serve would not be able to survive. This is especially true in 2005, when President Vladimir Putin is making increasingly bellicose pronouncements against NGOs, especially those engaged in "political" activity. Moreover, despite its shortcomings, the idea of the third sector remains compelling to local actors. Third sector has become an important part of the imaginary repertoire of Russian activists; it is a site of contestation and sense-making between money and morality, state and society. The next chapter shifts to explore democratization aid and civil society promoting projects from another angle. Picking up on the themes laid out in this chapter, I explore what "NGO-ization" has meant to Russian women's groups.

3   Gender Mainstreaming and the Third-Sectorization of Russian Women's Activism

> What can be legitimately political depends neither on people's perceptions of inequality nor on the wherewithal to organize, important though these are. It depends on what identities and activities can count as part of the public in various historical versions of a civil society.
>
> (Gal 1997:42)

Before I moved to Tver' in September 1997, I spent two months in Moscow, renewing my acquaintance with women activists I first met in 1995 when I began the project of mapping Russian women's NGOs. This gave me the opportunity to explore the effects of third-sector grants and funding on the women's movement. During this period I visited most of the main women's NGOs in Moscow and interviewed their directors and some of their staff. These activists were Valentina's peers, women with whom she was at least peripherally acquainted. Many of them had been involved in the first forums of the independent women's movement at Dubna, and in the early 1990s they found themselves on the frontline of engagement with donor agencies. Agencies such as the Ford Foundation and the MacArthur Foundation, which arrived in Russia in the early '90s, established their headquarters in Moscow. They had a new mandate to support women's groups and sought them out. Foundation representatives were particularly glad to make the acquaintance of highly educated, Western-oriented feminist women such as these, and invited them into the first collaborations.

I spent most of the time with one women's NGO, an information center, situated in a four-story building in a Moscow neighborhood about a one-hour journey by Metro from the center. This organization was one of the earliest beneficiaries of foreign aid; it had received a large grant from the Ford Foundation in 1992 after the second Dubna forum. Like the Humanitarian Institute in Tver', it had become a kind of clearinghouse, a resource center specifically for the women's movement. Its primary role was to collect and disseminate information (about grants, conferences, events, and activities of other women's groups), and to encourage the expansion of the Russian women's movement through distributing grants and running seminars on topics such as women's leadership, networking, and NGO development. Twice a week I made the hour-and-a-half journey on the Metro across the huge city from my apartment in the north to the comfortable, well-equipped offices where the organization was housed. Once there, I helped staff translate documents from English to Russian. Often these were electronic bulletins pertaining to new transnational campaigns; sometimes these were draft grant applications that needed to be translated into English. This offered me a good vantage point on the contemporary women's movement, or at least, that part of it which had close links with foundations and donor organizations. Although I never became as intimate with these women as with my friends in Tver', we had warm relations. Indeed, when they learned that I was supporting myself in the city by tutoring English, a small group of these women activists hired me to give weekly English language conversation classes. I maintained these relationships after I moved to Tver' and throughout my fieldwork, returning to the center fairly regularly. As the nature of my work in the city became apparent, the center women accepted me as a representative of Zhenskii Svet (jokingly referring to me as a *provintsial'ka*—a provincial woman). They greeted me as Valentina's envoy and asked me to carry materials back to her—brochures, newsletters, and other publications they put out. As our crisis center project got off the ground, they provided useful clues and tips about funding sources and helped us make contact with people.

Through my time at the center, I got to know what aid and the third sector meant to Moscow-based activists and how it had transformed their activities. At first glance, it looked great. Surely these women were "activists without borders," to draw on Margaret Keck and Katherine Sikkink's influential account (1998),[1] successful pioneers, testimony to the new freedoms and scope for political action post-1989. However, once again I found that this success was a source of ambivalence and that the move from activist to third sector insider entailed some uncomfortable shifts in identification. These women straddled complex sets of relationships, between foundations, international NGOs, and their sister groups in the provinces. Although sitting pretty in material terms, many of the women I spoke with chafed under the terms of engagement with foundations. The logic of foundation support was such that groups quite simply could not afford not to participate in major campaigns. Although they might have been skeptical about some of the campaigns, they were drawn in as evaluators, trainers, or grant administrators. Many of my interlocutors in elite Moscow women's organizations clearly felt less empowered and in control ("activists beyond borders") than baffled and confused. They struggled to master the new codes, uncertain of the appropriateness and efficacy of their activity. Rather than unconstrained by boundaries, they felt locked into a very uncertain environment and trapped in new relations of dependency, where the paymasters who facilitated their activity (by providing both material resources and protection) might move away at any time.[2]

Ambivalent Insiders

Maria was one of my key interlocutors at the center; I worked with her most regularly and we became friends. She is a veteran activist of the women's movement and first became active in the late '80s when a feminist discussion group set up in her institute. It was made up of women who were both excited about the potential for reform and concerned with the processes of socioeconomic change and their impact on women. Maria had worked at the center since it was founded, commuting daily to Moscow from her home in a nearby provincial city. Since attending the Fourth UN Conference on the Status of Women in Beijing in 1995, she had been very active on the international feminist circuit and frequently traveled abroad to represent the organization at the invitation of various groups working on women's issues. In Moscow, a good proportion of Maria's work involved sifting through the various electronic bulletins from international women's organizations, selecting materials to translate and disseminate to groups in the regions. Frequently baffled by the kinds of issues raised, she occasionally asked me to assist her in translating some of the key terms that would pop up (such as "sustainability," "grassroots"; one of our favorites was a campaign to issue women "passports for dignity"). One day, as we sat together at her computer, she turned to me with a grimace: "I have a master's degree and I know two foreign languages, but I live in a two-room apartment with my two sons, husband, and mother-in-law and have no hot water. Am I a grassroots woman?" This term, which she associated with rural, third-world contexts, did not seem appropriate to Russia or to her life. We would laugh hilariously at some of the mismatches between the rhetoric of transnational campaigns and of foundation mandates and Russian reality, and on occasion I assured her that some of the project-speak was incomprehensible to native speakers of English, too. She was familiar with the guiding principles of the development industry, knew them far better than I, and would tell me about the latest trends as she understood them, particularly after her trips abroad to attend meetings of international NGOs.

At the same time that she had mastered the rhetoric, however, she was uncomfortable with her role and frustrated with the exercise of translation. Her job required her to be deft in learning key words and concepts, to pick them up, apply them in grant applications, and explain them to other activists in seminars. However, she was skeptical about their utility and applicability. Through our conversations, she developed an interest in cultural anthropology. She told me that she felt like an anthropologist, trying to find her way around in this new field. Through her narratives, I got a sense of the changes that the women's movement had experienced in the course of the last decade. Her position meant long hours, working to deadline, and a sense of tremendous responsibility (the "social responsibility" of the third-sector rhetoric), as well as some guilt at being (relatively) handsomely remunerated. She was uneasily aware of the gulf that had opened up between herself and her colleagues and local women's groups. While she sat in a comfortable, well-equipped office and drew a hard currency salary, her colleagues in the provinces and friends from her hometown struggled to meet local problems with a chronic lack of resources. Disparities such as these had led to a breakdown of solidarities within the women's movement. Once when I asked her about her relationship with regional affiliates, she replied, thoughtfully, "Basically it's good, but I receive a salary and they don't. I swing between a guilt complex and being confident in what I am doing."

In the course of our conversations, I listened to her struggle between the two identifications that her work entailed—women's movement activist and third-sector worker. They were frequently in conflict. Like many of the activists I spoke to, Maria was nostalgic about the earlier phase of women's activism before foundations had arrived and begun to sponsor their activity. She told me that for her, the first Dubna forum represented an attempt to create a new solidarity among women. The independent forums marked a commitment to egalitarian, nonhierarchical relations between women. It was a time of easy exchanges, she told me, when women were willing to travel to other cities to lead seminars, to attend group meetings, "to get to know each other, not as 'trainers' or 'big sisters' but as equals." This was over. She now found herself engaged in a bureaucratic and constrained type of activism that was shot through with new hierarchies. In essence she had become a gatekeeper of third-sector resources. During my biweekly visits to her office I had numerous occasions to pursue this topic with Maria and her co-workers. As we sat drinking tea and eating cookies, or the fruit that they brought from their *dachas* (country houses), I asked them what they thought about the changes brought about by collaboration with foundations. I found these women struggling to make sense of their new environment, puzzling to understand the role of the third sector and its implications, and to figure out the often contradictory roles that foundations played. They told me that although foundations were ostensibly committed to ideals they shared, their policies frequently undercut these ideals. Some of the women said they were disturbed and frustrated by the fact that agendas were set outside, in Washington. They commented on the fact that issues such as domestic violence and trafficking became "fashionable," regardless of what was happening on the ground, and how their ability to maintain themselves depended upon keeping abreast of international currents.

In June 1998 I returned to Moscow from Tver' in order to attend a training seminar at the center. It was attended by about twenty women from different cities in the Russian Federation, representatives of women's groups that were part of their network. The office was transformed, crowded with new black office chairs. Maria and her colleagues facilitated the seminar, coaching the provincial women representatives in the technologies of organizational development (to write grants, keep accounts, write reports). Watching them, I could see that they were clearly invested in what they were doing and sincerely wanted to support these fledgling organizations. Yet behind the scenes, I heard them question the terms and concepts that guided their activities. Maria said to me, "Sometimes I think that it's just an economic game! We will never be able to figure out the aims of the foundations, what drives their policy." She continued, "Maybe the third sector and nongovernmental sphere are just a load of rubbish (*erunda*)?! What's the difference between this and business? We all pretend we know what the third sector is, and where we are going, but maybe it's not true! Maybe this is just professionalization! All we have is speculation, slogans—like civil society! What is it? Why is it any different from business?" Our English language lessons provided me with a further opportunity to pursue these topics with them. On one occasion, we read anthropologist Susan Gal's text on the gendered nature of the concept of civil society (1997); Maria and her colleagues were enamored of her critique and decided to devote a seminar to the topic.

In the course of our acquaintance, I witnessed Maria seesawing between these positions. She was still moved by the language of civil society and captivated by its promise; at the same time she was troubled by its social reality. In late spring 1998, I met with Maria shortly after her return from a meeting in New York. She told me she was inspired by the levels of cooperation she had witnessed between NGOs of other countries, particularly by the work of an African coalition that worked to find strategies to combat structural adjustment, and she wished that Russian NGOs could make similar alliances in order to better put pressure on the government. She told me that upon her return she had brought this issue up with colleagues within the women's movement and that most of them responded with amazement at her idealism. One woman said to her, "What are you talking about? A grant is money, and as soon as a person receives money, becomes the director of a project, she forgets about feminist principles! Principles are in conflict with this activity! We can't live on values! While I have no money, it doesn't matter what I do, nobody hears me. It's only when we have a budget that people start to respect us." They pooh-poohed her suggestion that alliances should be formed on the basis of trust, saying, "Trust? Trust in what? We need to be professionals!" She added, thoughtfully, "It's difficult to argue with their point of view. . . . Democracy—is just a slogan! In Russia the word is discredited, is taken to mean a free-for-all, the freedom to do what you like without any obligations or responsibility. Even politicians barely use the word any more."

What to make of Maria's predicament? How did she come to be in such an ambivalent position? Maria's situation typifies the form and logic of political activism encouraged at Cold War's end. She is the beneficiary of a new global infrastructure for women's activism that set up since 1989, a node in a complex architecture that links women's NGOs with UN conference and donor agencies. The contradictions she experiences typify the logic of this new form of activism that anthropologist Annelies Riles has characterized as "network politics." The network form took off after the 1985 UN conference on women, when funds were channeled into creating networks in preparation for Beijing; the network was the "official organizational form" for the parallel NGO forum (Riles 2001:48). Networks (in this case, networks of women's NGOs) claim to advance the interests of the grassroots; however, in Riles's depressing characterization they are "closed" and purposeless. In her account, network activity is a "means to an end and an end in itself" (2001:51). Information and resources "flow" through organizations or individuals who are essentially passive and have little scope to influence the content or direction of their work.

In many ways, Maria looks like a consummate network insider. However, she departs from Riles's characterization in key ways. The Fijian nationals who staff the women's NGOs Riles examines appear to be unconcerned about "women" or "gender" except as bureaucratic categories, distanced from activism and local concerns. Perhaps due to the fact that Russian women's activism is so new and is in an earlier phase of network integration, Maria is still very much engaged, as my account shows. She is aware of and concerned by the contradictions of her activism and still struggles to make "gender" matter. She did her very best to use the resources her job afforded her to be responsive to local groups' needs and tried to direct her critical observations to foundation representatives. As we got to know each other better, she told me about a paper she was writing and directing to one of the representatives of a U.S. foundation, which raised a series of critical questions about their policies. She yearned for the opportunity to take time out from her work to do research and write up her reflections. The next section traces how she came to be in this position of ambivalence. In Russia, perhaps unlike in Latin America or other global contexts, the story of network integration is not a story of the cooptation of the grassroots. Feminism in Russia has always been a form of elite identification, and the local and the global have always been mutually constituting in Russian constructions of feminism.

"Gender" and Russia

As I have explained in the previous chapter, civil society discourses suggest that social groups and interests would naturally rise up and express themselves once the socialist state collapsed. It was assumed that women's groups would follow the same trajectory. This assumption was manifest in the policy documents of foundations and donor agencies. In the words of a USAID report, "In many countries, women's voices are still not as powerful as men's. . . . However, civil society offers a very powerful means of overcoming constraints and promoting women's comparable collaboration in decision-making" (cited in Henderson 2003:91). However, to the consternation of many North American and Western European feminist scholars and activists, in Russia as in other post-socialist states this did not occur. Although there were small pockets of women activists organizing independently, this did not have a mass character and was regarded with skepticism by most people. To recall the quotation from Susan Gal that I began the chapter with, "What can be legitimately political depends neither on people's perceptions of inequality nor on the wherewithal to organize, important though these are. It depends on what identities and activities can count as part of the public in various historical versions of a civil society" (1997:42). Women's organizing only assumed a mass character in the mid-'90s; this took place as the so-called democratic and liberalizing reforms generated new gendered forms of marginalization and social exclusion in Russia.

For the historical reasons I have outlined in the introduction, the state socialist gender regime was distinct from that of liberal democratic states. In state socialism, gender was not politicized as it is in liberal democracies: crucially, there was no perception of gender discrimination. Gender was certainly politicized, but in a different way. Gender arrangements were a source of dissatisfaction, but this dissatisfaction was directed at the socialist state for its perverse form of social engineering, which had supposedly emasculated men and *over-emancipated* women (Gray 1989; Tolstaya 1990).

This lack of fit was immediately striking to me as I began my research. I found that mention of my topic (Russian women's activism) drew blank stares or barely suppressed incredulity among my Russian friends who were not associated with NGOs. Despite the shifts that concerned Western feminist scholars, they viewed the gendered reforms of the period (extended maternity care, legislation that encouraged women out of the workplace) as the righting of Communist-era perversions. Talk of the women's movement and women's oppression smacked of Soviet-era rhetoric, mandated political involvement, and the quota system and recalled official ("artificial") women's political structures.

So Who Were the First Women's Groups?
Phase One: Dissident-Era Feminism

Given these adverse conditions, who were the first independent women's activists who greeted foundations when they arrived in the early 1990s? What motivated them and what did they hope to achieve? In the late socialist period, "gender" and other terms and concepts of Western feminism came to make sense to a small group of Russian women—the highly educated academic women like Maria and Valentina. They ultimately spearheaded efforts to form a women's movement and played a pivotal role in liaising with foundations and bringing these gendered interventions to Russia.

The stirrings of what is now referred to as the second wave of Russian feminism began in the late 1970s and early '80s and is associated with the period of dissidence that resulted from the Khrushchev "thaw." During this period, some women journalists and writers began to document their own lives, in ways that contradicted the official representation of Soviet womanhood. The first feminist *samizdat* publication was the journal *Al'manakh: Zhenshchinam o Zhenshchinakh,* edited by Tatyana Mamonova, which circulated in dissident circles in Leningrad in 1979; it dealt with issues such as discrimination against women in politics, abortion, the appalling conditions in maternity hospitals and women's prisons, violence against women, issues that officially did not exist in the USSR (Marsh 1996:286).[3]

Like other forms of dissident writing (poetry, fiction) that questioned official ideology, this work was suppressed, and the editors were imprisoned, then exiled to the West. But as state socialism unraveled, feminism sprang new shoots, again in very elite and marginal circles. In research establishments and institutes, a few scholars gained access to feminist literature; though not available to the general public, English-language editions of feminist texts could be found in *spetskhrany,* closed archives of main libraries. Some young women scholars, mostly based in prestigious research establishments in Moscow or St. Petersburg, were given the freedom to write dissertations on women's issues (Posad-skaya 1994:10). As I have explained, Valentina was one of these pioneers. With the support of her advisor, she traveled from Tver' to Moscow twice a week, sat in the library, and took notes from English language editions of feminist texts— *Sexual Politics* by Kate Millet, Juliet Mitchell's *Women's Estate*.

Thus far, this portrait is perhaps unexpected from a Western feminist per-spective. Feminism did not appeal because it spoke to a sense of gender-based "discrimination." Indeed, this early interest in feminism (and the ability to pur-sue it) was the project of an urban, mostly Moscow-based, well-connected privi-leged few.[4] Feminism and "gender" came to make sense to this small and specific group of women for distinct reasons.

Feminism represented a vital way of reconnecting with progressive European thought and debates, through literature and personal connections. Indeed, for many scholars feminism and interest in women's activism provided an oppor-tunity to reexamine Russia's role in European history. Many scholars I came across were interested in prerevolutionary Russian women's activism, particu-larly the work of early Russian suffragists, who were active on the international stage and very much in touch with German and English feminists.[5]

Although it drew on Western feminist texts and concepts for inspiration, this late-Soviet feminism differed from second-wave U.S. and Western European feminism in significant ways. It was a distinct, antipolitical project that focused less on structure than on the individual achieving internal (psychic) change, often expressed as "self-realization," or "freeing the personality." Early groups focused on consciousness-raising. By this, they aimed to effect change first within themselves, and then they hoped to be able to bring about moral change in society. And this feminism was directed less against men, or a patriarchy, than the Soviet state.[6] For example, the complaints raised by the writers of the women's almanac about women's position in society were leveled at the state (for its shortage economy, which did not provide tampons), not at men or a pa-triarchy leaving aside the issue that it was clearly a male-dominated state. To the extent to which they did protest men, it was a protest against Soviet man—the weakened, effete, pathetic creature that the state had supposedly brought into being.

An example may help to illuminate this. One of my women's movement ac-quaintances in St. Petersburg had been active in dissident circles in the late 1970s and 1980s. As I asked her about those early years, she recalled her first attempt at translating an article for *samizdat*. Like many others who opposed the state, she had carved out a marginal but comfortable existence for herself in the cracks of the system. Working as a caretaker, she spent her days reading and translating German and English language literature. She would join her male colleagues in beer and vodka parties, happily one of the boys, and was active in dissident circles in her spare time. She told me she was terribly anxious about the quality of her first translation—would it be good enough for her peers? However, while the translation made the grade, the subject matter was met with derision. She had chosen to translate an article about feminism. What struck me as I listened to her was that she had so clearly not expected this. Although she was concerned about the quality of her work, it had not occurred to her that the subject matter would give rise to any objections.

Although extremely marginal in the Soviet Union, this feminist activity caused great excitement in the United States and Western Europe. Mamonova, virtually unknown in the USSR, was touted as the leader of an unofficial neo-feminist movement and toured the United States sponsored by *Ms.* magazine in 1980. She made contact with women's groups and lectured widely on the position of Soviet women; her first post-exile publication, *Russian Women's Studies: Essays on Sexism in Soviet Culture* (1988), included an enthusiastic back-cover blurb from Gloria Steinem.[7] But these expectations were not and could not be realized. Like other dissidents, these Soviet feminists did not represent a nascent civil society waiting to rise up and engage in civic activities and democracy. They were small circles and did not have broad legitimacy. Beyond this, they didn't necessarily want to expand beyond this into a movement. While second-wave U.S. and European women's movements were driven by a desire to achieve solidarity among women, the dissident or "antipolitical" Russian feminism was expressive of a *denial* of a specific form of collective identity in favor of embracing the individual. These scholars and writers combined an interest in feminism with a marked distaste toward mass politics. Their feminism was profoundly non-mobilizational, and few groups were truly open to newcomers.

Phase Two: Democratization, the Re-politicization of Gender and the Emergence of the Russian Independent Women's Movement

Democratization is a time not of the discovery, but the creation of women's otherness.

(Watson 1997:28)

This next phase of Russian women's activism has been extremely well documented by U.S.- and Western Europe–based feminist researchers (Bridger , Kay, and Pinnick 1996; Buckley 1992; Einhorn 1993; Kay 2000; Sperling 2000). It was marked by the catastrophic worsening of the position of women as a group and by the emergence of an independent women's movement. Here, I tell my version of this story, emphasizing the role of the highly educated feminist-oriented brokers.

As scholars of post-socialism have noted, the reforms and democratizing transformations that took place at this time had a markedly gendered character (Gal and Kligman 2000; Einhorn 1993; Watson 1997). In the Soviet Union and Eastern Europe, state-socialist gender arrangements and policies were overturned in a series of legislative moves. At the same time that he spoke of stimulating civil society and empowering the citizenry, General Secretary Mikhail S. Gorbachev enacted a series of reforms that encouraged women to move out of the public sphere to fulfill what he famously called their "purely womanly mission" as homemakers (Pilkington 1992). Maternity leave was extended and protective workplace restrictions to women were brought into being. Barring isolated feminist critiques, these reforms had broad support in Soviet society, and this consensus continued into the post-perestroika period. The breakup of the Soviet Union in 1991 and the introduction of neoliberal economic reforms accelerated these gendered processes. Democratic and market-oriented reforms hit women doubly hard. They lost both jobs and welfare provision through structural adjustment. What is more, since women remained responsible for the bulk of domestic work (cooking, cleaning, shopping, child care), the burden of coping with the consequences of these policies (increased prices of food, goods, and services) fell largely on their shoulders.

While women as a group were marginalized and impoverished by market reforms, and at the same time feminist ideas were met with popular hostility, some feminist scholars were propelled into a new and intimate relationship with the state.[8] As women were excluded from the public sphere, new federal and regional committees and departments were set up to promote their interests as a marginalized category of the population. As the USSR "opened" to the West and joined the international community, it took on more international obligations. In the early '80s, the USSR ratified CEDAW, the UN Convention for the Elimination of All Forms of Discrimination against Women. During the late Gorbachev and early Yeltsin period, a "national mechanism for improving women's status" was developed.[9] This meant that data on the position and status of women had to be collected. The Soviet state now required specialists who could undertake this work and speak on such issues at international conferences. Feminist scholars suddenly found themselves in demand (Sperling 2000:111).

The Moscow Center for Gender Studies was founded in this spirit. It set up shop within a prestigious state institution, the Institute of Socioeconomic Studies of the Population of the Academy of Sciences, and its researchers were invited to contribute on public policy issues. Politicized by the policies I have described, which led to alarming rates of female unemployment, the feminization of poverty, and a marked drop in women's political representation within the new democratic legislative and executive structures, feminist scholars used their positions from within or alongside state structures to research and critique the path of democratization. The LOTOS group (the League for Emancipation from Social Stereotypes), out of which the Moscow Center for Gender Studies (MCGS) grew, worked out "a thorough feminist examination of the social schemes introduced in Russia (socialist, perestroika, democratic, the market system) from the point of view of their gender programs" (Posadskaya 1994:2), concluding that perestroika was "a period of postsocialist patriarchal renaissance" (1994:4). In 1989, the group was able to publish these critiques in an article submitted to the Party-sanctioned paper *Kommunist*.

At this point, knowledge of Western feminism and the concept of "gender" became a resource that enabled them to generate new forms of capital (Gapova 2003). These feminist scholars began to win the grudging respect of Soviet officials: although it was locally despised, this form of knowledge had currency in international circles. However, "gender" was more than this. As the effects of market-oriented economics were felt, "gender" became a powerful rubric through which these women began to make their own lives in the context of radical social dislocation and new stratification. Popularized through the work of these first Moscow-based scholars, the word now began to spread through seminars and workshops they ran. As Belorussian feminist scholar Elena Gapova put it, the term "[gave] a name to the problem, it responded to certain anxieties that they—or we?—had as (post)communist women." It helped to "organize the texture of personal experience" at a time of major social upheavals and new stratification (2003:6). At the same time, other, non-urban, non-elite women's groups began to mushroom all over the Russian Federation. These were mostly survival groups; the majority of these women's organizations did not have a structural critique of gender relations, and would have looked upon feminist ideas with great skepticism (Bridger, Kay, and Pinnick 1996). Implicitly or explicitly, they sprang up as a form of protest against the direction of political and economic reform in Russia. Such groups included organizations for women with large families, professional groups such as the group Women in Education and Science and the well-known Committee of Soldiers' Mothers that campaigned to stop hazing in the military and against the draft.

In 1991 Moscow-based feminist activists made the first attempt to unify the disparate women's groups, initiatives, and organizations in the First Independent Women's Forum (held in Dubna, a city outside Moscow). The first Dubna forum was attended by around two hundred women, including Valentina and other members of Zhenskii Svet, representing forty-eight organizations all over Russia. It brought women into contact with each other and stimulated interest in the emergent women's movement. The main topic of the meeting was women's worsening sociopolitical position in Russia, and its slogan—"Democracy minus women is no democracy."

The independent women's movement shared many of the characteristics of dissident feminism. Despite the first efforts to bring about unity at Dubna, groups remained small, elite, non-mobilizational and anti-institutional. In tracking the history of the Russian women's movement, many have commented on the rifts and squabbles within and between organizations; it is a movement notoriously split and divided (Richter 1999; Sperling 2000). These first feminist groupings were marginal, small, mostly concentrated in university circles, and can best be described as very loose gatherings of colleagues and friends. There was very little communication or coordination between them. As Valentina put it, "Each group tried to do everything, on the basis of intuition. This was a spontaneous reaction against what was happening, it was not organized." Attempts to create more formalized connections met with considerable difficulty, even resistance. Anastasiia Posadskaia, the first director of the Moscow Center for

Gender Studies and one of the convenors of the Dubna forum, said that in spite of the common ground participants found, the majority of them remained reluctant to collaborate and unify at that moment. She characterized the mood thus: "We have our group. You have your center. You have your support group. We have already found each other. Why should we organize this? For whom?" (Racioppi and See 1997:144).

Crucially for my story, the Dubna forums won the nascent Soviet women's movement international attention. Feminist scholars and activists from Western Europe and the United States attended the forums and entered into dialogue with Russian women for the first time. These connections led to numerous intellectual and private exchanges and collaborations; activists began to think of themselves as belonging in a global movement. As Posadskaia put it, Dubna "was an attempt to see ourselves and our problems as part of the global female social spectrum, with a right to our own voice in the making of the new global order" (Posadskaia 1994:5). These connections also led to the institutionalization of the movement; the first offers of financial support to Russian women's groups were made during this time, mostly from private individuals and small feminist donor organizations.

During my fieldwork in 1997 and 1998, I spoke to some of the women who were active in the women's movement during this period. "Independence" was a key word in their recollections. They used it to convey their sense of excitement at organizing with other women for the first time, and to express their pride in belonging in the nascent movement. They also used it to express a sense of personal empowerment that they achieved through their activity. As one woman put it, "We were able to do so much, without funding, or grants!" While some spoke with some irony about their prior "naïveté" and the "chaotic" nature of communication between groups, others looked back on the fluidity of the time with nostalgia and fondness. However, at the same time, this period contained the germ of future discontent. By 1992, when the second Dubna forum took place, some activists had become concerned by the implications of Western connections, which were growing increasingly strong. In 1992, the Ford Foundation awarded the organizers of the Independent Forum a large grant in order to set up an office from which communication between women's organizations would be coordinated. The forum, which had been a loose coalition, became institutionalized as an organizational entity.

Phase Three: Gender Mainstreaming at Cold War's End

Aid to Russian women's groups began in the early 1990s with a fairly modest dribble. In the mid-'90s it became a torrent; all the main agencies in Russia that promoted civil society development began to target women's groups for a portion of this aid. This was in part due to recognition of local conditions—agencies were aware of the gendered shifts I have described and concerned by the marginalization and impoverishment of women. But, as with support for civil society, this policy switch had as much to do with shifts in global development agency agendas.

As I explained in the introduction, "gender" became a new guiding concept of the development industry in the '90s. Feminist lobbying within the UN system, which began in the 1970s,[10] gathered steam and gained pace in the post–Cold War era, culminating in the Fourth World Conference on Women, Beijing, 1995. The UN made recommendations, which although not legally binding had powerful effect. Most significantly, a concern with "gender" was "mainstreamed" into the agendas of main lending institutions. "Mainstreaming" signified the integration of attention to women in all aspects of agency operation (Buvinic 1996). According to the new wisdom, women's rights, or in the new terminology, "gender equality," was important for the development of markets and democratic transformation. "Gender" became a standard with which to measure the development or democratic status of states, just like social capital and civil society. As one World Bank publication puts it, "Gender equality is a core development issue—a development objective in its own right. It strengthens countries' abilities to grow, to reduce poverty, and to govern effectively. Promoting gender equality is thus an important part of a development strategy that seeks to enable all people—women and men alike—to escape poverty and improve their standard of living" (2001:1). Foundations and agencies were swift to embrace this new mandate, and it was soon manifest in their policies. By 1997, to my surprise, although the concept of "women's rights" and the struggle for gender equality had little local legitimacy in Russia, it was commonplace among international agency staff, as this example illustrates.

One day in late spring 1998, during one of my trips to Moscow from Tver', I was invited by some of my Russian friends to attend a photography exhibition in their neighborhood. Upon arriving, I learned that the exhibition, a Scottish-Russian joint venture, was to be opened by a representative of the Moscow office of the British Council. Valentina had just been contacted by a British Council agency representative and invited to apply for a grant, and I thought it appropriate to engage in a little networking. Our plan to set up a crisis center was under way and we were seeking the support of donor agencies. Fortified by a couple of slugs of cheap champagne poured by my Russian friends (acquaintances of one of the photographers), who were eager and, I suspect, somewhat amused to see me in action, I approached him and mentioned my work with the group and the work they were undertaking. A florid, besuited man in his late 50s with a bell-like upper class accent, he seemed an unlikely feminist, but to my surprise, he was eager to talk to me about this issue. Nodding his support for the topic, he eagerly intoned, "We must get women on board! Without them it is hopeless!"

The British Council was not alone; its policies reflected a general trend among bilateral donors. During the '90s, the United States, Canadian, and German governments and the EU also channeled significant funds to Russian women's groups. USAID was one of the major donors, targeting women's groups as part of their Women and Development program.[11] Private foundations such as the Ford Foundation, the MacArthur Foundation, and George Soros's Open Society Institute were also very active.[12] The Ford Foundation was a pioneer of this aid; between 1994 and 1999 it spent $2 million in grants to strengthen and institutionalize the Russian women's movement (Henderson 2003:121).[13] Donor support significantly changed the face of women's activism. In many ways, it looks like the "success story" agencies claim. Women's organizations began to proliferate and collaborate ("network") as never before. Foundation support enabled Russian women activists to go global, too, as Maria's case illustrates. Agencies sponsored their attendance at events such as the UN Fourth World Conference on Women in Beijing (1995). By all accounts, this conference was a pivotal moment for Russian women's organizations. Agencies such as the Ford Foundation provided travel grants in order for activists to be able to attend the Beijing NGO forum and funded a round of preparatory workshops and seminars, as well as research and report writing. In the months preceding the conference, Russian activists became consumed by this activity.

In the late 1990s, a small circle was well integrated into transnational campaigns. Much of their activity was geared toward the transnational feminist network and the need to implement international norms, such as CEDAW, in Russian politics (Sperling 2000:220–256). These activists brought the concepts of gender, empowerment, sustainability, and civil society to the attention of politicians and to the vocabulary of Russian activists.

However, although foundation support solidified the movement, it deepened the rifts between its constituent parts. In the late '90s there were somewhere between one thousand and two thousand women's NGOs in Russia (Richter 1999:6). These included groups that deal with a wide variety of issues, from women's rights to women's professional societies. The majority of these, however, had no connection with each other, or with donor organizations. Contact with foundations was monopolized by a small elite band. Thus, at the same time that the movement expanded, it also narrowed, exhibiting the same tensions and contradictions of the third sector more broadly. Encouraged by the foundations, the independent women's movement rather contentiously formalized around a set of Moscow-based resource and information centers—the Moscow Center for Gender Studies, the Information Center of the Independent Women's Forum where Maria worked, and the U.S.-NIS Consortium of women's organizations. These three functioned as information centers and clearinghouses; their very raison d'être was to facilitate communication and the exchange of information, and to encourage the formation of networks through the Russian Federation. To this end, they supported regional organizations through the dissemination of literature and grant monies and through maintaining electronic mailing lists. They were entirely dependent on the support of foundations, though they were provided with minimal support from Russian state structures. Their overheads were high, since rent in Moscow was terribly expensive and they supported permanent staffs.

From the outset an elite phenomenon and mostly clustered around university departments, in the 1990s the "movement" became even more rarefied and distant from the lives of the majority of Russian women. As James Richter described, foundations brought about a women's movement that was hierarchical, bureaucratized, clientelistic, mistrustful and secretive, and increasingly distant from ordinary Russian people. "If anything, Western assistance has widened the distance between the Russian third sector and the rest of society by creating a cadre of professional activists involved in their own networks, speaking their own language and pursuing their own goals" (1999:35). This caused much disquiet among the ranks of Russian women's movement activists, as several scholars have documented (Hemment 2000; Henderson 2003; Kay 2000; Richter 1999; Sperling 2000). Long-term activists Regentova and Abubikirova provide a scathing insider account of these changes (1995): "The foundation system has in practice replaced the previous state system of ministries and departments, as far as the third sector, including women's organizations, is concerned. The foundations' functions include distributing funds. They act through a bureaucratic apparatus that they created themselves. It is precisely in this sense that one can speak of the formation today of a new *nomenklatura*—within the women's movement" (1995:13–14). Women's movement activists were commonly perceived to be more concerned with pursuing their career than with transformational goals. At the same time, members of the old Soviet elite adapted well to this new environment.

"Gender mainstreaming," which in many ways looks like a feminist's dream, has had ambivalent outcomes, just like the civil society building project I described in the previous chapter. As my example of Maria shows, "gender" has become a bureaucratic category, a form of expert knowledge. Gender mainstreaming marks the continuation of what Adele Mueller has called the "bureaucratization of feminist knowledge" within the development industry. Ostensibly intended to empower local women ("grassroots women"), it has benefited a small elite and given rise to new hierarchies. Gender mainstreaming and the new emphasis on "women's issues" operates as a mode of power that constitutes some women and some issues as deserving of support and excludes others (Mindry 2001). As a professional feminist, Maria became a gatekeeper who had to implement and encourage campaigns that were externally defined, excluding others that are "too local" (Mandel 2002) from consideration. Gender mainstreaming was supposed to elevate "women's issues" to the attention of agencies—instead, here we see that the flow is reversed. Maria and her colleagues no longer debated the path of reform, but had become inwardly focused, kept guessing about the logic of grants and funding to the exclusion of local constructions. Gender mainstreaming was supposed to "empower" women—yet even those who are salaried and reap considerable benefits feel constrained and disempowered within these structures. Meanwhile, most women's groups and most women in whose name they organize are even worse off. Maria was painfully aware of this new and unsatisfactory division of labor—where the other women's groups are encouraged into service provision, made responsible for too much. She spoke about women being "used up" by their involvement in this sphere, "my heart aches when I think of how many excellent women I know who work in the third sector are ill. It takes such a lot from you, there is such uncertainty, we all get ill after a few years." She longed to quit her own job, saying that it was in contradiction with the circumstances of her own life, it demanded too much. Her colleagues urged her to keep at it, that she had to be responsible. "Yes, I'm responsible, we must be responsible, but why only us? And what about our families?"

Zhenskii Svet and Valentina's Perspective

From my vantage point in 1997 in the provinces I picked up critical commentary about the women's movement, as I had done about the third sector. Some of the Zhenskii Svet women were acquainted with Moscow-based activists. While they generally had good relations with them, they did not like the changes they saw and did not feel included. One of my Zhenskii Svet friends derisively referred to the Moscow feminist activity as a *tusovka* (a friends' hangout), or as a *mezhdusoboichik* (an insider's do), implying it was closed to outsiders. I understood their frustration. While it was easy for me to gain access to seminars and conferences as a foreigner, it was much harder for my Russian colleagues. The information flow was not very efficient (at this point only Valentina had email access and several of the women did not have home telephones) and finances did not permit many of them to make the three-hour bus trip very often. My friends who did make the trips in returned disappointed by the way women they had known for years, and considered peers in the movement, had transmogrified into professionals, mastering the art of public relations and self-presentation, armed with glossy calling cards and not shy to monopolize the attentions of foundation representatives. Relations between the capital and the provinces were often strained; provincial women activists frequently muttered that their Muscovite colleagues never made it to work before 11:00 AM, commanded high wages, and could afford exotic holidays.[14] At the same time, Muscovites grumbled about how hard it was to get anyone to do anything in the provinces, how they never submitted their reports on time and failed to stay in touch by email.

Valentina occupied an ambivalent position on these processes. She was well connected in Russian women's movement circles; she had attended the Dubna women's forums and had been a very enthusiastic participant in some of the early collaborations with international agencies. She had engaged in a kind of networking, attending the women's leadership seminars that were held in the early '90s and run by visiting foreign feminists. She had worked with Moscow-based activists in some of the first collaborative projects with international foundations (notably, she co-directed the first Ford Foundation–sponsored Summer School in Gender Studies that was held in Tver' in 1996).[15] Yet she had consciously resisted entering into the formalized structures that characterized the movement. She was part of the network insofar as she was integrated into its information flow, but she did not seek to cement her belonging by applying for grants or becoming a salaried NGO professional.

Valentina remembered the moment when the first big Ford Foundation grant arrived. Along with other women's group representatives, she was invited to attend a planning meeting in Moscow to discuss the grant and what to do with it. She told me she was initially eager to collaborate; she was interested in engaging with foundations, and with the technology and science of organization they brought with them. She was excited at the thought of winning resources to support the women and girls involved in her organization. But the more she saw, the less comfortable these changes made her. She watched former colleagues begin to interact as donors and recipients and knew she did not want to enter into these types of relationships. "I realized that the purpose of the meeting was to distribute funds," she said, "and I decided to go home." She remembers that "one of the girls who later became famous" (as she recalled her) stopped her in the corridor and asked her why she was leaving. "I told her that I had no projects to write, I understood that it was not my thing. I knew that the work we were doing here didn't require money, or making trips to Moscow. I didn't have a project, didn't have a team, I wasn't ready, I didn't want to do this!"

To some extent, it was distance from Moscow that made her opting out possible. The university offered an umbrella or a roof for her; although it did not provide significant material support, she was able to foster and develop new initiatives under its wing (such as the Evening School in Gender Studies). She had been able to stay at a provincial pace, to maintain her profession, and to retain a critical edge on the processes of third-sectorization she saw affecting the women's movement, making a luxury out of material impoverishment and her peripheral location.

But beyond this, her reluctance expressed critical resistance to the processes of formalization—this was what I was drawn to. As I have explained in the previous chapter, for Valentina, participation and belonging in the formalized NGO sector represented constraint, a *loss of freedom*. According to her logic, to enter into this world would be to sign oneself over, to give oneself away. She always talked about her *obshchestvennaia* (societal) work as a way of resisting formalization. It was a way of avoiding being owned or compromised by belonging in a structure. She was concerned about the drive to unity and the logic of expansion that characterized the "network" form of activism. Unity, she would argue, only makes sense around specific issues. She spoke eloquently about the negative local effects of this center-driven tendency. When she spoke to me and to others about the history of the group, she referred to the "travel agency" phase of Zhenskii Svet, which coincided with the buildup to the Beijing conference. At this time, donor agencies and Moscow-based NGOs urged local groups to register and formalize in order that they could boost Russian women's representation; they offered travel grants to assist Russian women to attend the Beijing conference. As local women saw that resources were attached to women's activism, local attitudes toward Zhenskii Svet changed. Some local women had begun to participate in the group because they saw feminism as a ticket to ride, and had no further interest in the ideas or following through. She was mortified when a young woman traveled to Tver's sister city at the invitation of German crisis center activists but did not share information about her experience when she returned home, or pursue the idea any further. This, she felt, was not only a waste of precious resources but it amounted to a "profanation" (*profanatsiia*) of feminist objectives.

One evening in early December 1997 I attended a Zhenskii Svet meeting. It was International Human Rights Day and so Valentina, who made a point of noting and celebrating international events such as this, facilitated a discussion on the theme of human rights and what constitutes human rights. As we sat in the library, drinking tea, the women made their own suggestions about how the human rights situation could be improved locally. They suggested a law to protect small businesses (which are often women-led), that the state should be held accountable and should pay wages, that taxes should be abolished on charitable donations. At the end of the meeting, Valentina suggested an *aktsiia* (political action)—to send New Year's greetings cards to the new deputies, with a list of these demands. The women all agreed, "*nado shumet*'!" (we need to make a noise), as Lena put it. One woman, a writer I had not seen at meetings before insisted that we needed to build a coalition, arguing that "nobody will listen to us if we write as individuals or separate organizations." Valentina disagreed: "We can unify around concrete projects, but these can only be temporary alliances." She asked us about Women of Russia, a national women's party that apparently had a local branch in Tver'. "Does anyone know the representative in Tver'?" Nobody except Lydia did. This replication of Soviet-style organizations was her worst nightmare.

In 1997, Valentina occupied a highly ambiguous position. She had been a broker of the early exchanges, but was uneasy about what was now taking place in the name of civil society and women's rights. I came to see that she was straddling a complex set of relationships. Typifying the trends I have outlined, she was now feted by both foundations and local elites. She was invited to apply for a number of grants during the time I was in the city: she was approached by the Moscow office of the Open Society Institute and invited to co-direct a summer school in human rights in Tver' by the Ford Foundation; at the same time, the governor's office invited her to set up a new commission on women's affairs and to join the board of a new regional human rights commission. In early spring 1998, she was invited onto the steering committee of the Women's Assembly, the new regional umbrella agency founded by Liubov' Svedova, the president's representative to the *oblast'*. This brought her into contact with some powerful local women, many of them former members of the Soviet elite who now occupied administrative positions, or who had reconstituted themselves as businesswomen. It was a privileged yet precarious position to be in. And at the same time, as I have said, there were more and more demands to do something more concrete from within the group. Valentina wanted a center, but did not want it to become a "network," disembodied, careless of its roots and local concerns. And she was quite clear that she did not want to become an NGO professional.

My fieldnotes from this period document a lot of talk about a women's center both during Zhenskii Svet meetings and in our one-on-one discussions. We discussed the possibility of grants and Valentina distributed information she had received online to those who were interested. Some of the women felt that Valentina was squandering her cultural capital and should make more of it. My notes reflect my own confusion as I tried to find my way between these issues. A woman's center in the city would be wonderful—a "roof" (*krysha*), a space for the diverse projects offered by the Zhenskii Svet women to happen, money to support them in their activities. And yet, who would run it, and what would it become? There were numerous discouraging examples in the city—both the women in the administration and the new third-sector professionals (who turned out not to be so distinct) had brought bureaucratic, top-down organizations into being. Despite talk about inclusion and supporting the "women's movements" [*sic*], meetings of the Women's Assembly were too often small and restricted to already acquainted, well-appointed women. This "umbrella organization" appeared to be merely a launch pad for the political career of its founder that did not serve the interests of local women who, inside and outside formal organizational activity, were engaged in what Valentina insisted was "*obshchestvennaia rabota*" (societal work). In both arenas, the spirit of organizing, the commitment to openness, lack of hierarchy, debate, and self-realization were gone. And yet—not engaging was clearly not an option.

It was a watershed moment, as Valentina acknowledged in our joint presentation at Cornell:

> In 1997 [when Julie came] it was another situation. It was three years since the last women's world conference, and maybe you know, our Russian government had to implement several documents of that conference into their activity, and they were very active in organizing different committees, women's committees, there were lots of orders of our president from above as usual. And I began to think it's not enough to resist only this patriarchal modernization, modernization of patriarchy, but it's very important to be involved in the processes of changing. But how?

She continued to say that she recognized the demand from within the group for something more, for a "socially important project," perhaps a women's center. By then, a lot of women had been through her education project; "because of this training program, women were ready to do something else, more concrete perhaps," she said. "We trained people in women's leadership schools, computer courses, so on and so on, but what then?"

4   Global Civil Society and the Local Costs of Belonging: Setting up a Crisis Center in Tver'

"You have to be very patient," the fox answered. "First you'll sit down a little way away from me, over there, in the grass. I'll watch you out of the corner of my eye, and you won't say anything. Language is the source of misunderstandings. But day by day, you'll be able to sit a little closer . . . "

Antoine de Saint-Exupéry, *The Little Prince*

By early April, contrary to the Fox's advice, I was quite *im*patient. Nine months into my fieldwork in Tver', I was frustrated that I'd not done anything participatory. Chastened by the unsatisfying experience of writing the UNIFEM grant, I felt that my collaborative intent had failed. On the other hand, other aspects of my fieldwork were going swimmingly. It was easy, almost too easy, to gain data about international support for women's activism. Over the last months, I had attended numerous seminars, meetings, and conferences in Moscow and other cities; I had an increasingly sophisticated grasp of the ways things worked—of donor priorities and foundation mandates—and I had a wide range of acquaintances within NGO circles. I had traveled to other cities and met with other provincial groups and I had seen how they flourished, drawing on donor support in often unexpected ways. I was particularly excited by what I had seen of the new women's crisis centers and what donor support offered them.

Yet despite my best efforts, this all seemed to be taking place separately and apart from my work with Zhenskii Svet. Participant observation had enabled me to gather rich data; I felt sure that it would be of value to my friends, yet I found it strangely difficult to share it with them. It was hard to get them to come and see for themselves, since they did not have the time or money to travel, often at short notice, to attend events in other cities. While I was able to drop everything, they had responsibilities that kept them in Tver'. In between Zhenskii Svet meetings, the women were busy hustling to make ends meet, engaged in elaborate informal economic arrangements—exchanging a child's coat for a medical consultation, vegetables for care.

Caught in the midst of my own contradictions—the internal contradiction of participant observation—I was growing increasingly frustrated with the group.

Upon my arrival in the city, I had been thrown off by the informality of Zhen-skii Svet, baffled by its lack of structure and coherence, and the erratic way in which it met. In so many ways, it defied my expectations of what a "group" should look like—there was no membership, no regular meeting place, no phone number or address or clear division of labor. I had come to be captivated and intrigued by these same qualities; as I got to know the history and activities of the group I came to understand that it was an extremely creative response to local conditions. Yet now that there was clamor for change among group members, I was exasperated again. How would we formulate new plans, and who would lead and undertake them? Although quick to voice their discontents, the women in the group tended to defer to Valentina and did not take steps themselves.

After one morning of intensive fieldnote writing, I left my apartment to get some air. I set off down the main pedestrian street, past the kiosks that sold newspapers, past the vegetable stands and past the "gypsies" (Roma) buying gold outside the jewelry store on the main street, and found myself wandering into *Dom Moda* (House of Fashion). This formerly monolithic Soviet-era store was now divided into different departments, each with a very different feel. On the ground floor were brightly colored Russian scarves, hosiery, and knitwear, while upstairs there were racks of imported, mostly German clothing. Like many local women, I used to come in to browse, to gaze admiringly at the outfits on the racks. This store, like other privately owned stores in town, felt like a museum: one could look, but the items displayed were out of grasp. This form of shopping made for a pleasant if ironic kind of recreational activity. To my surprise I saw Valentina, who was doing exactly the same thing.

She told me that she had just come out of a wonderful class with her social work students; they had talked for three hours and she had not been able to get away from them. Together they had decided to turn their class into a kind of participatory seminar, and she invited them to set their own agenda for the semester. Her students had a project in mind: they wanted to set up a kind of youth center in the city, tapping youth-oriented city resources Valentina had told them about. To this end, they decided to invite a member of the administration in charge of youth affairs to their next class. Delighted by the serendipitous meeting and by her upbeat tale, I invited her to join me in my walk. We set off to the riverbank. I remember feeling intoxicated by the freshness of the April air, and by the spontaneity and unusualness of the occasion—it felt fresh, a departure from our tradition of meeting in the department, the library, or her apartment.

On the way we talked, and I spoke of my frustrations. I told her how I had been remembering our first conversations in 1995 and felt that I had drifted far from that original goal. I told her of my sense of frustration after the UNIFEM experience and my confusion with the group: it seemed we were going round in circles. How could we formalize our activities? What would this look like? There were so many loose ends we had been playing with, so many possibilities—it

Women selling at a street market, Tver'. Photograph courtesy of Frank Hein.

seemed it was time to take on what she had called a "strategy of involvement" (that is, to work with local authorities), and yet how? To my surprise, she eagerly agreed. As we reflected on our activities of the last months, we realized the extent to which we had been focusing on events outside the group—the founding of the Women's Assembly, the presence of third-sector grants and funding—with the result that we had lost our own sense of purpose. And as she talked, confiding her own worries and concerns, I realized that this crisis of the group was also a personal crisis for Valentina. She was overwhelmed by peoples' needs and expectations. Contrary to her intent (her dislike of hierarchy and refusal of the role of "leader"), she found that Zhenskii Svet women frequently deferred to her. Furthermore, other local women approached her for assistance and guidance on topics that ranged from intensely personal crises to requests for assistance with moneymaking schemes (hearing of her activities, some local women assumed she had easy access to "Western" resources and could help set them up in business!). Her home phone had become a kind of unofficial *telefon doveriia,* or hotline, and her doorbell was constantly ringing. When she began Zhenskii Svet, she, like many societal activists, had been ready "to do it all," as she put it. In the late '80s and early '90s, when everything was uncertain and in flux, it made no sense to have a "mission statement"; there were no clear boundaries to the group, and no clear boundaries to demarcate her role within it. The boundarylessness that had made sense then, now threatened to consume her. At the same time, she was highly ambivalent about the alternative (becoming an NGO professional). Caught between these two models of activism, she was unsure what to do.

By the end of the conversation, something profound had taken place. We had decided to hold a seminar, to call together a small group of the most active women to undertake a process of intra-group clarification. We were committed to moving ahead, but did not know how. Before we could decide on a course of action, it seemed important for individual participants to figure out their stake or level of investment in Zhenskii Svet. The conversation was transformative insofar as it authorized our collaboration and enabled me to become more directly engaged in projects with members of the group. It enabled the Zhenskii Svet women to ask things of me, to deploy, or "exploit" me, in Valentina's ironic terms, as a foreigner-outsider, by sending me to knock on doors and sweet talk local powerbrokers. And the conversation brought about another transformation: it gave rise to a new stage of intimacy between us. The shift to activism was inseparable from the process of "taming," inseparable from the process of making ties. Despite our friendship, I had always been a little in awe of her. Out of respect, I had persisted in addressing her with the formal term for "you," "*vy.*" Now, overcome by emotion and the new sense of intimacy our conversation had left me with, I shyly asked her if I could address her with the familiar term, "*ty.*" "Goodness," she said, "I thought you would never do it!"

In May 1998 we gathered together for our first collaborative seminar. Although we planned to hold the seminar one weekend in Valentina's *dacha,* we eventually met in my apartment due to poor weather and the fact that women couldn't afford to give up two whole days to travel to the country. The seminar was postponed on a number of occasions and several of the women originally invited couldn't come. The eventual participants were the four women I was closest to—Lydia, Lena, Valentina, and Oktiabrina. We conceptualized it as a retreat, a step out of routine and daily life in order to give group members the opportunity to critically reflect upon their activism. I ran it as a "search conference," adapting a common methodology of participatory research (Crombie 1987; Cabana, Emery, and Emery 1995). Our discussion was structured around three broad questions designed to assist the group in clarifying its goals and aims: where did we come from? (the group's history); where do we want to go? (the ideal); how to get there? (the action plan).

In addition to these stated objectives swirled motivations that couldn't quite be articulated: I wanted to clarify my relationship with Lydia after our failed collaboration, to bring information about the crisis center network to the group and perhaps to find someone to pursue the project of setting a crisis center up in the city. I realized Valentina was partly motivated by the desire to be freed of expectations she could not meet. She knew that some of the Zhenskii Svet

Oktiabrina and Valentina discuss the history of *Zhenskii Svet* during a seminar in 1998.

women were moving from educational projects (where her heart lay) to more socially oriented projects concerning women's health and training. She couldn't do it all, and she remained determined that while more formal projects could take place, Zhenskii Svet itself should remain independent.

During the seminar, discussion spilled over with revelations and recollections about the history of the group. The women discussed changes in the group, from the early days of organizing when Zhenskii Svet was little more than a cluster of Valentina's students, to what Lena mischievously called the "travel agency" phase when local women had flocked to the group for the wrong reasons—not out of interest in women's issues or activism, but because they saw it as an opportunity to travel to the West. They discussed other activities in the city, too—the new vogue for things nongovernmental, the proliferation of local "gender" projects, and the elite former Communist Party insiders who wanted to "play the women's movement." By the end of that day, we had achieved something substantial. We had a shared and enriched perspective of the history of the group and had reached a broad consensus: the women agreed it was time to formalize the activities of Zhenskii Svet in some way and to found a women's center. This would be a real "concrete, socially oriented project," as Oktiabrina put it, that would both sustain existing projects and enable Zhenskii Svet women to devise new ones. Valentina insisted, "and it must keep its original name— Zhenskii Svet. You see, our idea is linked to the two meanings of the word *svet:*

globe/world and light—Zhenskii Svet is above all a project of enlightenment" (*prosvetitel'nyi proekt*).

In the months that followed, we met several more times. Our collaboration was a bumpy process, unraveling and reconfiguring, reflecting our different objectives and motivations. Our original goal—to found a women's center— morphed into three projects, or "directions" as the women called them: a publishing house, led by Lena, a "crisis center" for women victims of sexual and domestic violence, led by Oktiabrina and me, and a Center for Women's History and Gender Studies, led by Valentina, which built on the educational work of Zhenskii Svet and the Evening School in Gender Studies. All of these involved making outside alliances, taking steps toward some kind of formalization and seeking support from both international foundations and the local administration. Our collaborative process enabled us to take these deliberate steps in the name of Zhenskii Svet, to draw on its resources both by inviting current and former members of the group to participate and by invoking its rich history of activism in the city. Lena conceptualized these "directions" as "rays of the sun"—separate, but linked and mutually sustaining projects that radiated from Zhenskii Svet.

In this next section, I focus on one of these rays, the project to set up a crisis center in the city, in which I was centrally engaged. In this account, two threads of my analysis come together—the critique of international gendered interventions and the story of the constructive political project I engaged in with members of Zhenskii Svet. The decision to set up a crisis center in the city involved entering the third sector and taking part in a campaign that was testimony to the "success" of gender mainstreaming—the transnational feminist campaign against gendered violence. The story of our project is a story of two competing constructions of "crisis" and two competing catchalls; it is the story of how we made a strategic decision to embrace an international model at the expense of local concerns, and of our subsequent struggle to make gender matter. I show that this decision entailed significant costs as well as benefits. In setting up the crisis center, the Zhenskii Svet participants moved away from their deeply held commitment to independent, informal forms of organizing to enter the third sector and to embrace a new identity as NGO professionals. They shifted to a new vision of politics, from working determinedly outside the state, to working with it, using international foundations as a wedge.

All Paths Lead to Violence

Violence against women was a persistent sub-theme of my research. A concern with gendered violence was part of my own feminist trajectory; I had worked in women's crisis centers for victims of sexual and domestic violence in England and the United States and hence was interested in Russian responses to the issue. I originally decided to base myself among Zhenskii Svet because the group had listed a crisis center as one of its activities in the online announcement I had originally seen (in return, my experience of working in crisis centers was one reason why Valentina was eager to take me on). Although by 1997 when I arrived to do my fieldwork there was no actual crisis center, a conception of "crisis center" percolated in the group. It dated from the early '90s when Valentina had traveled to Germany for the first time. She had visited several crisis centers and was greatly impressed by them. Subsequently, some of the activists she met there proposed a collaborative project to set up a crisis center in Tver'. However, the project had fallen through: to Valentina's chagrin the Zhenskii Svet participant who had initially expressed interest backed out and the German activists gave up when their grant did not come through. Now my presence, questions, and expressed interest had caused some of the women to engage and reconsider the idea. In the end however, despite this early interest and history, violence against women became an issue around which our activism coalesced not because it was considered the most important issue facing local women, but because it had political currency. In 1997 both sets of our potential sponsors, international foundations and Russian local officials, were persuaded by this issue and deemed it worthy of support.

Gendered violence has long been a concern of local women's movements. In the United States and Western Europe, the battered women's movement was a prominent component of second-wave organizing. The first women's crisis centers were survivor-led grassroots organizations. The battered women's movement was an explicit challenge to a bourgeois patriarchal set of relations that relegated women to the private realm. The provision of shelters—secret safe houses where women victims of domestic abuse could take temporary refuge—was central to these early campaigns. Psychological counseling and support groups were offered as a challenge to a repressive, patriarchal system of relations that prevented the expression of women's solidarity. Elsewhere, women's groups organized around local manifestations of violence—in India, around campaigns against dowry deaths, in Latin America against the state-sanctioned violence perpetrated by authoritarian regimes.

However, until the late 1980s, gendered violence was a feminist issue and was not regarded with much seriousness at the international level. In the late '80s and early '90s this changed when, due to the efforts of activists of the international women's movement, the issue of violence against women went global. By 1997 violence against women was not only a feminist issue that concerned women's groups, it was an international development issue, too. Making use of the global apparatus I have described in earlier chapters, feminist activists pushed the issue to international prominence at UN conferences during the '90s. "Violence against women" emerged as a "framing" (to use the language of social movements theory) that had the power to unite women from the North and South in a global campaign. It was an effective catchall that encompassed a broad range of practices, hence bringing about dialogue between women from different locations.[1] Its success at the international level was largely due to the innovation of linking women's rights to human rights, bringing together two powerful constituencies for the first time—human rights activists and feminists. The UN Fourth World Conference on Women in Beijing, 1995, was a pivotal moment for the success of the framing. Combating violence against women emerged as a central policy agenda both of the international women's movement and of international development.[2] The campaigns galvanized support across diverse constituencies, among politicians and donors. After Beijing, many major U.S. and European foundations made violence against women a funding priority, channeling funds to NGOs that addressed the issue. The Ford Foundation played a significant role in determining patterns of funding, leading the way in funding campaigns against violence against women. While in 1988 major U.S. foundations awarded eleven grants totaling $241,000, in 1993 they made sixty-eight grants totaling $3,247,8000 (Keck and Sikkink 1998:182). By the late '90s, concern about violence against women had become a kind of common sense, a mainstream campaign that few could object to. As one American male coordinator of a crisis center training I attended in 2000 explained to his Russian trainees, "[In the United States] we've found that domestic violence is an easy theme to go to the public with. People give readily. We're at the point where it's politically correct to support this type of organization."

From Crisis Society to Crisis Center

In the mid-to-late-'90s, these transnational campaigns took root in Russia. At the time of my research in 1997–1998, the campaign to combat violence against women was one of the most prominent campaigns of the Russian women's movement. The issue was supported by many of the international foundations that support women's nongovernmental activity, and almost all of the main women's organizations participated in it in some form or another.[3] When I attended several crisis center conferences during 1997, I was stunned to see almost all of my Moscow-based women's movement acquaintances, as well as representatives of the main international foundations and agencies (the Ford Foundation, the Open Society Institute, the American Bar Association, the British Embassy, Amnesty International). "Violence against women" was the topic of many high-profile visits: in the '90s both Hillary Clinton and Madeleine Albright visited the former Soviet Union and addressed women activists on the topic of gendered violence. At the time of my research there were over thirty women's crisis centers (*krizisnye tsentry*) in Russia, offering free psychological and legal services to women victims of sexual and domestic violence. They worked together in a network in a well-orchestrated national campaign. The transnational feminist campaign was successful in Russia not only due to the considerable sums of money put into it, but because it brought another key resource to women's groups—a clear model around which to organize. For activists, the crisis center model, based on rape crisis centers in the U.S. and Western Europe, offered a blueprint and a framework. Neat, easy to learn, it had become a kind of do-it-yourself NGO kit. Foundation support financed the production of easy-to-use materials—brochures, posters, and handbooks, many of which were translated from English or German, including the one that Lydia had come across in 1996 titled "How to Start and Manage a Women's Crisis Center." The book was edited by Russian scholars and crisis center activists Tat'iana Zabelina and Yevgeniia Israelyan and put together by the Youth Institute's Center for Women, Family, and Gender Studies. The Canadian Embassy funded its publication. According to one of its authors, five thousand copies were distributed to nascent crisis centers and women's NGOs (Zabelina 1996). The Information Center of the Independent Women's Movement was involved too. In 1997 it published an analytic document that discussed the draft legislation against domestic violence.[4] This model was accompanied by skills and methods that could be transferred and taught, enabling the idea to spread. These were techniques taken from Western European and U.S. crisis centers—nondirective active listening skills, crisis counseling—and were backed up by a broad feminist paradigm that offered an explanation for gendered violence: here, rape is seen not as a sexual act, but as an expressions of male dominance and power. This conception offered a robust counter-model both to old Soviet ideological explanations for interpersonal violence and to new "expert" explanations that placed the blame on women for "asking for it."

During the Soviet period there had been little discussion of the topic of sexual or domestic violence, since it contradicted official ideology. Soviet ideology asserted that socialism would eradicate all forms of human exploitation and crime. Like other forms of violent crime, rape was generally regarded as an anomalous act of sex maniacs or common criminals, those who were either psychologically ill or represented the relics of bourgeois morality (Attwood 1997:100). Quoting the Soviet Encyclopedic Dictionary of 1980, Russian feminist scholar and crisis center activist Tat'iana Zabelina writes that the entry on violence (*nasilie*) makes no mention of actions against the individual. Instead, violence is defined as a property of class and inter-state relations (1996: 170). Soviet law was, however, comparatively tough on rape. The Criminal Code of 1922 first recognized rape as a crime, which carried a maximum penalty of fifteen years imprisonment or even the death penalty (Attwood 1997:101). However, by all accounts, these laws were very rarely invoked. Domestic strife, meanwhile, in all its forms, tended to be dealt with by the collective—trade unions, workplace-based party committees, the *zhensovety* (women's councils) (Zabelina 1996). This changed during perestroika, when sexual violence became a hot topic of debate. Discussion of this formerly taboo topic was legitimized by Gorbachev's policy of *glasnost'*, or openness, which entailed the lifting of Soviet-era restrictions on the media. *Glasnost'* uncovered a plethora of social problems that had been concealed and denied in the Soviet era, such as prostitution, sexually transmitted diseases, drug abuse, and youth gangs. It also led to the discussion of topics that had formerly been taboo, notably sex and sexuality, and led to the introduction of sexually explicit publications and broadcasts for the first time (Gessen 1995). Data revealing increased incidence of rape and sexual violence caused great alarm.[5] This new trend was interpreted as a sign of broad societal and sexual dysfunction, and attributed to Soviet-era "perversions" of gender roles. During this period, Soviet legal scholars and criminolo-

gists portrayed rape as motivated by a naturalized male lust or anger and pre-
cipitated in large part by women's provocative behavior (Atwood 1997). The
suggested solution was a return to supposedly "traditional" gender norms. In
some cases, scholars went so far as to blame women victims for being either
provocative or masochistically drawn to a form of sexual humiliation. According to this narrative, women and the Soviet state were seen as cronies, to be
equally blamed.

With the dissolution of the USSR, new discourses and a new explanatory
framework for interpersonal violence began to circulate as international norms
and standards were introduced and discussed. Small groups of feminist-oriented
activists played a pivotal role in influencing public discourse, as I have described
in chapter 3. Some of them were particularly concerned by shifts in discourse
during this period, and condemned such representations of women as misogy-
nist (Posadskaya 1994; Voronina 1993; Zabelina 1996). Drawing on Western
feminist writings, Russian feminist scholars provided counter-explanations for
the increased incidence in rape and domestic violence and introduced the paradigm of violence against women (Khodyreva 1996; Zabelina 1996). They interpreted rape and domestic violence not as sexual acts but as expressions of male
dominance and power. The solution, in their analysis, was gender-sensitive education that would challenge what they called the myths and stereotypes of female passivity and masculine lust, and hence the roots of this violence. Moscow
and St. Petersburg-based activists had set up the first women's crisis centers in
Russia in the early '90s after learning about the notion from foreign feminists.
The first center to deal with domestic violence, the Association No to Violence,
or ANNA, was set up in Moscow in 1993. In an interview, Marina Pisklakova,
the director, explained that she had become aware of the issue of domestic abuse
through her work as a journalist for the Soviet era women's magazine *Rabot-
nitsa*; however, she did not interpret it as a problem of larger social significance
until a colleague at the Moscow Center for Gender Studies informed her of the
Western feminist literature on domestic violence. She then visited a crisis center
during a trip to Sweden (Richter 2000:18).[6] Switched on to this "new" issue and
its social importance, Pisklakova and her colleagues began to do research and
publicity work, bringing the issue of gendered violence into public discourse
for the first time (Pisklakova and Sinel'nikov 2000).[7] The UN Fourth World
Conference on the Status of Women in Beijing, 1995, marked an intensifica-
tion of this work.[8] Several Russian activists attended the NGO forum and returned to Russia empowered by the National Platform for Action, where violence against women featured prominently. Although old attitudes certainly
prevailed, these new constructions began to take root.

In my research during 1995–1998, I was struck by the ubiquity of the notion
of "crisis center." The concept percolated among provincial women's associations and groups, much like the notions of civil society and third sector. I came
across many women (excluded from trainings and unfamiliar with the international model) who expressed their intent to set one up, or described their work
(unconnected with sexual or domestic violence) to be "something like a crisis

center." Further, "crisis center" had entered the lexicon of government officials and social services personnel. Illustrating the power of the post–Cold War global politics I have described, the Russian government was now obliged to make provisions for the protection of women. Local administrative officials were mandated to take steps to provide services to deal with women's issues, including the newly defined issue of domestic violence.[9] At least at the level of lip service, there was official support for a crisis center in Tver', as Valentina had begun to realize.

I was impressed—clearly, the prominence of the campaigns marked the success of feminist transnationalism and gender mainstreaming. Russian crisis centers raised public awareness of an issue that had formerly been denied, providing specialized services to women victims of sexual and domestic violence for the first time. But once again, although crisis centers were clearly doing valuable work, I found that the Russian campaigns combating violence against women were a contested terrain and that the work of the crisis center network was marginal from most peoples' lives. Participant observation at seminars and conferences and in individual crisis centers alerted me to some intense and troubling mismatches. First, there was a gulf between the internationally formulated campaign and local understandings. Most Russian people do not recognize the formulations "violence against women" or "domestic violence." Crisis center activists in one provincial city informed me that questionnaires handed out on sexual violence were returned blank, respondents complaining that they just did not understand the questions. Although there is plenty of conflict in the private realm in Russia and I do not for an instant wish to downplay its significance, neither men nor women regard it as a "gender" problem, a problem between men and women. The solutions proposed (hotline counseling, counseling, shelters, legal prosecution) do not persuade. For historical reasons, Soviet people were nervous about admitting to the existence of problems in the home, since this led to unwelcome state scrutiny.

The rhetoric of antiviolence campaigns posits sexual violence as an inevitable outcome of the gender antagonism that is a universal condition of patriarchal societies. Although heralded as a new universal, a truly transnational issue, the campaigns to combat violence against women have Western liberal democratic roots. They presume that women are both economically dependent on men and stuck in the private sphere. The battered women's movement assumed the existence of the nuclear family and posited the home as an autonomous unit. This was not true for Soviet women, who were brought into the workforce and guaranteed formal equality by the socialist state. Crisis centers presume a set of bourgeois property relations, too. However, property was nationalized in the Soviet Union, and there was no ideology of private ownership to give Soviet citizens the illusion of domestic inviolability. Many Russian citizens still live in the notorious communal apartments, sharing kitchen and bathroom facilities with their neighbors. What is more, few married couples live autonomously as nuclear families. Chronic housing shortages mean that many people live with extended family, grandparents, in-laws, and siblings. For all these reasons, domestic conflict most commonly expressed itself in the form of tension over rights to living space, interpersonal strife, or alcoholism. Although patterns are certainly changing with the introduction of a free market—indeed, recent crisis center network research indicates a high prevalence of gendered violence among Russia's new rich—lack of housing remains a chronic problem. Indeed, this helps to explain why women's shelters have not taken off in Russia. I met many crisis center activists who were keen to establish shelters. However, they acknowledged that local conditions did not permit. First there was the difficulty of obtaining premises from local authorities. Second, it was unclear where to relocate women once they had been admitted. If in Western Europe and the United States the shelter is a temporary refuge, a stopgap for women and their families before they find their feet, in Russia people have quite literally nowhere to move on to.

Privately, many Russian activists involved in the campaigns admitted that they did not think gendered violence was the most pressing issue facing Russian women. In the light of major socioeconomic upheavals such as the decay of the free healthcare system, the erosion of state-sponsored day care, and a sharp decline in living standards, they were concerned that the issue had such high priority and that so many resources were put into it. I was struck that many of those engaged in the ideological work of the antiviolence campaigns (organizing the conferences, publishing materials) even *objected* to them. One of my friends, Irina, who worked for an organization that supported antiviolence campaigns, rolled her eyes upon learning that I was working with a group to set up a crisis center. "Crisis centers, crisis centers! That's all you can think about. But let me tell you, there *are* good Russian families, you know. I know that there is really a serious problem in America, but in Russia it is different."

The critical anthropologist in me was alarmed by these effects. At the same time that I was deeply concerned about the issue of sexual and domestic violence and thought the work of the crisis centers extremely important, I was concerned by the cultural imperialism of the campaigns as they played out in Russia and their blindness to local knowledge (Hemment 2004a). Irina's comment attests to the fact that women activists often felt unheard. As with other democratization initiatives, the anti–gendered violence campaigns took place within the climate of liberal triumphalism that saw post-Soviet Russia as a blank slate and conceptualized the project as reeducation (Wedel 1998). Her comment reflects the bitterness of post-Soviet citizens now positioned as "less developed." Where gender is a marker of development, failure to conform to international standards is a signifier of gender primitivism. Moreover, I began to see how the framing of violence against women had alarming discursive effects. It not only screened out local constructions of events but deflected attention from other issues of social justice also, notably the material forces that oppress women. During conferences and seminars, I noted that when Russian activists attempted to expand discussion of "violence" to encompass other issues, such as economic or structural violence, agency representatives seemed to reject these out of hand. I found that many North American or Western European feminists dismissed discussions of economic factors (such as the crisis of living space, unemployment) as either Communist holdovers or as rationalizations for male perpetrated violence. These insights could have been fed into the campaigns, enriching them, yet I didn't see it happening. North American and Western European foundation staff were clearly dedicated to women's rights; however, the logic of the framework and pervasive climate of liberal triumphalism (according to which all things Soviet were discredited) did not permit them to heed local women's constructions. Within the campaigns, economic issues and structural violence became unnarratable. In this way, I saw that the campaigns contributed to the neoliberal restructuring process I have described in earlier chapters.

The framing used by the international campaigns has the ideological effect of obscuring the fact that violence against women is structurally endemic within liberal-democratic capitalist regimes. It is not so much the case that liberal democratic "civil" society is not violent but that the system allows for the existence (and occasionally encourages the provision) of services to mop it up. Making gender and violence a marker of development obscures a fact that both crisis counselors and their clients know very well—that all forms of violence, including gendered violence, have been exacerbated by structural adjustment, the very liberalizing project that was supposed to bring civility to Russia.

As I considered the appropriateness of the skills and technologies that accompanied the campaigns, I realized that they had troubling effects. In the context of violent economic dislocation, crisis center techniques of nondirective active listening served to educate people away from structural factors to take responsibility for themselves, making political protest against these economic policies less likely. These strategies can be seen as exemplary "technologies of citizenship"; they combine the same coercive, disciplinary function as the model of the third sector I examined in chapter 2 (Cruikshank 1999; Hyatt 2001). Techniques of nondirective active listening require callers to come to their own solutions. Crisis centers provide information and consultations (on legal issues and social services) but aim to "empower" clients by helping them to take part in the defense of their rights and make their own decisions. In Russia, the same formula takes on new inflections; the post-Soviet project of reeducation is most explicit. While most centers offer free legal advice, their main message is frequently what *not* to expect from the state. The director of one center told me, "Their first question is always—what will the state do for me (as a battered woman) if I get divorced? I explain that they have little realistic chance of getting help." She told me that in survivor-support groups, she worked to make women aware of these material and political issues, to recognize that the state is not going to help them, and that the only way forward was to help themselves. "Some women say they don't think they should have to work, or help themselves, it is a man's duty. I work with them on these illusions." Like "civil society," "violence against women" succeeded as a framing in development circles due to its catchall quality. The problem with this was that once again, it was emptied of its original intent—in this case, distanced from its roots in social justice campaigns.

My ethnographic research alerted me to these complex and contradictory effects. I puzzled over these thoughts as I returned from crisis center meetings and conferences. But then, what use was this critique? I understood why activists rushed to join the campaigns. Whatever their misgivings, they could not afford the luxury of disengagement. And as I continued in my research and became more attuned to what was going on around me, I began to see things differently. First, the rhetorical persistence of "crisis center" was not merely a result of top-down donor pressure. The crisis center concept did have local resonance, but for different reasons than those presumed by the transnational campaigns. Here, the keyword was not violence (*nasilie*) but crisis (*krizis*).[10] In the '90s, the whole of Russian society was perceived to be in crisis—with good cause. In addition to the perception of social and economic breakdown, the Russian crisis was also perceived to be a psychic condition. My fieldnotes taken during crisis center conferences and seminars note that the speakers—often doctors or social workers—frequently used the term "crisis," and referred to the "neuroticization" of society.[11]

Further, I came to see that this alternative, broader construction of crisis center did inform their activities (as it informed the idea of crisis center that my friend Lydia embraced). While international aid has had a powerful impact on new activities in the nongovernmental sphere, it did not determine them. Wittingly or unwittingly, activists had reformulated the international model. As I spoke with activists and traveled to different centers, I saw that Russian activists were able to make good use of these international resources, translating them in order that they made sense locally. Between 1995 and 1997, before the action research project in Tver', I visited crisis centers in St. Petersburg and several other cities. These visits provided alternative insights and left me with quite different impressions of the antiviolence campaigns than those I received in Moscow. Despite the fact that they formally adopt the crisis center model (which they often referred to as the "international standard"), many of these centers had much broader programs in response to local needs. As the director of one provincial crisis center said to me over coffee, "We go to these Moscow-based seminars, workshops, and conferences, but our agendas are still driven by local concerns." Because these centers were raising the issue of violence against women for the first time, only a relatively small proportion of clients called to discuss it. All the counselors I spoke to confirmed that when they first opened, a wide range of people called their hotlines. Men called as well as women, and, strikingly, a lot of pensioners—in sum, those who felt marginalized and vulnerable. I was told that people called to speak about diverse issues—unemployment, unpaid wages, loneliness, alcoholism, loss of children to the military service, as well as domestic or sexual violence. As one Petersburg-based activist put it, "There is great confusion now, the old system is broken down, but it's not clear what is emerging. People are confused, and there is a great demand for information. They don't know what to ask for, who to speak to, how to name their problems." Centers have responded to this in different ways; some speak to all callers, others only to women victims of violence. One center in Sergiev-Posad abandoned its women-only focus for a few years in response to local incomprehension.

Counselors in all the centers I visited informed me that women who did call to speak about gendered violence frequently related it to a range of other materially based issues, such as unemployment, impoverishment, and cramped living space. In response to this, counselors focused on the woman in a broader social context, particularly on the family. Activists in provincial cities, whose centers often provided the only women-oriented services, concluded that it made no sense to specialize too narrowly. They insisted it was impossible to separate the problem of domestic or sexual violence from other issues women faced. In general, I learned that counselors afforded a high priority to clients' material problems. In one St. Petersburg center, survivor support groups placed great emphasis on practical steps women could take, sometimes resulting in members of a group going into business together.

In April 1998, I traveled to Pskov to visit a crisis center after having met its founder at a seminar in Moscow. I learned that this group had very different origins from Zhenskii Svet. Their solidarity and common purpose was based not on feminism or university connections, but on family ties. The crisis center was a project of the Independent Social Women's Center, a women's group that was founded and run by Natalia V. and her two daughters (one a trained social worker). It drew on the connections and cultural capital of Natalia, a former Communist Party member who had worked within Soviet-era administrative structures before being elected to the city *duma* (legislative body) in 1994. Natalia had become involved in the Russian women's movement in the mid-'90s following a trip to the United States. There, on a month-long USAID-funded training program on NGO management, she had met some leading Russian women's movement activists who had persuaded her to get involved. This was a turning point; inspired by what she had learned about civil society and the potential of nongovernmental groups, she quit electoral politics to found her own women's *obshchestvennaia organizatsiia*.

In 1998, when I visited it, the center was celebrating its third anniversary. It was an impressive women-run project with a permanent staff of seven, and thirty-one volunteers, sustained by a combination of city support and international grants. It ran a series of projects—a women's health group, a legal aid project, a press service, a support group for elderly women, and the crisis center.

The crisis center, run by Natalia's daughter Elena, seemed to me to be especially dynamic. It brought local women into dialogue with activists all over Russia and brought funding to the center. It not only provided a service for women in crisis, raising awareness of the issue of domestic and sexual violence in the city for the first time, but it provided local women with jobs and the opportunity to volunteer and to gain valuable work experience that better equipped them for the labor market. I returned to Tver' inspired by this provincial center, which seemed an ideal role model for us. I was impressed by the vitality and dynamism of the volunteers and staff I met and by the sense of solidarity and common purpose between them. It seemed to me that although they were certainly doing some important work with the issue of domestic and sexual violence, this was secondary to the main work of the center, which had more to do with the generalized sense of "crisis." Like Zhenskii Svet, the Pskov center acted as a kind of workshop or support center for local women who, like my Zhenskii Svet friends, found themselves downsized and devalued in the new democratic Russia. And like Zhenskii Svet, the Pskov center was as important for the women staff and volunteers as it was for their clients. Indeed, the line between client and volunteer was often fuzzy. Elena told me some former clients returned to work unpaid as counselors on the hotline, or to do office work. In her view, they chiefly returned for *obshchenie* (social intercourse, personal contact), encouraged and inspired by the atmosphere and dynamism of this women's collective. Clearly, there was significant scope for local innovation within the crisis center network and the antiviolence campaigns.

Strategizing Aid in Tver'

As Valentina and I pooled the information we had learned over the last months, we realized that a crisis center was the most likely way to achieve the dream of founding a women's center in Tver'. My research had given me a sense of the rhythm and pace of the nascent network; I realized it was at a moment of expansion and sought new collaborators in order to found a National Association. To assist in this process, several international agencies were offering start-up funds to fledgling centers. Moscow-based crisis centers offered trainings, assisted by foundation support. These taught not only crisis counseling and nondirective listening skills (the hallmark skills of crisis centers), but also management, NGO development, and public relations. Meanwhile, Valentina realized that in Tver' local conditions were ripe. Through her work on the governor's commissions and at the Women's Assembly she had learned that partly out of obligation, partly out of personal commitment, some local officials were looking to support a crisis center. Forthcoming elections made this moment particularly opportune—the mayor was preparing for reelection and was eager to win the support of local women. Though her requests for support for a women's center fell on deaf ears, talk of "crisis center" caught powerbrokers' attention.

Oktiabrina

Oktiabrina[12] emerged as a key interlocutor during the weeks and months before our first seminars. I shared my discoveries with her and nurtured secret hopes that she would be interested in working with me on the crisis center project. As I have said, Oktiabrina was a newcomer who seemed to have great potential. She had gone through the Zhenskii Svet "corridor" with great enthusiasm and was now looking to find her own niche. She and I were drawn to each other because of our closeness in age and the fact that we were both newcomers to the city. In her self-presentation, Oktiabrina liked to emphasize her humble, unpretentious origins. She was not a "university type," as she put it, unlike Valentina and many of the other members of the group. Her mother was a librarian and her father an engineer, until he was disabled in an industrial accident. From the portrait that she drew of her parents, it was clear that they had little cultural capital, but that they were staunch believers in state socialism and its promise. They had brought her up to be truthful and honest; she was a good *Komsomolka* and had a strong sense of fairness. It came as a shock to her, therefore, to be confronted by the unfairness and hypocrisy of the Soviet system. She told me that she had first become aware of it when she applied to study in the prestigious department of education at the local university. While waiting in the corridor to be interviewed, she overheard conversations between teachers and parents that clearly communicated the workings of *blat*. While she had to study hard for entrance exams, the door was open for the sons and daughters of Party and state high-ups. In response, she withdrew her application, announcing to her parents that she couldn't become a teacher, since it would entail telling children stories about the USSR that she now knew were untruths (that it was the best country in the world, that it was fair). She told me that she had decided to study medicine because it represented something authentic and unambiguous to her. "Medicine is real," she told me. "When I see a problem, I want to do something to resolve it." In this way, she expressed the idealism and sense of social responsibility commonly manifested by Russian physicians. It is important to note that the Soviet medical profession was quite differently configured than in the United States or Western Europe. Doctors were not highly remunerated; during the Soviet period they received lower salaries than many manual workers, a fact that persists. As a result, the medical profession is feminized, with women comprising the majority of practitioners. Further, although they did have a great deal of social prestige—and the ability to generate capital through informal practices due to their position as providers of needed services—medical doctors did not have the same expert authority as in the West. Like other specialists, doctors were prevented from attaining professional status by the party-state (Rivkin-Fish 2005:23–28).[13]

Oktiabrina always impressed me by her vitality, optimism, and generosity. She took me under her wing as a fellow newcomer to the city, and invited me to join her and her family in different social events. She invited me to her young daughter's school play, to the theater, and on picnics. As we got to know each other better, she told me more about her life. Her confidence and general poise was such that I was completely taken by surprise to learn of the chain of events that had brought her to the city. I learned that she and her husband had moved from Siberia because they could no longer afford to live there. After working unpaid for six months in the institute where they were employed, they made the decision to sell and move to Tver' where his parents lived. They sold the pleasant two-room apartment they had moved into as newlyweds and deposited the money in the Tver' Universal Bank, before flying to Moscow. When they tried to access these funds from Tver' a few weeks later, they discovered that the bank had collapsed and their savings had disappeared. Three years on, they had given up all expectation of receiving compensation and lived in a cramped and shabby one-room apartment that they rented on the edge of town. Even medicine let her down. In the lean post-socialist conditions she had struggled to find a professional niche; this was no mean feat for someone outside the networks of patronage and connection. For a while she worked at a private clinic, but she quickly became disenchanted catering for wealthy clientele. She even tried working in "commerce," as she put it, selling the imported dietary supplements that have flooded the Russian market since the early 1990s. She quit in disgust after a few weeks, however. Selling a product she thought was unfairly expensive and unnecessary made no sense to her. Disenchanted by her attempts to make money, she decided instead to prioritize professional satisfaction. She told me that if she could not make much money, she had decided that she might as well do something that interested her. To that end, she took courses in two forms of alternative medicine that were becoming increasingly popular in Russia, acupuncture and hirudlogia, or leech healing, and began to practice at the local hospital.[14] Her earnings were meager, however.

Oktiabrina had learned about the existence of Zhenskii Svet through a newspaper article. She was inspired by the activities of the group and its philosophy and quickly formed friendships with some of the other group members. She attended some of Valentina's lectures and some sessions of the evening school, wherein she learned about women's history, the international women's movement, and about what she called a "gender approach" (*gendernyi podkhod*), of which she thoroughly approved. She understood it to mean that men and women do not have to be constrained by their sex and that gender is a social construction. It was clear that group involvement had brought about changes in her thinking about her own life. Retrospectively, she defined her relationship with her husband as a *partnerskoe otnoshenie*, a "partnership of equals." They had moved to Siberia as newlyweds and she had given birth to their daughter shortly afterwards. Far from relatives, they could not count on the support of extended family as was customary in Russia. In this environment, they learned to work together. She proudly told me that they shopped and did chores together, and that he helped with childrearing and liked to cook. She was determined to be a strong role model for her daughter, then age eleven.

When I met her, Oktiabrina was looking for a niche, a place to which she could bring her considerable energies and which would allow her independence. "I'm not afraid of hard work," she told me, "the main thing is that I am committed to what I do." She dreamed of being able to bring about a unity between what she called her hobby (issues of women's health, the women's movement) and her career. The idea of setting up a crisis center appealed to her because it most closely approximated the "concrete social project" she had dreamed of being involved in. Her own economic vulnerability meant that she was attuned to the plight of the women in the city and she wanted to do something practical to meet their needs. Furthermore, as a doctor whose work brought her into intimate proximity with issues of women's well-being and health, she was persuaded by the issue of domestic violence. She had noticed that many of her women patients had bruises under their clothes. "It was obvious that some of them had violent spouses, but there was no way to talk to them about it," she said.

Through our meetings and seminars, we discussed these possibilities and came to see a crisis center as an ideal umbrella project. It offered a way to strengthen and institutionalize some of the more socially oriented programs offered by Zhenskii Svet. The crisis center could be a potential base from which already existing projects could be run and new ones could be devised. In our discussions, we thrashed out a vision and a plan for what the crisis center would look like. We ultimately decided—and my input was crucial here—that in order to be viable, we had to embrace the "international model" of violence against women and focus on sexual and domestic violence. This meant temporarily moving away from the broader conception of generalized economic violence that some of the women (including Lydia) supported. In practice, the women hoped to be able to address these wider issues and saw the crisis center as a kind of diagnostic. As Oktiabrina put it, "We don't yet know the extent to which domestic violence is the most important issue facing women." After reading the book *How to Start and Manage a Women's Crisis Center*, Oktiabrina said that she had a lot of respect for the crisis center model, but that she had a lot of questions about it too: "Seventy percent of all problems now in Tver' have a material basis. I'm not sure what crisis centers can do to resolve that." She conceptualized the crisis center as a pilot project through which we could learn more about women's real and most pressing needs and a new site from which to continue the educational and enlightenment work of Zhenskii Svet: "When women come for assistance and consultations in connection with real problems in their lives, then we can tell them about their rights. Then it's not abstract, but has some real basis."

Our Project and the "Exploitation of Western Intellectual Resources"

Beginning in late May 1998, Oktiabrina and I, coached by Valentina, set about our preparatory project to set up a crisis center. It was clear that in order for the crisis center to work, we would need the support of the local administration; a crisis center required stable office space and a telephone, resources only city officials could provide. At the same time, we clearly needed foundations—for access to training and know-how and material resources (computers, photocopying). We had a lot to achieve in the two months that remained before I flew back to the United States and we wanted to use the time well. Through the PAR seminars we were able to pool our resources, to present and refine the project and invite others to join us. We were able to recognize and define our individual and collective resources, to figure out a division of labor and a way to deploy them. My task, as I have explained in earlier chapters, was to liaise with both local powerbrokers and foundation representatives—to use my foreignness and the access it allowed to win them over.

In the weeks before and after our first seminar, Valentina sent me to "interview" and smooth talk some of the members of the city administration she knew to be favorably disposed towards the crisis center project who were influential in the allocation of resources to nongovernmental groups. She suggested that I introduce myself as a former crisis counselor and researcher writing a book, interested in the perspectives of women in the administration. "Their doors will open for a Western visitor," she told me, "but never for me." Sure enough, she was right. A phone call to Irina Mikhailova, the director of the state Social Protection Agency whom Valentina had been trying to reach for days, yielded an invitation to meet and to give a presentation at an upcoming conference on the family and the state. It emerged that Mikhailova had recently returned from a visit to Germany where she had visited a crisis center for the first time. Enthusiastic about what she had seen, she invited me to talk from my experience of crisis centers in the United States. Valentina was delighted, since she knew that the conference would be attended by some key powerbrokers in the *oblast'* and city administration. We wrote a carefully crafted speech that emphasized my ties both to Zhenskii Svet and to international foundations and emphasized my willingness to collaborate with the local authorities to set up a crisis center. I delivered my paper to an audience that included the deputy governor to the *oblast'* and the president's representative, Liubov' Petrovna Shvedova. This woman had significant power in the city, and I hoped to be able to make contact with her.

Shvedova sat at the head of the conference as I gave my presentation and seemed to be listening attentively. However, she and the members of her entourage mysteriously vanished during the lunch break before I could reach her. Despite my best efforts, I was unable to track her down—the institute's dining hall, where I had naïvely hoped to be able to find her, was empty, and it seemed she had vanished. I thought I had failed my mission; however, all was not lost. At the beginning of the afternoon session, an elderly man wove his way towards me through the crowd—Shvedova's assistant, bearing her gold embossed business card. "Liubov Petrovna awaits your call," he said.[15] This phone call, once accomplished, led to the eventual support of the Women's Assembly. Shvedova assigned two of her subordinates within the administration to work with us and pledged to lobby the mayor to find us rent-free office space.

Meanwhile, Oktiabrina and I set about getting integrated in the crisis center network. I recognized that one of the most important things I could offer her was acquaintance with some of the main players. The more I had seen of the third sector and foundation-sponsored women's NGOs, the more I had realized how crucial acquaintance was. For Oktiabrina to succeed, she had to become integrated into this *tusovka* (scene/hangout). Ironically, I, the outsider, was in a position to facilitate this. Ever the pragmatist, Oktiabrina realized that she had a lot of learning to do before she could proceed. She drew up a list of priorities:

to visit crisis centers, to sit in on consultations, and speak with staff and volunteers. In May and June we made several visits to Moscow to visit the crisis center ANNA. Due to the excellent networking abilities of its founder, this center now served as a lynchpin or clearinghouse organization, liaising between foundations and other crisis centers, organizing conferences and running training programs for provincial centers. I had introduced the Tver' project to the ANNA staff at a recent crisis center conference; this had yielded invitations to visit and pledges of possible inclusion on future training programs.

The ANNA staff received us gracefully. As I say, our project coincided with a moment of expansion for the network, and so they welcomed newcomers. They were especially pleased to meet provincial newcomers. Donor fatigue with Moscow and St. Petersburg had led to a new trend to support provincial groups. The deputy director, Irina, gave us an overview of the work of ANNA and the network more broadly, telling us that they based their work on the Western model but adapted it to suit Russian circumstances ("Why reinvent the wheel?" as Irina put it). She told us that through telephone hotlines and individual consultations, center staff and volunteers provided free and confidential legal and psychological counseling to female victims of sexual or domestic violence. Some centers had organized support groups for women victims. Irina told us that counselors (ideally) underwent eighty hours of training, run by staff of the most experienced centers with input from feminist psychologists, scholars, and lawyers. They were trained in nondirective listening skills, crisis counseling, and suicide prevention, and they attended feminist-oriented lectures on the myths and stereotypes of rape and domestic violence. She told us that most crisis centers also did educational work, which she called *likbez*, ironically recalling this Soviet abbreviation for "the liquidation of [political] illiteracy." She explained that the ANNA staff ran seminars and trainings not only for regional crisis centers, but for policemen, lawyers, and doctors too, in cities all over the Russian Federation.

As we visited the different centers, Oktiabrina sized up her new peers and contemporaries within the crisis center movement. She was greatly impressed by the professionalism of many of the women she encountered and by the scope of the work they were doing. "It's real," she said, as we left the offices of ANNA, "a new kind of social expertise." It was clear to her that they were filling a void and providing services (for free) that had never before been offered. She was impressed by the feminist paradigm of the campaigns, its "gender approach" that provided a framework for understanding domestic and sexual violence without blaming women victims. It was consistent with the gender education she had received through Zhenskii Svet and had found to be so powerful in making sense of her own life. She was greatly impressed by the levels of support the campaigns were able to offer activists. In June we traveled to Pskov on an official internship or training visit sponsored by the Tver' Women's Assembly, and I introduced Oktiabrina to Natalia and her colleagues. The women spent long hours in the kitchen talking about the specificities of provincial nongovernmental work (the art of collaborating with local authorities, how to attract volunteers, and the political economy of grants and funding). At the same time, they exchanged tales about their romantic and professional lives, deferring to each other at different moments (Natalia appealed to Oktiabrina as a doctor, and consulted her about her ailments, and Oktiabrina listened raptly as Natalia told us her insider tales—her time as a city deputy, what the authority structures looked like from within, her battles from within the administration). These two women now united in the women's movement had strikingly different backgrounds and life courses.

As we made these trips, we learned a great deal about the work of crisis centers and about networking. Our self-presentation improved as we gained in confidence and grew steadily more persuaded by the project. In her interactions with the women she met, Oktiabrina spoke about Zhenskii Svet with an increasing sense of inclusion and personal investment. She spoke with pride of its history and educational projects. Our preparatory project cemented both our friendship and our sense of belonging in Zhenskii Svet. And as we honed our networking skills, a subtle shift took place between us, and our roles changed. I had been the facilitator of these encounters and introduced her to people. But while I was able to get us in the door, she was able to form different kinds of relationships and make more durable connections. While the Russian activists I had met through my research regarded me warmly and I was granted a kind of insider-status due to my close association with Zhenskii Svet, I was still an outsider, a foreign researcher seen to be primarily pursuing my own ends. Oktiabrina was in the trenches with them, and while I was leaving, she was in it to stay. I noticed how the activists I had introduced her to spoke to her in a different way; they chose to present different, deeper information that included personal details about their struggle to balance family life, and about the political economy of grants and funding.

It was a whirl of activity, and a lot of fun. "It feels like we're in a film with an unknown director!" she exclaimed once as we left the offices of ANNA, after having received the pledge of inclusion on their next counseling training program; "We are not guiding the plot ourselves, but doors keep opening for us— and while they do, we're going to keep pushing through!" For me, the high point of our breathless two-month-long preparatory project was our trip to the Moscow office of the American Bar Association, which marked Oktiabrina's first encounter with foreign agency representatives.[16] I was acquainted with Kristen, a young American woman who worked there as the lone "gender expert." Despite the existence of a Gender Issues program, gender was less mainstreamed in these offices; I gathered that many of her colleagues considered her work to be peripheral to their broader mandate. Still, she used her small budget to work tirelessly with the crisis center network, assisting Russian lawyers to work with crisis centers in support of women victims of sexual and domestic violence. I called Kristen in May, knowing she was soon leaving Russia, and asked if we could drop by. She readily agreed, inviting us to her farewell party. We arrived to find things in disarray; a typical North American office party, with most people still at their desks. Kristen invited us to sit a while with two newcomers—her successor, Dianne, a lawyer and long-term women's activist from New Mexico, and her colleague, a human rights lawyer from Texas. They were in Russia for the first time and seemed rather overwhelmed and at loose ends. At any rate, they were glad for the diversion we provided. Enlivened by Oktiabrina's presence—Kristen had introduced her as the director of a new crisis center project in provincial Tver'—they invited her to tell them about herself and the project via their interpreter. We suddenly and unexpectedly found ourselves at center stage. As I receded into the background, Oktiabrina held forth, speaking eloquently about Zhenskii Svet, the excellent "school" it provided and how we had a ready pool of "well-adapted" feminist-oriented potential volunteers through the group. Two hours later as we stood by the elevator, invitations to seminars and offers of financial support ringing in our ears, we looked at each other with round eyes. "It's like a film!" she said, shaking her head, "Yes," I replied, "and you are the heroine: provincial woman! (*provintsial'ka*)."

The ABA proved to be a terrific source of support for us. Dianne, utilizing guerilla tactics she had honed during her work within the battered women's movement in the United States, was adept at cutting through red tape and stretching budgets. She helped us negotiate a modest grant that enabled Oktiabrina to buy office equipment and a computer; later she procured second-hand furniture from a U.S. office that was closing down, telling Oktiabrina it was hers if she could get to Moscow and pick it up. Meanwhile, we had been included on the next ANNA-run crisis center training course.

This foreign agency support was of crucial importance in Tver', where we were able to use it as a bargaining chip in our negotiations. Clearly ABA support and offers of office furniture and supplies was contingent upon office space. This now became the task. One morning in July, I set off to the buildings of the *oblast'* administration to check on the progress of our project. After we had exchanged pleasantries, Shvedova picked up the phone and dialed direct to the mayor. "Valentin Pavolovich," she began, "as you know, the Women's Assembly looks upon you quite favorably (*ne ravnodushno*). I ask you to receive Julie Hemment and Oktiabrina Cheremovskaia and to assist them in their crisis center project by finding them office space." Ten days before my departure to the United States, Valentina, Oktiabrina, and I met the mayor to discuss our project. We left his office with a pledge of free office space and two and a half paid staff positions.

Thus it was that we embarked upon this new "strategy of involvement," as Valentina called it. Our collaborative participatory project led us to do that which at the outset I had not at all expected or desired; in setting up a crisis center in the city, we entered the third sector of NGOs. The decision to undertake this project was a significant shift for the group and its members. It marked a move away from perestroika-era antipolitical formulations of societal activity and activism, toward the formulation put forward by international agencies; it was a step away from the *obshchestvennoe dvizhenie* (societal movement) to the third sector of NGOs. For the members of the group, especially for Valentina, this involved profound and costly personal shifts, too. It marked a shift from her deeply held commitment to voluntarism and the principle of enthusiasm, to a new vision of herself as an NGO professional. It marked a shift to a new vision of politics, from working determinedly outside the state, to working with it, using the foundations and the support of international agencies as a wedge. It marked a shift from her refusal to exploit her intellectual resources and networks of acquaintance within the women's movement to the measured, strategic deployment of them. In many ways it was a high-risk strategy, yet the stakes were high—and as Valentina put it in July 2004 when we sat reading early drafts of these chapters and recalled this period, "You can't stand still—like the CPSU (Communist Party of the Soviet Union)." And we went in with our eyes wide open.

The crisis center, *Gortensia* (literally, hydrangea, but named upon Valentina's suggestion in honor of Hortensia, a noblewoman in Ancient Rome who spoke out against militarization), was set up in the fall of 1998, directed by Oktiabrina and staffed by a group of interested women she pulled together who were prepared to start work on a voluntary basis. Valentina, Shvedova, and I were appointed to the board of directors. We had made substantial gains; we made important political alliances with both sets of powerbrokers that are crucial to the success of NGOs—actors within *vlast'* (the local administration), and the representatives of international foundations. The mayor's office had promised us rent-free office space, a telephone, and the salaried positions. The American Bar Association and ANNA, the Moscow-based crisis center clearing house, had pledged small grants for equipment and training.

Ours was a success story: a community group played the game of information and accountability politics (Keck and Sikkink 1998) to bring pressure on the local authorities to recognize a social need and made a successful bid for tender. This is the endpoint of civil society discourse, which in a fairytale way assumes that "they all live happily ever after." In Putnam's terms, this cell will begin to generate social capital, which is perceived to be a general good. According to this logic, the story ends here. I could have named this a "successful" outcome of a participatory project and stopped at this point; however, the ties between us did not permit me this comfortable resolution. The outcomes, predictably, were contradictory. I left Tver' in August 1998, leaving Oktiabrina to navigate the decidedly less exciting and breezy experience of becoming a professional, transnationally engaged women's activist. I have followed the project as closely as possible over the last years, during brief return trips (summer 1999, winter 1999, summer 2001, and most recently summer 2004) and through a couple of meetings we have had in the United States. As I have followed the project, I have watched Oktiabrina's shifting identifications as she has struggled to manage this transition, as she has navigated relationships with our two sets of beneficiaries—the local authorities and international foundations—and as she has labored to make gender matter.

5   A Tale of Two Projects

"If you tame me, my life will be filled with sunshine. I'll know the sound of
footsteps that will be different from all the rest. Other footsteps send me back
underground. Yours will call me out of my burrow like music. And then, look!
You see the wheat fields over there? I don't eat bread. For me wheat is of no
use whatever. Wheat fields say nothing to me. Which is sad. But you have hair
the color of gold. So it will be wonderful, once you've tamed me! The wheat,
which is golden, will remind me of you. And I'll love the sound of the wind
in the wheat."

Antoine de Saint-Exupéry, *The Little Prince*

Once again, I find myself at odds with the fox's predictions; at this stage in our
relationship, taming proved to have a much more complicated dynamic, and we
experienced only intermittent sunshine. If, in the preceding chapter, structure
seemed to be something we could dance through, here our collaboration took
on a quite different momentum. This chapter provides a portrait of the two
Zhenskii Svet projects—the Crisis Center and the Center for Women's History
and Gender Studies—between 1998, when the bulk of my fieldwork ended, to
2004. The transition to professionalized NGO work was neither smooth nor unambiguous for either Valentina or Oktiabrina, but the two projects followed
rather different paths and had divergent fates. While one project (the Center for
Women's History and Gender Studies) took off relatively easily, the other (the
crisis center) experienced a very bumpy and stressful start-up. At the same time
that I map the projects, I map the shifting contours of my own participation in
them. Initially foreseeing a very active role for myself beyond the field—as grant
writer, advocate—I was forced to change gears as my own center of gravity
shifted back to the United States. Here, I was dropping in and out of the political
"conversations" (Gibson-Graham 1994:220) we had begun together and struggling to keep up with them. Perhaps because of the changed nature of my participation in the projects, I have found the story most difficult to narrate, and I
have been pushed more than ever to think about the ethics of representation
(Fine et al. 2003). I offer this account of my own struggles not for the pleasures
of disclosure, but in order to contribute a discussion of the implications of departure, both from the field and from fieldwork relationships, a topic that has
been of concern for, though relatively little explored by, feminist anthropology
(Behar 1996; Berdahl 2000b; Enslin 1994).

In telling this tale of two projects, I have elected to focus on two themes.
First, I draw attention to shifts and change within the political economy of

grants and funding. Our experience underscores that neither are all funders equal, nor are all the campaigns that they finance. Second, I focus on the topic of informal acquaintance and its continued importance in the post-Soviet era. Those who are persuaded by the civil society message and the promise of the third sector in Russia face numerous compounded obstacles: poverty, bureaucratic red tape, lack of transparency and clear rules or regulations, and the persistence of Soviet-era patronage systems. How one experiences this depends centrally on one's location and the cultural resources one can muster. The transition to formalized activity involves cultural processes also. Some of the themes that emerge are the grave importance of cultural capital, connections, the ability to access information and the right people and resources, and the ability to massage and finesse these relationships, too. And I want to emphasize that these informal relationships are important not only to post-Soviet subjects, but to the Western European and North American people who work in donor agencies, also. A subtheme that emerges is the importance of acquaintance between donors and recipients, Russian activists and foreign agency representatives.

Summer 1998: The Projects Take Off as I Plan to Depart

We had easily won start-up support, but we needed to reinforce this if the projects were to be sustainable. The different projects had different needs. While the Center for Women's History and Gender Studies was provided basic infrastructural support by the university (office space and salaries for teachers), the crisis center was in a very different position. Strikingly, Oktiabrina had no salary; she had refused to take up one of the salaried positions offered, partly due to a lack of fit (they were designed for "specialists in social work"), partly because she was reluctant to compromise her independence, which she felt that taking on a municipally-sponsored position would entail. While Valentina began seeking materials and resources (books, support for conferences), Oktiabrina and I focused on securing running costs for the crisis center. During that summer, we made a number of grant applications, seeking support for both projects. Since many of the foundations, even in the late '90s, required applications to be completed in English, I took on the bulk of the writing. Valentina and I put in for a couple of Open Society grants for the Center for Women's History and Gender Studies,[1] and we began to look for potential sources of support for the crisis center. I knew from my participation in the crisis center conferences that many of the embassies were actively supporting crisis centers and decided to try the British Embassy, my own.[2] At the same time, we prepared to apply for a new Open Society grant, which organized and funded exchanges between activists of crisis centers in the former Soviet Union. The OSI Host-Visitor Exchange Program offered an apprenticeship model that felt particularly appropriate; we were delighted to find a grant that specifically supported newcomers to the crisis center network. Naming the project Crisis Center for Women— Women's Light, we sat down to brainstorm. Again, it had to be written in English, so I undertook the bulk of this work, liaising with one of the Moscow-based program officers, a friend and long-time women's activist I had gotten to know while undertaking research in Moscow.

Despite our shared concern and skepticism about funding agencies, I cannot deny that it was a dizzying and gratifying time. Writing grant applications eased my sense of anxiety about leaving the projects and my friends at such a sensitive stage; it was a new role I hoped I could continue to play from the United States. We were optimistic that funding could enable us to accomplish the goals we had set. Valentina hoped it would release her from other projects to focus on the educational work she held most dear. For Otkiabrina, it promised a new world and a new future when she could realize herself in the city and achieve the socially oriented project of which she had long dreamed. And applying ourselves to this new art of project crafting was fun. At this stage, we were clear that we were doing this on our own terms. We were a team, with a tight sense of history and shared purpose, derived in part from the discussions that took place during our seminars. The narratives we crafted emphasized the long history of Zhenskii Svet and its work, and the grants we put in for were small, concrete, and right on target. We felt confident that we were in the driver's seat, seeking support for projects we had defined in ways that did not compromise our integrity or independence.

And together, we were learning to work with the authorities; we had made useful allies who were helping us in our negotiations on behalf of the two projects. Olga Mikhailovna and Liudmila Pavlovna were mid-level officials who worked for two of our benefactors within the local administration; Olga Mikhailovna was as an aide in the mayor's office, and Liudmila Pavlovna worked within the regional administration under Shvedova, the president's representative to the *oblast'*. Originally assigned to work with us, they went beyond the required parameters to extend warmth and sympathy. Both socially oriented, newly interested in the women's movement (now dignified by the participation of local women entrepreneurs and officials in the Women's Assembly), and interestingly, both also recent newcomers to the city,[3] they found what we told them about Zhenskii Svet compelling and were interested in supporting the two projects.[4]

In the midst of this hustling, Valentina began to experience a very different form of relationship with international foundations. The cultural capital she'd accrued and the reputation she had gained through her work with foundations so far led to the series of invitations I mentioned in chapter 3. In the spring of 1998, Valentina was approached by Mary McAuley, head of the Moscow office of the Ford Foundation, and invited to host and direct the upcoming Summer School in Human Rights. And in July, shortly before my departure, she received something more substantial: an invitation to apply for an individual grant to support her work in setting up the Center for Women's History and Gender Studies under the auspices of Tver' State University. These grants, which guaranteed a decent stipend and money for travel, were rare and precious.[5] This was testimony both to the special place she occupied and to changes within the Ford Foundation. Through the workshops and conferences she had organized and participated in, Valentina had established herself not only as a serious and committed feminist activist and scholar, but as a good manager, too. At the same time, this was a period of reflection and reevaluation in the donor community, and I suspect that the principled distance she had held from grants and funding had also won her respect.[6]

I happened to visit Mary McAuley at the Ford Foundation at this time, and she asked me to carry the application materials back to Valentina. Back in Tver', Valentina sat down to write up a formal request using the guidelines she had received. Since the document had to be written in English, I assisted Valentina in drafting it. Together we sat and thought up a series of consultation meetings to advance the project, with feminist scholars she was acquainted with in Buffalo, N.Y., New York City, and Ithaca, N.Y. It was this individual grant that enabled her to visit me at Cornell—the time we made a copresentation and she quoted from *The Little Prince.*

In August 1998, I left Tver' for the United States to take up a writing fellowship at Cornell University. Although I felt upbeat about the projects, it was dreadfully hard to leave. And as I contemplated the implications of moving from participant to analyst, global political economic events forced me to refocus my attention on the changes my friends were facing. A few days after I left Tver', the Russian economy crashed, causing investors to flee in droves. In England I read hair-raising accounts of the devastation this caused, the losses incurred as people lost their entire savings. Liberal triumphalism, which had characterized press reports throughout the '90s, was replaced by the more somber tones of reevaluation: What had gone wrong? *Who lost Russia?*[7] I worried dreadfully about my friends and our new strategy. Would the financial support be safe? What if the international agencies left, just as the projects were getting off the ground?

December 1998 and Post-Crisis Russia

I returned to "post-crisis Russia" in December 1998, to find a new, more fragile environment. My activist friends in Moscow were shaken and fearful about their status—would the international foundations cut and run as so many foreign investors had done? But I found that in Tver', there was less concern. Although people talked freely of "the crisis," there was a sense of distance from it. Shielded from the economic fallout by the fact that they had never experienced monetary gains, my Zhenskii Svet friends spoke with some irony about it. However, they were preoccupied with new and more pressing difficulties.

While Valentina was engaged in preparatory work for the Center for Women's History and Gender Studies (negotiating with university administrators, preparing to travel to the United States), Oktiabrina was negotiating her own position. She found herself caught between two paymasters—the international foundations and the local authorities. These had very different norms of interaction and expectations, and she was required to study and learn to work with both.

More so than Valentina, whose "partner institution" (the university) she already knew, Oktiabrina had to learn to work with *vlast'* (the local organs of power, or the authorities). Despite the assistance of our allies in the administration, she found it an uphill struggle. In ways that recalled my Moscow activist friend Maria's account of adapting to the world of projects and NGOs (chapter 3), she told me of her struggles to find her way in this new field. We had expected that the transition to NGO work would require some learning. After all, this was a brand new profession and form of activity. But she had discovered that getting to know the authorities was an educational project in itself. She told me that *vlast'* had their own "rules of the game"; for someone who was not brought up in these circles, they were hard to fathom and penetrate. And unlike the literature of the third sector, this knowledge was not packaged and distributed.

I asked Oktiabrina to explain what she meant. Over tea in my room at the university hostel, she itemized the hurdles she had encountered over the last months. In order for it to be recognized as a "real" project, and to receive the support and funds already pledged, she had to undergo a series of complicated bureaucratic steps. The mayor's office required a series of formal letters from her that laid out her requests (office space, telephone). She then had to petition the municipal property committee in order to lay claims to specific rooms. The mayor's office had initially suggested a form of collaboration that she could not accept (that she register the organization not as a societal organization—*obshchestvennaia organizatsiia*—but as a "noncommercial partnership," a legal designation neither she nor anyone else understood). She received contradictory advice from the people she consulted and wasn't sure what to do. When she finally decided upon the correct course of action (her Moscow-based crisis center colleagues insisted that she must found an *obshchestvennaia organizatsiia*), she hit other bureaucratic walls. The formal registration process itself was full of hurdles. With a grimace, she explained the complicated legal documentation she was required to assemble before she could register: a charter, a letter from the director of the building confirming that she had permission to use the rooms, and a signed document confirming the identity of the founders. She encountered a complex web of material and psychological hurdles to these seemingly straightforward tasks. First, the director of the building was in hospital and she could not get the signature for one month. Second, she found it hard to write these formal letters; she wasn't sure what they should look like and had no mastery of the necessary bureaucratese. Finally, she had no word processor or typewriter and had to borrow from friends. When she finally submitted the documents, she ended up playing an exhausting game of tag with the justice administration, who kept finding different faults with her paperwork, which was returned to her several times. Eventually, Liudmila Pavlovna, our ally in Shvedova's office, assisted her by calling the office. "You see," she said, when this tactic worked, "they needed a phone call," an intervention which, though helpful, only underscored Oktiabrina's outsider status and lack of connections. Oktiabrina finally submitted the documents in early December and expected to receive registration in January. She told me that the nightmare wasn't over—the next steps were to open a bank account and to register at the tax inspector's office. These promised to be complex bureaucratic procedures also, and entailed some financial commitment, since opening a bank account involved fees.

I was amazed to learn of these structural impediments and marveled at Oktiabrina's staying power. She had to accomplish all these tasks to establish the right to receive what she had already been promised. There was no transparency to guide her, no rules and regulations to help her find her way, certainly no website detailing these steps or explaining the format her applications should take. And despite the mayor's support, she received constant messages that she was incompetent and inferior from lower level officials, and even veiled threats that her center might be taken away from her.

These delays were not only painful to endure, but they had consequences and almost upset relations with our other set of benefactors; we came close to losing the Soros Host-Visitor grant because the paperwork took so long to complete. When I called her from Tver' in December, my friend in the Moscow office told me rather sharply, "If the organization is not real, then the application is invalidated." This unsympathetic comment underscored her lack of awareness of provincial conditions and the uphill struggle Oktiabrina was facing, revealing once again the gulf between Moscow and other cities.

Meanwhile, as Oktiabrina struggled to make it exist on paper, the "real" work of the new center continued. In August she and Lena, a former student of Valentina's, had attended a weeklong telephone hotline training in Moscow run by ANNA. Excited by the course, she pulled together a group of interested women who were prepared to start work on a voluntary basis. Some were students, but most were women she had known through her work at the hospital. She led seminars based on the training she had received in Moscow. These were both skills-based (active listening and crisis counseling skills) and substantive (on the "myths" and "prejudices" around domestic and sexual violence). At first they gathered once a week in the cramped office she shared with another doctor at the hospital where she worked. They then met in the dark, unheated, empty room that they had been allocated by the mayor's office, discussing and debating the issues with enthusiasm. Like Oktiabrina, these women were looking for a niche, for meaningful, socially oriented forms of employment. They were drawn to the project because they were compelled by its newness, its focus on women, and by Oktiabrina herself. Her enthusiasm and sense of mission were compelling.

In contrast with her difficulties with *vlast*, Oktiabrina had achieved a relatively easy accord with her new colleagues within the network of crisis centers. She thought highly of the individuals she encountered in her work and had a good working relationship with the agency representatives she had met. The direct collaborations we had negotiated were working out well—the ABA representative had visited Tver' and run seminars the fall; Oktiabrina spoke highly of the ANNA training she had attended, and of subsequent trips and trainings they had led in Tver'. However, she chafed at the uncertainties of the donor-

Zhenskii Svet participants and university colleagues gather at Valentina's apartment, winter 1998.

recipient relationship she found herself in and was critical of the broad logic and decisions she saw being made. In November, she had attended a Joint U.S.-Russia Conference on Family Violence in Moscow. The delegates were greeted by a fax from Madeleine Albright wishing them well in their struggle. However, this high-profile event had disappointed her; on the Russian side, crisis center staff and volunteers were greatly outnumbered by representatives of *vlast'*—representatives of the Ministry of Internal Affairs, regional social services, and educational ministries. In terms that recalled anthropologist Don Kalb's critique of civil society projects as a "celebratory banquet" for elites (Kalb 2002), she told me that the conference did not achieve much and that the lavish expenditures were a dreadful waste; "They could have used that money to set up a regional crisis center and to keep it running!" She told me she felt uncomfortable about all the jostling and hustling for resources that she saw going on. The Muscovites grabbed all that they could, swooped in on the foreigners, giving out their business cards left, right, and center. She lamented, "I understood how important it is to have the [English] language—without it, I was totally at a loss and had no way of making contact with these people."

This was a vulnerable stage in the crisis center's development. Indeed, the structural circumstances and rules of the game as determined by both foundations and local authorities kept Oktiabrina in an insecure position vis-à-vis both sets of power brokers. She told me that she had caught wind of local jealousies—people had asked her suspiciously, "How did you get to the mayor?" Now that the structure of the center was in place and on the books, she was afraid that someone else might step up and displace her. She had devised a cunning way to protect herself from this—she realized that she could use me as a "defense shield" against these local appropriations and against suggestions for the center that she did not approve. In invoking me and our relationship—"Julie would not support that!"—she was subtly reinforcing the fact that the project and support of foreign agencies depended on her own participation in the project.

Summer 1999: Unraveling

When I next returned to Tver' six months later, I found a very uncertain situation. It seemed to me to be a time of unraveling, when the fate of the crisis center looked unsure and the contradictions of trying to set up a professional NGO in these uncertain provincial circumstances appeared almost insurmountable. Oktiabrina was experiencing something far different from the easy rhythms of the early stages of the project; the "invisible director" appeared to have packed up and gone home. And the contradictions of my own participation in the project felt acute; my fieldnotes capture my uncertainty as I struggled with different tasks: to catch up with all that had happened since I had been away, to comprehend the processes in motion, and to support my friend and partner Oktiabrina.

On the one hand, I learned that great strides had been made: the center was open every day; it had five full-time staff, four of whom had salaried positions, and several volunteers (many of whom were Valentina's students). Six of the women had undergone the ANNA crisis counseling training program. The ABA/CEELI and Open Society grant money had come through and the center was modestly furnished—with chairs, a couple of tables, shelves packed with booklets and leaflets from the Russian women's movement (bulletins of the Moscow-based Independent Women's Forum, several copies of the journal *Vy i my*—You and We) and crisis center materials. There were pictures on the wall, including posters from the campaign "Say No to Domestic Violence," and a potted hydrangea. The center was well equipped, with a computer, printer, photocopy machine, TV, video player, and camera. It looked every inch the provincial NGO, yet Oktiabrina and her colleagues were prevented from doing much of their work and faced some serious structural contradictions and constraints.

First, despite the mayor's order, there was no telephone. In fact, there was only one public telephone in the whole building; crisis center staff had to go downstairs and wait in long lines to use it and, of course, there was no possibility of taking incoming calls under such circumstances.[8] Hence, they were unable to set up a hotline. Oktiabrina experienced this as a major roadblock and felt that the rooms were nearly useless without it. The women had been trained specifically as telephone counselors and were less able to handle face-to-face clients.

She would have liked to hire a professional psychologist who could have run groups and done face-to-face in-depth counseling, but the salary levels she had been awarded were the lowest (and "cheapest") on the books—designed specifically to support social workers, they were worth only 330 rubles. It was impossible to attract experienced professionals at such wages. Equally, she was prevented from taking on the legal aspect of the crisis center project, because she could not afford a professional lawyer. Until they had a phone Oktiabrina did not see the virtue of advertising the center widely, and they had received relatively few clients accordingly. Many of these clients had heard about the service by word of mouth because they knew one of the staff or volunteers, or they had come in to the office by accident. Prevented from what she considered the real business of the center, the work she had been prepared to do, she improvised, choosing to focus instead on the educational aspect of the anti–gendered violence campaign. She and her co-workers had given awareness-raising talks on domestic and sexual violence in schools, at the university, and in local factories. However, they were frustrated and felt constrained from undertaking the work they considered most important.

Another key problem was a structural contradiction that derived from the center's status. Although it was registered as an independent nongovernmental organization (*obshchestvennaia organizatsiia*) and headed by Oktiabrina, the salaried positions were provided by the administration of the municipal Social Protection Agency; *her* staff members were *agency* employees.[9] This led to a number of difficulties. Despite her formal independence, Oktiabrina was dependent upon this agency. Indeed, she was required to submit monthly accounts of the center's activities to the director, work which she felt was not only burdensome and time consuming, but pointless, since they had very different values and the director did not understand the work of a crisis center. Later, when I visited Tver' in 2004 after the crisis center had closed, she showed me the dense piles of documents she kept stored in a cupboard in her apartment; these were the accounts required by the local authorities, which she was obliged to keep for ten years. Further, the agency made considerable demands on the time of her salaried staff, requiring them to spend two full days a week at the agency working on the phone. Oktiabrina explained to me that they were not able to do crisis counseling there, since the phone they had access to was a *kontaktni telefon,* that is, a kind of general information number that people call to make appointments. There was no privacy, and there were always lots of people milling around. The demands of the Social Protection Agency director not only prevented her staff from focusing on the work of the crisis center but also undermined Oktiabrina's own status. She was left in an ambiguous position and had no clear authority. These contradictions had led to a series of run-ins with the administration of the Social Protection Agency; Oktiabrina was frustrated and felt that the director was behaving high-handedly and making unreasonable demands on her staff; the director felt that she was "ungrateful" and not pulling her weight. Since the work was incomprehensible to her it was also invisible, and she was suspicious that the rooms were being wasted and that nothing was being done. Hence, she occasionally sent her representatives to check up on the crisis center.

These tensions became apparent to me through my interactions with Oktiabrina and her staff in the context of the first seminar I ran at the crisis center. Two of her co-workers, Ira and Olga, had just returned from the Social Protection Agency, offended at the way that they had been addressed by the director. They felt caught in the middle of two often contradictory sets of demands—those of Oktiabrina as director of the crisis center, and those of their other boss. It was an uncomfortable discussion, and I felt bad for Oktiabrina. The ironies of being director of such a project were multiple. First, her partner institution—the Social Protection Agency—had very different goals and origins and did not understand the work of a crisis center. Second, unlike the Center for Gender Studies, which was based on an already existing form of solidarity, she was faced with the task of creating a sense of unity and solidarity among her staff. At this stage, none of the staff had attended Zhenskii Svet; they neither had the "gender approach," nor bonds of loyalty to the group and its history. Under these circumstances, it was hard to establish a clear division of labor. Struggling in this new terrain under quite stressful circumstances, she ended up taking on most of the work and was clearly overwhelmed and exhausted.

We didn't talk much about the content of the work (the gendered violence campaigns) that summer. As I look through the notes and jottings I took during that time, I see the extent to which I was preoccupied with issues of organizational development. The crisis center was a professional NGO; it needed a clear division of labor, clear priorities and goals. But Oktiabrina's circumstances were sharply at odds with the professionalism required of an NGO worker. She was putting all of her time and energy into the crisis center, to the detriment of her own material well-being. She was working full time at the crisis center unpaid, and thus she had no time to practice (and hence earn) through leech healing. Indeed, her new position was contributing to an unraveling of her professional expertise and qualifications. She explained that unless she took additional medical examinations within the next year, she would be disqualified from practicing. She spoke with frustration of her position within the contradictory topography of the NGO world she had entered, and was acutely aware of her marginal position vis-à-vis the center. Following the same logic described in chapter 2, many of the large international agencies preferred to concentrate their funds by supporting clearinghouses, which were usually based in Moscow or St. Petersburg; this meant that only small grants were available for provincial centers.[10] There were inconsistencies, too. While agencies did not provide funds to meet running costs (rent, salaries) for provincial centers, the metropolitan centers had their overheads paid for, and Moscow-based consultants received relatively substantial compensation. While she respected the individuals, she objected to the logic, "It's all based on acquaintance," she said bitterly, "they appoint the people they trust and they stay with them. As for voluntarism—well, it just doesn't make sense in our circumstances." The crisis center model she had signed on to by joining the international campaigns offered no clear guidelines; the "NGO kit" turned out to be inadequate.

And her work as director of a crisis center threatened to be derailed by her own crisis. The parallel story of summer 1999 was the story of Oktiabrina's own economic vulnerability. As I have already explained, Oktiabrina and her family lost their life savings shortly after arriving in the city in 1996, when the bank where they had deposited them crashed. Instead of buying an apartment as they had intended, they were forced to rent a small one-room flat. Ultimately they hoped to be allocated an apartment through her husband's workplace, but in the meantime, they had to make their own arrangements.[11] Earlier in the spring the lease had ended, and the landlord refused to renew it. Her husband and daughter had moved back in with his parents, in a small house outside the city that they shared with his sister and her family. Oktiabrina, who needed to be closer to town, had found temporary lodging in a hostel. She told me it was dirty, unpleasant, and unsafe. One of her neighbors there was an alcoholic, and she refused to let her daughter stay there. She had to move out again imminently, and she was desperately consumed by the struggle to find a permanent home for herself and her family. This was a struggle not just for a roof over her head, but for legal status too. While her husband was officially registered at his parents' house outside of the city, she was not registered anywhere. Without a *propiska* (residence permit), she was vulnerable—a "nobody," in her words—and had no rights.[12] I want to emphasize that once again connections could have offset this. The contradictions of the Soviet system were most acute when it came to issues of residency and living space. Following the dissolution of the USSR, populations were in tremendous flux, residency requirements notwithstanding. Those who were able to do so used *blat* connections to circumvent official restrictions and controls as they had always done, gaining either state-allocated living space or the opportunity to buy land or real estate advantageously. As a newcomer in the city, without a background in the institutions of the party-state, Oktiabrina didn't have these connections. But there is more to it than that. Mobilizing *blat* relationships requires not only a form of cultural knowledge, but a certain disposition, too (Ledeneva 1998:113–117).[13] Oktiabrina's new position as director of the crisis center put her in proximity to powerbrokers. She could have used these new relationships to her advantage; however she chose not to do so. Later, when I shared my analysis in this chapter with her during a return visit in 2004, she confirmed this. She told me that a couple of years into the project, in conversation, the mayor had asked her where she lived. She had refused to say. "I wasn't going to tell him I live in a communal apartment!" she exclaimed, "I told him that I was talking to him in a public capacity (*kak obshschestvennoe litso*) and that he didn't need to know my personal problems." In response to this, she told me with a smile, he had exclaimed in astonishment, "You're not very contemporary, Oktiabrina Evgenevna!" Her refusal to maximize her self-interest in the face of such obstacles surely begs interpretation. This was not due to some stubborn determination to remain materially impoverished, or because she did not think she was owed this support. Indeed, she—and the rest of the Zhenskii Svet women—felt that she was due support from the city, because of the service she was providing. However, to *ask* for this support was a different matter. Once again, in refusing to engage in these informal strategies with powerbrokers, Oktiabrina was refusing to play by what she called the "rules of the game." Engaging in this game would have entailed a kind of moral compromise that she was unwilling or unable to make. Exploiting these burgeoning connections would have felt inappropriate; it would have contravened both her own values and those embodied by Zhenskii Svet. Regardless of these nuances, however, at the time, Oktiabrina's structural insecurity lent an additional edge to her interactions and negotiations with powerbrokers. The people upon whom she depended for the future of the crisis center were the same people who had the power to allocate living space, as she was acutely aware. At the same time she was hustling and petitioning on behalf of the crisis center, she must have been thinking about her *lichnyi vopros* (personal issue).

My Zhenskii Svet friends were well aware of the predicament and met me with an urgent barrage of information. Deeply concerned about Oktiabrina, they were also becoming concerned about the crisis center and sensed danger. Valentina had caught wind of grumbles from some of our benefactors in the Women's Assembly, who were only too eager to take credit and lay blame. Valentina knew Oktiabrina was struggling in her dealings with the local authorities and empathized greatly. Over the years she had frequently encountered similar problems—lack of comprehension and hostility toward her work, and disdain on the part of officials. One day as the three of us sat in her kitchen drinking tea, she urged Oktiabrina not to take it to heart, to "just put up a screen between yourself and the job—don't pay any attention, or take it personally." However, this wasn't always easy, as the following incident reveals.

The Telephone

The most concrete issue Oktiabrina wanted to resolve was the telephone. She told me that the rooms were nearly useless without one and that she regretted accepting them. She was consumed by the paradox this presented. She told me how she had written letters upon letters, had been bounced back and forth from office to office, but nothing budged. Once again, she had been granted something, was entitled to it, and yet it wasn't there. She told me that she was considering paying to have a phone installed with the remainder of the American Bar Association grant, but couldn't get a definitive answer as to how much it would cost. She had been sent from office to office, and each person she had spoken to named a different sum. Furthermore, she was fearful of spending the money, since the mayor had guaranteed them this office rent-free only until the new year. What if they were turned out of the building?

As the importance of this issue became clear to me, I decided to focus my energies on it. Together, we brainstormed steps to take. While she consulted with local people, I contacted some of my Moscow NGO acquaintances. One of them, a Moscow-based American lawyer, who worked closely with crisis centers under the Women in Law project, was able to help us. Long experienced in working with the Russian authorities, Gabbi devised a clever solution. She would pledge money ($400) to have the phone installed, on condition that we were given a legal guarantee that we would not lose the office.[14]

One morning in July 1999, Oktiabrina and I visited Olga Mikhailovna, the mayor's aide who had been a staunch supporter of the crisis center project, and told her about Gabbi's pledge. She explained to us that it no longer depended on the mayor's office—the letter had already been sent out and it was now in the hands of the director of *Dom Byta*, the building where the crisis center was located; she was the pivotal person who could provide this guarantee. When we learned that the director had once taken classes with Valentina, we invited her along for this delicate negotiation.[15]

A few days later, Valentina, Olga Mikhailovna, and I gathered at the crisis center to meet with the director. The four of us chatted over tea and biscuits, exchanging pleasantries and asking the director about herself. The woman, who had a rather stern and forbidding demeanor and with whom I could well imagine it hard to find a common language, began to soften as we explained our dilemma. Could she help us resolve it? She explained to us some of the complexities we had not understood: our lease was secure for one year; meanwhile she explained that we did not have to pay to have a new telephone cable installed (as we had believed); there were three telephone points vacant in the building— two that belonged to a firm that had left the building, and a third belonging to a woman who had also left but who owed a lot of money. If we could reach an agreement with one of them and receive their official refusal, we could pay off their debts and take over the line. When she left, Valentina and Olga exchanged smiling glances. They gently chided Oktiabrina and coached her to adopt a different strategy—"Did you see her reaction to us at first? And how it changed, how she warmed up to us later? You need to visit her, to be diplomatic, make her feel included." Olga Mikhailovna urged her to defer to her: "You need to go to her as if to your mama, tell her all the little things that you do, include her, ask her advice, invite her to things." Valentina nodded eagerly and made additional suggestions—we could form a political council of the crisis center, and invite her and some of the administrators of the Social Protection Agency onto it; we could invite them to meet with Moscow trainers when they visit, it would make them feel included.

I watched as this delicate cultural choreography unfolded. To them it was obvious what was necessary and where Oktiabrina had gone wrong—but of course, this did not take into account the painful structural contradictions she was facing that lent a sharp edge to these encounters. As previously, she was refusing to play by the rules of the game, to abide by the Soviet era contract: "You're the boss and I'm the fool." As a recipient of state-sponsored largesse, she was required to be dependent and grateful. But her pride and independence, the characteristics that had earlier led her to withdraw her application to study in the education department and had later prevented me from grasping the severity of her economic situation when we first met, made it hard for her to do this.

In setting up the crisis center, Oktiabrina was entering the "new profession" of the third sector that was propagandized by the literature I've examined in chapter two. However, she clearly found this move less liberating than constraining. Many of her difficulties stemmed from the fact that she was struggling to change her expertise and to retool. She felt unsure of herself, of how to comport herself. Further, the new profession was not understood. What had worked for the well-connected, *Komsomol*-affiliated Galina, director of the Humanitarian Institute, did not work so smoothly for Oktiabrina. In the absence of already existing networks and *nomenklatura* connections, the local officials she encountered saw her not as a bold pioneer of an important new sector but as a hustler; hence she was met with derision and superciliousness. Indeed, this was reinforced to me when the director returned ten minutes later with a document she had promised us. Mollified by our conversation, she was softer, more open, and in passing confided that she had problems with her health. Oktiabrina took over, moving into the more familiar professional mode of doctor, and as she did so, the woman relaxed and her demeanor changed. In soothing, professional tones, Oktiabrina asked her a series of questions; she invited her to sit down next to her and clasped her hands, and began to squeeze her pressure points. She made some recommendations and the women parted happily. I was struck by the ease with which this latter interaction took place and by the transformation it effected in both women. In the course of this interaction, the director of *Dom Byta* softened, and Oktiabrina moved in her eyes from being an irritating petitioner, to a person deserving of her attention and humanity.

During the summer of 1999 I felt I hit the wall of my own competence. We had begun this together, but now Oktiabrina, my partner and friend, was grappling alone with issues and processes that I did not understand and could not do much to help her with. As outsider, I had been able to facilitate her acquaintance with other outsiders (foundation representatives), yet what use was I here? My Westernness had been a useful resource that enabled us to gain audience with local powerbrokers, yet here it had no currency; these issues were of a quite different magnitude. Overwhelmed, I struggled to figure out what to do. It was clear to me that, until Oktiabrina had a stable home, it was pointless to do much with the center. At the same time that I was running a couple of seminars at the crisis center, I joined her in a round of property viewings and negotiations with real estate agencies.

My goal in holding the seminars was to get to know crisis center staff and the issues they were facing, and to offer my energies to them and figure out how best I could continue to collaborate. However, I found them vastly more difficult than the seminars I ran the previous year. The main difference was that whereas in 1998 the seminars grew organically out of a set of months-long interactions, this year I was a fly-in consultant, trying to facilitate discussions among a group of people I did not know. No longer an insider, I was out of touch, struggling to piece together the story of the last twelve months. Further more, my role was unclear. Warmly introduced as co-founder, I had a clear historical role, but who was I now? A consultant? A friend? An ethnographer? Or merely a well-wisher, passing through? Through the seminars, I could begin to see some of the problems facing the group. However, it was quite beyond my competence to be able to do much about them. This was pushing at the boundaries of both participatory action research and anthropology—and the contradictions of my position felt acute. I yearned for some of the skills of a PAR practitioner (facilitation skills, organizational development), but even if I had had them, it might have been impossible to use them effectively. By this stage, I was too embedded in the project and in relationships with some of the main players. Here, taming meant that I was fiercely partisan in my loyalties and saw things from a decidedly partial perspective.

Through the seminars, I learned that gendered violence was very much on the periphery of the project in the first months of its existence. The first clients who came to the center were either already personally acquainted in some way with staff members or were chance passers-by. These women did not talk about domestic violence but discussed instead a variety of other, mostly materially based problems. When I asked them about their plans for the near future, Oktiabrina and other staff and volunteers talked of setting up a variety of other projects within the center to meet local women's needs—a "work therapy" club—designed to help local women go into business together and consider economic strategies; a social club; and seminars in cosmetology and women's health. These were ingenious solutions that recalled the work of some of the other centers I had visited.

One evening, we left the crisis center to take a walk by the Volga. The evening was lovely; it was cooler than it had been and the riverbank was crowded with young families and couples promenading. As we walked, I tried to elicit Oktiabrina's feelings about the crisis center. I told her that it seemed she didn't get much satisfaction or pleasure from it; I was afraid that it would become a burden to her. As I look back on this discussion, I realize I was telling her that she didn't have to stick with the project out of any sense of responsibility, or loyalty to me. She insisted that she got a lot from it and that she was convinced of the importance of the work. In fact, it had helped her through some of the really hard times she had experienced and she was excited about the possibilities. She knew she had a lot to contend with—she told me that she wanted to learn management skills, and she lamented that she still did not know English.[16] She was tired, it was hard to focus when she had so much going on. She told me, the foreigner, for whom she had done so much to make feel at home in Tver', that *she* felt foreign (*chuzhoi*) both in medicine and in the new women's NGO sphere she found herself in. However, her passion remained, and she remained determined to make it work.

The Center for Women's History and Gender Studies

Meanwhile, the Center for Women's History and Gender Studies was continuing to follow a very different path. An impressive team was taking shape around Valentina, consisting of Lena (the manager) and three of Valentina's graduate students who had taught courses at the evening school. Indeed, she told me proudly that there were four "family pairs" involved in the center. Her own husband had long provided computing support; now the three husbands of her young colleagues were also involved in a variety of different ways. They had recently completed the hard work of registering the center when I arrived;[17] although arduous, the work was eased significantly because undertaken by a team. But most notably, they had just received word of a substantial Ford Foundation grant that would support them for two years. Valentina's center was one of only three Centers for Women's History and Gender Studies to be supported in Russia, under the Knowledge, Creativity, and Freedom program. Once again, Ford had invited her to apply. Impressed by all she had achieved on her individual grant and the work of the evening school, *they* had called *her*. Mary McAuley had visited her at her dacha a few weeks earlier to arrange the details; she was leaving her post as head of the Moscow office and wanted to be sure this was first established. Valentina was delighted; the Ford grant provided running costs, salaries, and materials and enabled her to support the work of her impoverished university collective. She planned to split her salary and give a portion of it to her office manager.[18]

One sunny day in mid-July 1998, Oktiabrina and I joined Valentina and her young team for a celebratory "seminar" at her dacha. After talking and making plans, we swam in the nearby river, ate a picnic lunch, and played. It was a fun day—there was much to celebrate—and everyone was carefree and relaxed. There was something organic and solid about this—an easy camaraderie among the women, structured of course by the university and relationships formed through this. They were held together by bonds of affection that derived from the structural relationships within which they had grown. Valentina was former teacher and a beloved mentor to these young women, as she was to many of the women in the city whose lives she had touched.

Bolstered by Ford Foundation and other agency support, Valentina had been able to skillfully finesse relationships within her department and the university administration. Via the Center for Women's History and Gender Studies she was able to support her impoverished university collective even as she pursued her goals of providing gender education.[19] At the same time, she tried to turn these skills and connections to support Oktiabrina and the crisis center.

That summer, the three of us put our heads together to try to figure out ways to bridge the two projects and allow them to better support each other. Valentina had recently been approached by another international donor agency, the British Council. A British Council representative had traveled to Tver' to visit after learning about the evening school in gender studies from the representative of a different foundation. The representative loved what she saw of the evening school and was excited about the crisis center project; she suggested that Valentina put in for a grant that would support the two projects simultaneously. Together, we drew up a proposal (which I wrote up in English) that emphasized the link between the two newly formed nongovernmental organizations and was tailored toward securing support and resources for the crisis center. Our stated goal was "To achieve a solid volunteer base with a background in gender education and to train a cadre of women leaders who are able to pass on the skills that they have learned to other women in Tver' city and in the surrounding regions." To this end, we proposed a series of gender education classes and women's leadership classes to be offered by the teachers of the Center for Women's History and Gender Studies, followed up by seminars led by visiting British crisis center activists.[20]

We hoped to be able to grow the project, and there was initial discussion of expanding it to provide running costs of the crisis center. Unfortunately this did not come to pass, mostly because the British Council insisted that Valentina remain the project director. She told me that despite her repeated requests that they consult with the director of the crisis center, Oktiabrina, they had only wanted to do business with her. Valentina told me that she understood this, and that it made sense, but she was clearly disappointed. Her goal throughout had been to focus and limit her activities, to move away from trying to do everything, to doing the work she loved best and was best suited to, yet here, she was being pushed into the lynchpin role that she objected to. I was struck by the irony. Despite the transparency they preach, foundations are equally reliant on networks and acquaintance, to the extent that they refuse to trust those who are nominated by their trusted beneficiaries.

2000–2003—Multi-sited Meetings

During 1999–2000 I was consumed by the job market and by writing up my research and did not manage to return to Tver' either during the winter break nor the summer. Through Valentina's emails, I heard good news about the crisis center. Oktiabrina had won a small grant of $4,000 from IREX to assist with the running of the center. She had used these funds to purchase a second computer and to hire professional psychologists and lawyers to run consultations at the center. Ten months after the crisis center opened the telephone was finally installed, in August 1999, with money our American lawyer friend had negotiated for us from the International Women's Club. This enabled the center to finally open its hotline; it was now open from 9:00 to 6:00 every day except weekends. In the fall of 1999, they had begun running a couple of support groups. Meanwhile, Oktiabrina was traveling to Moscow to attend monthly seminars on the legal aspects of domestic violence at the American Bar Association. After the bumpy and stressful start-up she had achieved a kind of equilibrium, and the project was gaining momentum.

Oktiabrina and I met in Boston in March 2000, when she was attending a training program organized by a U.S.-based nonprofit organization, Project Harmony.[21] She was part of a group of fifteen Russian men and women—lawyers, police officers, doctors, and NGO activists from different cities—who were visiting the United States on a program tailored to professionals who worked on the issue of domestic and sexual violence.[22] I joined them at the end of their two-week stay. It was exciting to see Oktiabrina in the United States (which she had visited once before on a lightning tour organized by the Library of Congress, but we had not been able to meet). Tables turned, I was the outsider and I slept in her hotel room, which she shared with one other woman lawyer. I was generously invited as a friend of her project to sit in on their seminars. It was clear to me that this was a good program; there were two fluent Russian speakers facilitating, the seminars were fluid and dynamic, and they had assembled a good team of professionals on the Russian side. Oktiabrina was pleased with the training, which she said was extremely well put together, and she got a lot out of her co-participants, whom she found to be bright, interesting people.

When the seminar had ended, Oktiabrina and I left the hotel to walk in the Public Gardens. As we walked, she updated me on some of these more recent activities, and I was struck by how differently she spoke and how upbeat she sounded. She told me she had put in a second application to IREX, this time requesting $9,000. She showed me photographs of the latest events and I noticed that there were new people involved. These were new professionals she'd been able to attract—psychologists and lawyers, who ran weekly sessions at the center. In addition, she had several student interns from the psychology department, students who had been sent along by Valentina. The university connection was a significant bonus—the students who came were smart, energetic, and "well adapted" to the issues of gender violence, having taken classes at the Center for Women's History and Gender Studies.

She told me that the client base had changed as soon as the telephone was installed, and they now received fifty to seventy calls per month from women who had learned about the center from advertisements. Indeed, according to their accounts, between June 1999 and October 2000, the center received 759 phone calls, of which 160 pertained to domestic violence, and held 397 face-to-face consultations (129 on legal issues and psychological issues). The educational-outreach aspect of the work had really taken off—this was a place that she felt deserved most energy. "We need to get involved in preventative work," she told me; "it's so important to get the message out to young people." To this end, they had run 36 trainings with university students and in middle schools, and given individual lectures in local women-run businesses, women's clinics and in schools. In addition to this, they held five round tables, at women's clinics, institutions of higher education, and police stations. They had undertaken public relations work, too—actively engaging with the media to publicize the work of the center and draw attention to the issues.[23]

Oktiabrina exhibited increasing self-confidence, both in her own position and in the validity of the crisis center narrative. I asked her to tell me about the issues clients raised. She told me that many came to discuss problems in their relationships with the people they lived with—alcoholism or conflicts over living space upon divorce. I asked her how many of these people had experienced domestic violence. She paused to consider and told me that in each case there was "an element of domestic violence." However, this was loosely defined. One woman came to speak of problems with her mother, another about difficult relations with her sister. The rest came to discuss issues with their spouses. She told me that she was surprised that women were willing to come forward and to talk about their problems, however they defined them, and that she was surprised too that people did speak about forms of domestic violence. "The need is real," she told me.

It was clear to me that the work conducted in the center both embraced and exceeded the gendered violence narrative. Oktiabrina was doing some of the critical work she had intended—the work of diagnosing, figuring out the main problems of local women, and reconfiguring and adjusting the work of her center to suit. In so doing, she was providing a valuable service to the women of the city.

I was equally struck by the new way she spoke about her two sets of benefactors. She had begun to work with local powerbrokers, people she had previously felt estranged and distant from. She told me that she had begun a formal collaboration with the Humanitarian Institute, which she had previously regarded with a great deal of skepticism. Now she told me, "Katya's doing a good job. She really knows what's going on. They have a lot of resources there, why not collaborate?" She had recently organized a round table on domestic violence and invited senior members of the city and regional administration. She told me that her next step was to make inroads to the governor's office: "It's all very well dealing with the city administration, but in future, we really do need to work at the regional level. That's where the resources are." I looked up from the notes I was hastily jotting and smiled at her, "You've come a long way, girl!" We laughed.

On the last night of the stay in Boston the group was invited home by one of the project leaders, a former police chief I shall call Tom. He drove us out in a minivan to his home, a large, open-planned house in an attractive new development with fabulous views of the surrounding hills. We were greeted by his smiling wife, who welcomed us and proudly showed us the drapes she had made for each room. The Russian team, which I'd come to know as quite boisterous, suddenly became awkward in this affluent and unfamiliar suburban setting. Maxim, a lawyer in his thirties, announced that he was experiencing culture shock. The men and women perched tentatively on cream-colored sofas, uncertainly accepting the drinks and snacks offered; several of them pulled out cameras and took photographs of each other. Their discomfort was palpable and our hosts looked embarrassed. Tom urged me to explain in Russian that their affluence was hard won—that they had only recently moved to this house and that they had worked hard for it. I did so, aware how incomprehensible this must sound to these lawyers, doctors, police officers—mature, well-qualified professionals who could never achieve such material stability and comfort through their own labor. It was an uncomfortable moment; until this point, I had seen Maxim and his colleagues connecting with their American hosts as equals, but now they suddenly felt alienated and felt diminished in the midst of this luxurious domestic setting, which surely must have recalled the America they knew from soap operas. Through their participation in this project and their engagement in the campaigns, they had taken a leap of faith, yet here things broke down. Despite the best efforts of Tom and his wife (who tried to connect by talking about the importance of their work, and how much "strong" American and Russian women had in common), the sense of disconnect remained. But beyond this uncomfortable juxtaposition, I was unsettled by something more. I suppose it was because here the cultural project that accompanies democratization was laid bare. On this trip, under the auspices of the campaigns to combat violence against women, something else was being sold. Once again, the exchange took place in the name of women's rights and the struggle against violence against women that originated as a project of the radical women's movement. Yet here, it was stripped of its critique of patriarchy and the bourgeois family. Moreover, it was part of something else. Like the Tupperware parties that Daphne Berdahl discusses in her ethnography of post-reunification Germany, it was selling a consumerist ideal that was unattainable (Berdahl 1999: 196–197).

Valentina and I met in the fall of 2000 when she was in the United States. I was able to use my university resources to invite her to visit, and she stayed with us in Northampton for a week.[24] We gave another joint presentation, picking up themes we laid out in our talk at Cornell to my new department. It was a treat to be able to reconnect. As we poked around the Northampton coffee shops and bookstores, she updated me about the recent events of the two projects; Oktiabrina, Lena, and one other were about to set off for England on the British Council exchange; meanwhile, the Center for Gender Studies was consolidating its position within the university and continued to win support from granting agencies.[25]

My next trip to Tver' was a short one; in June of 2001 I made a flying visit of two weeks. Heavily pregnant and entering my second year of teaching at the University of Massachusetts, I knew I could not offer much in a practical sense. The trip was about honoring ties.

The crisis center was much more solid and had a good cadre of staff. They were doing a lot, and Oktiabrina seemed much more secure in herself and her dealings with the administration. They had recently won the second IREX grant, which enabled them to maintain their activities and provided small stipends for the staff and volunteers. Oktiabrina's grant application, "A new bud on the flower of the hydrangea," also proposed running a series of training workshops and seminars for a group of women in Mamulino, an industrial housing estate outside Tver', in order that they could set up a filial of the crisis center.[26] The center looked more solid; it was now well equipped with two computers, a Xerox

Staff and supporters of the crisis center Hortensia, winter 1998.

machine and some good-quality office furniture, donated by the American Bar Association. The center had a lot of energy about it. In addition to the foundation proposed projects, it ran diverse and creative activities—art therapy sessions, support groups, self-defense classes. The sense of solidarity and community was impressive.

Oktiabrina's domestic situation was much more stable too. In 1999 she had managed to purchase a room in a communal apartment, near the center of town. Although the situation was far from ideal, the other inhabitants of the communal apartment were quiet and mostly absent. One room belonged to a young man who lived with his parents, while the other belonged to a woman who only occasionally visited.[27] Oktiabrina and her husband were hoping to be able to buy one of them out. At the same time, they were trying to secure accommodation through her husband's workplace at the GAI (traffic police). Not to overstate their stability: indeed, her husband, Konstantin, had adopted a rather drastic strategy to this end—he had signed up for a three-month tour of police work duty with his division in war-torn Chechnya, from which he had recently returned. One night, after we had appreciatively finished the dinner he had prepared for us, he showed us pictures and told stories of his time there. No supporter of the war ("It's all about oil!"), he told us he had signed up partly out of a sense of duty, partly to increase their chances of getting housing.[28] Later, as Oktiabrina escorted us back to our hotel, she spoke about the contradictions of her life—here she was, the director of a crisis center, and yet she lived in one room and had no phone. Could she call herself middle-class when their combined income was below the official poverty rate?[29] She told me how uncomfortable it was at work sometimes, when clients came to accept their free services who were evidently wealthy: "When a well-dressed woman with a cell phone shows up to help and I offer her free consultations, how am I expected to feel?"

Yet, she was sounding more solid. Most remarkably, I learned that she ran for election to the city duma. She smiled as my eyes widened and proudly showed me her campaign posters. She had been encouraged to run by one of the members of the Women's Assembly; although unsuccessful, she was proud of the attempt. She told me that she loved getting involved, and thought that she might run again.

Lena, our crisis center colleague from Pskov, was visiting for a couple of days during my visit. The two centers had maintained close ties and connections. Oktiabrina had organized a seminar to introduce both Lena and me to the co-workers. The women were eager to hear from her about the Pskov center. They were particularly impressed by the fact that the center had established its own independent economic base. Drawing on her connections in the local administration, the director of the center, Lena's mother, had established a sewing factory.

Despite the differences between the two centers, they were united by their professionalism and dedication to combating forms of gendered violence. They were united too by the way they were making sense of the contradictory terrain of NGO politics. They spoke at length about the policies of foundations and agreed that in some ways things were getting harder. They found the new emphasis on encouraging state/non-state partnerships unrealistic. First, it did not allow for their very different goals and ideological objectives. Second, it did not acknowledge the difficulties of securing local systemic sources of support. Several of the women regarded the new emphasis on social partnership by local officials as a sneaky means of displacing independent groups. As Sveta, one of the psychologists, put it, "We raised the issue and now we're pushed aside."

Lena, Oktiabrina, and I resumed this discussion later, when we met in the park. I told them that I wanted to address policymakers and NGO representatives in my writing and asked them to talk more about these themes.

In the course of our conversation it became clear that the two women were dissatisfied and baffled by foundation policies and felt unheard by foundation representatives. Although they felt that they were doing useful work, they were frustrated that so much time was taken up by bureaucratic activities. They both grimaced as they told me about the dreaded *otchet*—the time-consuming accounting procedures that agencies required of them. What is more, they felt constrained. Grants permit and exclude specific activities, down to the themes of trainings. Otkiabrina told me she had been excited by self-defense trainings she had attended in Pskov, yet she was not permitted to do them in Tver' since IREX did not support the idea. Lena explained that her center had recently been visited by agency evaluators and it was absolutely clear to her that they were not interested in the content of the center's activities; "They just need pretty numbers, they don't need to hear my thoughts about our work." Further, they were concerned that donors were moving away from supporting the theme of *nasilie* (violence). The new theme, she continued, was *torgovlia liud'mi* (human trafficking). Oktiabrina nodded, saying, "We have to be like chameleons to please the foundations. Even if you don't want to take it [trafficking] on, you have to!"

Finally, they had begun to feel a sense of futility about the work they had been encouraged into. They had successfully raised an issue that both felt was real and important, but at the same time, they were aware that it was nested within a host of other concerns. As with the other crisis centers I came across, they found that their clients came to discuss a wide variety of issues. Although they were frequently able to locate (or "uncover") an element of domestic violence in clients' accounts (whether it be verbal or psychological abuse, economic pressure, or actual physical violence carried out by spouses or male relatives), clients most pressingly made reference to material problems that affected both them and their families. Their work with women uncovered issues that they felt powerless to address—problems connected with unemployment, unpaid wages, the crisis of living space. "All we can offer is psychological support. It doesn't resolve the main issues," Oktiabrina lamented. "We can't solve the material problems." Lena agreed, saying, "The global attention to solving women's problems must be the business of the government! Housing, the police, the law—it's too much on our shoulders!"

Thus it was that the two Zhenskii Svet projects unfolded, following rather different paths. Conceived together and intended to reinforce each other, the two projects collaborated as much as possible. Valentina's students worked at the crisis center as volunteer-interns, gaining valuable experience with computers, counseling, and working with members of the public. Several of them wrote undergraduate theses on domestic violence, offering socially useful research to the city and the center. Oktiabrina and her crisis center colleagues gave occasional lectures at the Center for Women's History and Gender Studies on domestic violence, and some of the counselors subsequently entered the university to undertake graduate work based on their applied work. However, as we have seen, professionalization ultimately drove these two projects further apart. What conclusions can we draw from the comparison?

First, the stories tell us that the world of NGO professionalism is wide and differentiated. By the end of the story, Oktiabrina and Valentina were both NGO professionals, but very differently located within the landscape of NGOs I have mapped; they experienced different angles of the gendered interventions accordingly. Second, the story tells us that not all donors are equal, and neither are the campaigns they support.

On the one hand, Oktiabrina gained substantially. Belonging in the crisis center network has clearly given her a new sense of pride, purpose, and dignity, as she is quick to acknowledge. The network has been a source of emotional and psychological support as well; she maintains close friendships with several of her peers in other crisis centers. She has been able to travel, too, attending training sessions in the Russian Federation (Moscow, Pskov, and other provincial cities), within the former Soviet Union (Mongolia), and occasionally overseas (London, Boston, Italy). Oktiabrina is frequently sardonic in her commentaries about international agencies. During one of my most recent return visits to Tver', in the summer of 2004, we sat in a café discussing my struggles to represent our collaborative project. When I mentioned that I was using *The Little Prince* as a kind of talisman or motif in my book, she smiled and without missing a beat came out with exactly the same phrase Valentina had used in our presentation at Cornell: "You're responsible for those whom you tame." Pausing slightly, she added archly, "The foundations forgot that! If they want to change the world, they'll have to change their policies!" Such commentaries—specially tailored for the ethnographer—do not, however, prevent her from acknowledging the positive outcomes of foundation support and what she has gained from her engagement with them. Belonging in the crisis center network has generated significant cultural capital. Despite the considerable uphill struggle, she was ultimately able to turn her activities to local advantage. Through this story we have seen how she moved from being a vulnerable outsider to gaining a name in the city, even running for office in elections to the city parliament (as Valentina put it when she read this chapter, Oktiabrina has significant "political weight"). Yet as I have watched her, I have been struck by how far this is from the supposed NGO gravy train. Funds provided by international agencies were modest and of limited duration and did not permit her to focus exclusively on her crisis center work. As we've seen, foundations privileged network expansion rather than consolidation; quick to provide start-up funds to fledgling crisis centers, they failed to sustain them. Oktiabrina was unfavorably situated within this infrastructure. Although it was her provincial location that originally assisted her to win the attention of agency representatives, this same location prevented her from rising. Even at the height of the campaigns, resources were channeled to the Moscow-based organizations that acted as central nodes, and provincial centers only received funding for projects (limited duration training sessions and seminars) rather than running costs or salaries. This instability interrupted the work she had signed on to undertake. In 2001, she was increasingly persuaded by the importance of the work she was undertaking ("the need is real!"), yet aware that she was only scratching the surface of the issue. She had lots of ideas and wanted to expand their activities, yet she was constrained from doing so.

Our strategy of involvement was a decision to undertake a carefully choreographed dance with both sets of powerbrokers—*vlast'* and foundations. Our goal was to use international foundation support as a wedge, a persuasive device to gain local credibility and support. Certainly pledges of support from international agencies helped us in the early stages of our crisis center project; however, this only took us so far. Entering into strategic partnerships with the local authorities was one thing, but we had to maintain these relationships. As we have seen, official acceptance and support for the crisis center did not mean understanding—Oktiabrina had to do a lot of persuasive work, battling the incomprehension of mid- and lower-level bureaucrats and workers, toward both NGOs in general and crisis centers in particular. Unlike Valentina, or Katya (of the Humanitarian Institute), Oktiabrina did not have the clout or connections to offset the hostility that her work elicited. And when she finally did manage to achieve a kind of stability and equilibrium, the international donors walked away.

As I have shown, the campaigns against gendered violence looked like a good bet. In 1998 the issue was supported by most of the agencies that worked to promote women's rights in Russia, and by others besides (embassies, sister city crisis centers, and visiting foreign activists like me). However, the support that had looked so promising turned out to be fragile in the end. The "violence against women" framing, so successful at the global level, proved to be a fad, subject to political currents within donor nations. By 2001, support for the issue had begun to wane. Support provided by USAID (channeled through IREX) was scaled back considerably in 2001 due to shifting political priorities in the United States. As Oktiabrina and her colleague Lena noted, funds began to be shifted away from the campaigns against gendered violence, toward another, altogether broader campaign against "trafficking" in women and girls in the region.[30] Many crisis centers shifted their priorities accordingly, but begrudgingly. Like Oktiabrina and Lena, they are aware that the problem is broad, beyond their scope. As many scholars have discussed, this change in priorities can be seen as a shift toward policing fortress Europe/the first world (Berman 2003; Sassen 2002). Indeed, this drift continued. In 2004 I learned that former crisis center workers are being encouraged to adopt a new framing that perfectly captures the post–September 11 zeitgeist—to work on the "rehabilitation of terrorism victims" by providing counseling to victims of the August 2003 terrorist attacks in Beslan. While the importance of this immediate activity cannot be understated, this drift and the transmogrification of the issue speak to the weakness of the catchall strategy and should give feminists pause. As international foundations withdrew from the issue of gendered violence, they left some brave and risk-taking people in the lurch. In the end, Oktiabrina's story confirms the situation that my friend Maria described, where those who are on the periphery of the women's movement, engaged in service provision, are "made responsible for too much" and "used up." She was kept on a treadmill, consumed by issues of organizational survival and kept busy guessing at foundations' intent, which prevented her from focusing on the content of her work.

What of Valentina? In this chapter, I have shown that she also struggled with the centrifugal tension of network politics. Initially deciding to enter formalized work in order to limit and focus her activities, she finds herself drawn back into the lynchpin role she objected to. She didn't want to be an "NGO professional"—a gatekeeper and purveyor of projects—yet by the end she is drawn into this role. Despite her efforts to delegate and include her young colleagues in projects and plans, she was thwarted by agency representatives (trust emerges as a theme in this chapter, but not in the way Putnam proposes. Rather than a happy by-product of associational activity, it is a commodity in short supply). However, as we have seen, these negative tendencies were offset by a number of factors. First, unlike Oktiabrina, who was in all respects new, Valentina was consolidating old work and drawing on existing ties. In the Center for Gender Studies and Women's History, we see the continuity of her former interests and an institutionalization of work she had long undertaken in both her formal and informal activities (though Zhenskii Svet, the Evening School in Gender Studies, and her teaching at the university). Second, the university was a favorable location. As I have described in earlier chapters, the university had long served as a "roof" in enabling her to undertake community-based projects. Now, this took off. The foundation/university/NGO triumvirate made for a very successful partnership, and Valentina was able to negotiate these relationships well. As an educational project, the work of the Center for Women's History and Gender Studies corresponded with the long-term goals of the Ford Foundation in the region. The strength and consistency of Ford Foundation (and other agency) support won her respect within the university and allowed her to overcome any suspicion about the content of her work.[31] Indeed, there was an interesting symbiosis taking place between the agencies; she was able to use support not only to nurture her nascent center, but also to sustain her impoverished university collective. In return, the university provided "matching support" in the form of infrastructure (rooms) and personnel (staff). During my most recent visit to Tver' in July 2005, Valentina told me a story: during a gender studies conference she had organized, one of the Finnish delegates commented that it was nice to see that the university was tolerant of her Center for Women's History and Gender Studies. To this, the university rector stood up and declared, "It's not tolerance, it's love!"[32]

One could argue that this move to the university has narrowed Valentina's focus and activities. The Center for Women's History and Gender Studies is unambiguously a professional unit, a unit of academic feminism, no less. Is this not the depoliticization of social activism that some authors have discussed? (Messer-Davidow 2002). Agency support has provided funds for curricular development, the gender revision of textbooks, conferences, libraries, and latterly, publishing of academic texts. But at the same time, it has enabled her to continue her *obshchestvennaia rabota*.[33] First, she has been able to use funds to support the work of the Evening School in Gender Studies. Free, and open to the public, it offers classes taught on a voluntary basis by teachers and volunteers, continuing the educational-enlightenment work of Zhenskii Svet.[34] It is not a narrowly "academic" project; it holds workshops on topics such as human rights and domestic violence and discusses the proliferation of international marriage agencies in the city. Second, she has continued to encourage her students to do critical, community-based projects (such as interning at the crisis center).

I'll end here. The subsequent histories of both Zhenskii Svet projects provide further insights. Donor priorities continued to shift, and both projects were vulnerable. Between 2001 and 2005 the Center for Women's History and Gender Studies continued to thrive, sustained by the support of the Ford Foundation; however, this support is slated to end in December 2005, and what happens beyond is uncertain. Meanwhile, the crisis center closed in December 2003. The project lost a crucial local ally when the city mayor suddenly died. His death left Oktiabrina institutionally vulnerable, and she was unable to defend the center from hostile attacks and demands for rent payment from the city legislature. Meanwhile, the "shield" of international support proved to be inadequate, as we have seen. Oktiabrina was only able to secure modest and sporadic funding from foundations at the best of times, and starting in 2001, these agencies began to redirect their resources to the new hot topic of sex trafficking, as I have shown. The story of the two projects draws attention to a third-sector secret—that the foundation functions as a kind of invisible and precarious fourth leg, propping up the third sector model but writing out its own existence.

Conclusion

The unraveling of the Cold War gave rise to ambitious new projects for global renewal. In the immediate aftermath of the Soviet Union's dramatic collapse in 1991, idealism and optimism about the potential for global harmony were broadly shared by populations both inside and outside the former Eastern Bloc. This climate of hope reauthorized and brought new legitimacy to development interventions; it gave rise to the creation of a new apparatus for global activism, sustained by UN conferences and underwritten by the U.S. and Western European governments. The '90s was a decade of ambitious new development initiatives that extended beyond the global South into virgin territory—Central Eastern Europe and the former USSR. Universal strategies and one-size-fits-all solutions were enthusiastically exported all over the globe. Some of these were concepts that originated in progressive struggles for social justice—human rights, participation, women's rights, and gender. It looked like the victory of "the people" (or "civil society" as it came to be known) over states; indeed, the '90s was the decade of the nonstate actor, the NGO. NGOs were seen as the vital "connective tissue" (Wedel, 1994:323, cited in Hann and Dunn 1996:1) of democracy, and they were promoted by development agencies accordingly (Fisher 1997).

However, these global interventions of the supposedly post-ideological age were deeply ideological. The collapse of the socialist alternative gave rise to a new political climate characterized by the absence, or loss, of a progressive vision of a just social order (Fraser 1997a). This permitted a new neoliberal vision of development to take hold, a "New Policy Agenda" (Robinson 1993) that was "driven by beliefs organized around the twin poles of neo-liberal economics and liberal democratic theory" (Hulme and Edwards 1997:4). This vision foresaw an economic restructuring process and a redrawing of state/societal relations along neoliberal lines, where, ideally, civil society is strong and the state "cut back" like an unruly perennial. Left-oriented activists and commentators had earlier embraced the civil society concept as a counterweight both to governmental power and to abuses of the free market, yet the new version of civil society that came to dominate in U.S. policy circles was all about the establishment of markets. This new formula for development was particularly aggressively applied in Russia and other formerly socialist states, and it had dire results: the economic "shock therapy" that was prescribed by IMF advisors and international lenders led to the downsizing of state industries, the dismantling of the social security system, and sharp cutbacks in the healthcare system, leaving populations struggling to deal with unemployment, hyperinflation, and health costs without a safety net.

The gendered interventions this book examines were situated in this new context. "Gender mainstreaming" was a victory of feminist-oriented women's movements, the culmination of a decades-long effort to make women more central to development projects. Yet the gender projects it has authorized are compromised, bound up in this troubling political economy in such a way that undermines their intent. In Russia, gender projects have unlikely bedfellows, unsavory traveling companions. Women's rights and gender equity are promoted at the same time that welfare systems are cut back under structural adjustment.

In recognition of these complex and problematic outcomes, the pendulum has swung in recent years; whereas in the early '90s scholars expressed broad support for these interventions, by the late '90s it had become politically correct to critique "democratization." A new and robust scholarship has emerged to lambaste NGO and civil society-promoting projects. Anthropological studies have examined the perils of importing and imposing "Western" models such as civil society on the former Eastern Bloc, revealing the moments of rift, dissonance, and disjuncture (Creed and Wedel 1997; Gal 1997; Hann and Dunn 1996; Ottaway and Carothers 2000; Sampson 1996; Wedel 1998). Recent scholarship has critiqued the new infrastructure for international activism as fatally compromised, inextricable from the neoliberal agenda that has achieved hegemony in the post–Cold War era. Some dismiss the civil society concept as a primarily rhetorical device for democracy's missionary work (Comaroff and Comaroff 2001; Hardt and Negri 2000; Mandel 2002), a device that simultaneously rationalizes structural adjustment policies and facilitates the cutting back of state social provisioning (Alvarez, Dagnino, and Escobar 1998; Foley and Edwards 1996). Alvarez, Dagnino, and Escobar describe the new service-oriented NGOs as "APSAs" (apparatuses and practices of social adjustment)—band-aids, palliatives, hopelessly compromised by the role they play in stopping up the gaps of the free market (1998:22). Others have portrayed NGOs as vehicles for elite advancement rather than grassroots empowerment, characterizing those who work in this sector as a "comprador bourgeoisie" (Sampson 2002:299), a transnationally focused elite who have more in common with each other than with local populations or the social movements from which they sprang (Feldman 1997; Kamat 2001; Mandel 2002; Richter 1999; Sampson 1996). Worse, NGOs have been denounced as imperialist lackeys, midwives, and facilitators of Empire (Hardt and Negri 2000; Roy 2004).

Feminist scholars have begun to critically interrogate the ostensible successes of international feminism in the post–Cold War era. In this scholarship, global women's activism is disembodied from social movements, "a means to an end and an end in itself" (Riles 2001:49); the feminism and feminist concepts that have been promoted at Cold War's end are compromised by their complicity with imperial and/or corporate agendas (Gapova 2004; Mohanty 2003; Snitow 1999). Seen from this perspective, the mainstreaming of gender and what some have called "NGOization" is synonymous with depoliticization and demobilization of feminism and women's movements (Alvarez 1998; Lang 1997; Paley 2001).

The critique of international democratization aid was my own point of departure in my research; fleshing out the troubling outcomes of global interventions has been an important message of this book. I have examined three of the main export items: the third sector, civil society, and the "violence against women" framing. I have shown that the third sector does not deliver what it promises: rather than allowing a grassroots to flourish, the third sector provides a structural and symbolic framework for the reproduction of former elites of the Soviet regime. It facilitates the gendered distribution of power and resources and contributes to the formation of hierarchies, jealousies, and competition between groups. Further, complicit with the logic of neoliberalism, it pushes the responsibilities of the state onto local nongovernmental groups. In the absence of sustained state/governmental support, groups are left to deal with ever-widening problems, encouraged into activities that are unsustainable. As we saw in chapter 4, the feminist-oriented framing of "violence against women," when applied in Russia, inadvertently deflects attention from other issues of social justice, notably the material forces that oppress women. Further, it morphs problematically in the direction of police-state work, from trafficking, to terrorism. This is a troubling outcome for a movement that intends to challenge the global inequities that contribute to women's marginalization. The critique is of crucial importance, especially as the United States launches new projects in Iraq and the Middle East in the name of democratization and human/women's rights. In these troubled times it is more important than ever to keep asking questions of U.S.- and European-sponsored projects of "funding virtue" (Ottaway and Carothers 2001). Yet I have insisted that it is not enough. The critique in many ways is the easy part. It has a ready market; it sells copy and packs benches. But it is problematic on a number of counts.

First, these critiques potentially shore up conservative arguments that democracy and its appended values (civil society, human rights, women's rights) are just foreign imports and have no relevance for Russian (or other non-first-world) peoples' lives. These arguments have gained substantial ground in Russia in recent years. The Putin administration has signaled its hostility to independent NGOs, extending sanctions to groups it deems political. It has reserved especial disdain for NGOs that receive foreign funding, particularly since the 2004 "orange" revolution in Ukraine.[1] The policy implication of the critique of NGOs is, of course, that "we" should disengage and withdraw funding from such projects, leaving some very brave and risk-taking people in the lurch. Indeed, since the late '90s when I completed the bulk of my research, international donor support for civil society in Russia has decreased and funding to women's (and other) NGOs has been correspondingly reduced, in part due to shifts in perceptions of security post–September 11, in part due to the arrival of a Republican administration in the White House. Meanwhile, in the United States,

NGOs are under attack by conservative organizations and think tanks, which condemn them as creatures of the "Global New-Left" intent upon "hijacking democracy" (Evans and Evans 2003).[2] In short, the critique of NGOs has resonated with anti-democratic and anti-human rights forces and led to the withdrawal of funds from rights-promoting projects. Is this what a progressive critical scholarship should do?

A second problem is that the critique of international aid can obscure the potential for agency within these global exchanges. Some of the important and powerful critiques I've reviewed present activism as contentless, consisting merely of symbolic gestures. These analyses have the perhaps unintended effect of rendering independent organizing unthinkable. To my mind, this does injustice to the people who work in NGOs, many of whom are well aware of the problematics and trying to make their activism matter. It obscures the dynamism and negotiation that takes place within "network politics" at all levels. As I have shown, tracing the path of my friends as they moved from informal to professional forms of activism, the terrain is contradictory and complex. Yet they cannot afford to assume a purist position. The critique is of vital political importance—but what of the activists engaged in NGO work who are denied the luxury of such contemplation and who do not reap rewards or gain cultural capital through making it?

A final shortcoming that has preoccupied me at all stages of this work is that the scholarly critique of international funding is unreflexive and fails to acknowledge our own problematic location, as academics, within these processes. As a scholar of women's activism, I am also a product and beneficiary of gender mainstreaming. My work, even my critique, is supported and consumed by the same agencies. What then is my responsibility? How does acknowledging this fact influence the kind of data I present and my representational choices?

This book is located in a new phase of critical NGO scholarship, one that moves towards a theorization of international intervention that is determinedly global, reflexive (i.e., scrutinizing the contradictions of export models and acknowledging our own role as actors in the transition), and practice oriented.[3] The abrupt shift from "NGO-good," to "NGO-bad" blurs the distinction between NGOization as process, and actual NGOs and the people who work within them, many of whom are well aware of the problematics and struggling to make their activism matter.[4] My contribution has been to argue for the necessity of linking the critique of international aid to constructive political projects. In this book I have presented my own response to this challenging environment, my attempt to forge a more dialogical research process through participatory action research. The collaborative project I undertook with members of Zhenskii Svet propelled me into new intimacies and new proximities with some of the activists who confront the sharp contradictions of the global political economy in their daily lives. The relationships I forged with them and my own involvement in their work forced me to view these global gendered interventions differently.

First, let's take one of the main charges leveled at NGOs: the depoliticization of resistance. Does Russian women activists' engagement in global gendered interventions compromise them in this way? The story of post-Soviet Russian women's activism departs from other global contexts in key ways. While in Latin America, South East Asia, and other locations in the global South, NGOization signifies the cooptation of already existing popular struggles and the "demobilization" of social movements (Kamat 2002; Paley 2001; Roy 2004), in Russia and other post-socialist states, the trajectory is somewhat different. Here, social activism has very recent and fragile roots. During the Soviet period, independent social organizing was prohibited. The fluorescence of associational activity I have described as the "societal movement" was led by intellectuals and did not have a popular base. Feminism in Russia has always been a form of elite identification, and the local and the global have always been mutually constituting in Russian constructions of feminism. Women like Valentina and Maria, my colleague in Moscow, were brokers who were intimately engaged in negotiating first contact with international activists and agency representatives. I have shown that for a small group of highly educated women, embracing feminism and the concept of gender was initially a means of critiquing power and social relationships during the late socialist period. It was also a means of making connection with an imagined Europe. As the effects of democratic market-oriented reforms took root, this activism and the concept of "gender" had another purpose; it assisted women to make sense of the violent economic and social dislocations that were the result of market-oriented policies. As the stories of Valentina, Oktiabrina, and other members of Zhenskii Svet reveal, "gender" became a powerful explanatory framework that enabled them to reinterpret the past and to forge dynamic projects for personal and social change. Their societal work or activism was not only a means of being of service to others, but it was a strategy that enabled them to articulate and reassert their identities as socially concerned members of society. As material resources (grants and funding) became attached to women's activism and to the concept of gender, the nature of their activities inevitably shifted. It brought them into a different kind of realm, to engage in a different kind of politics. Deeply ambivalent about NGOization and the professionalization of the women's movement, they felt that they had little choice but to engage it.

Second, what about the discussion of NGOs as elite? Much of the new critical scholarship of NGOs and civil society points to local elite enrichment and corruption (Feldman 1997; Kamat 2001; Mandel 2002; Richter 1999; Sampson 1996). Certainly it is true that old elites have prospered in the "third sector," the new realm of NGOs that donor agencies have brought into being. It is an important part of the post-socialist story that I too am compelled to tell (as in the case of the Humanitarian Institute). It is important, insofar as it demystifies the image of the third sector as a new uncorrupted space. However, the story is more complex and there are other modes of interaction within this sphere. One contribution of this book has been to insist on the fragility of activists' position and stability. Through my account of the Tver' crisis center project, I have shown the ambiguity of belonging in the civil society of NGOs. Involvement in the nongovernmental sphere can certainly be regarded as a career strategy. To gloss this activity as "elite," however, is to screen out a great deal of complexity. The terms of engagement are rather constrained; donor agencies encourage groups into specific activities; activists spend much of their time maintaining themselves (writing grants, puzzling through the policies of funders, securing resources). Although it certainly provides local kudos, the NGO realm does not provide job security; NGO workers are often highly insecure. Unless they are truly well connected in former party or state circles, they operate outside state networks of patronage and support and are often materially impoverished, as Oktiabrina's case reveals. They are not eligible for state benefits such as pensions, and according to the logic of the system, they can actually stand to lose professional qualifications.[5] Far from being a gravy train, NGO work is frequently sustained by the financial input of spouses, children, and extended family and friends. An interesting point to note is that a high proportion of the women activists I got to know in Tver' (particularly the younger generation) had supportive husbands—Valentina proudly celebrated the fact that her Gender Studies Center comprised four married couples (where the husbands, including her own, provided computing and technical support, as well as material support through their own income). Partnerships forged with local power brokers are extremely fragile and often dependent on the symbolic presence of powerful outsiders. Activists are aware of the precariousness of the situation and continually fearful that foundations will move on or jettison projects.

Our collaborative project and the two Zhenskii Svet projects I have traced illustrate both the fragility of nongovernmental activity in Russia and the contradictions in the third-sector model that posits this activity as the core of democratic panacea. In our collaborative project we essentially played the third-sector game, presenting ourselves to city officials as a community group eager to take on the mantle for social service provision. It worked. Whatever its shortcomings, the third-sector model and the funds behind it have forced local politicians and officials to pay attention to independent community groups. We worked with both international agencies and local authorities, using international aid as a bargaining chip and a wedge. However, the differential fates of the two Zhenskii Svet projects illuminate something that third-sector promotional literature elides—that without international foundation support, the third sector is not sustainable.

Finally, what of the shift that my friends and I made? Does the story about the trajectory of Zhenskii Svet confirm or contradict the critical portrait of the third sector and network politics? Was our "strategy of involvement" a move for the better, or for the worse? Does it provide evidence of cooptation, or skillful negotiation? At base is a simple and urgent question—is it possible to achieve agency, that is, to hold on to projects that are locally defined and that matter, in the troubled NGO realm? What does it mean to ask these questions, and how can someone with as much investment in the projects as I provide answers? Beneath this lurks another urgent question: did I do more harm than good?

These are tough questions. Indeed, as a former participant and sometimes instigator of our involvement, I can only answer them partially. The ties, responsibilities, and taming that took place between us complicate this still further. My relationship with group members and my responsibilities to them influence the way I write, what I tell, and the way I theorize this activity. Here, I step aside from this perhaps irresolvable question to argue from another angle. My task has been twofold—to explore how NGOs are experienced on the ground by the people who are caught up in them, and to engage in a locally defined political project with them. Activists like Maria, Valentina, Lydia, and Oktiabrina, differently located within this structure for global activism, encounter these gendered interventions with their eyes wide open. We see them veering from optimism and passionate engagement to weary, sometimes cynical commentaries, but they retain their commitment to their work. Can we dismiss their successes and perceptions of empowerment as false consciousness, as yet more evidence of the success of disciplining technologies and the "production of neoliberal citizens" (Hyatt 2001b)?[6] These circumstances and this terrain call familiar categories into question—as Greenhouse, Mertz, and Warren have argued, "Ethnographies of political instability force us along with our subjects to rethink many key ideas, including our conceptions of agency" (2002:357). This book refuses the dichotomy of success/failure, and refuses to rest with the critique. Unlike scholars of NGOs and civil society who see no possibility of agency in this terrain, I have elected instead to write with hope.

As I have followed these groups, their members, and their shifting identifications, I have become aware that despite their fears, NGOization has not eclipsed their activities. Activists have been able to use resources creatively, to support a number of already existing projects. Although it is heavily influenced by agency mandates and the objectives articulated in Geneva and Washington, their work is not overtaken or determined by them. Through the crisis center and the Center for Women's History and Gender Studies, Valentina, Oktiabrina, and their colleagues were able to continue the work of Zhenskii Svet. The decision to formalize had myriad outcomes. While it was in operation, the crisis center acted as a kind of support center for local women; it provided a sense of community (*obshchenie*). It has provided practical training for the women who volunteered or worked there, both students and recent graduates and older women, many of whom had their first experience with computers and the Internet. The Center for Women's History and Gender Studies continues to act as a kind of umbrella project under which different initiatives thrive. Enabled by the "roof" the university provides and the funds agencies bring, it supports a number of nongovernmental, voluntary projects, and activities. Indeed, at the time of going to press, I have learned that Oktiabrina and Valentina are working to reanimate the crisis center under the Center for Women's History and Gender Studies' auspices by opening a hotline. The women's activism continues to be a critical project of engagement with the work of international foundations and the economic and social policies of the Russian government alike.

When I caught up with Valentina and her Center for Gender Studies colleagues in June 2004, I found that they had adopted an ironic term to refer to their activities and identities—they referred to themselves, humorously, as "*genderisty*" (genderists). As I understand it, this term, which sounds even more comical in Russian than it does in English, acknowledges the paradoxical play of this global exchange and their position within it. At the same time, it recalls the fervor and commitment of prior progressive/revolutionary struggles; they clearly see themselves as following in the footsteps of other social reformers such as the *dekabristy* (Decembrists, a group of Russian army officers who led a revolt against the Tsar in 1825) and the *sufrazhistki* (suffragettes). It indicates their acknowledgement of "gender as grant"—to recall Oktiabrina's ironic terms—and marks acceptance of its symbolic and market value.

These are ambiguous, complex, yet surely ultimately encouraging tales.

Who's Taming Whom?

That was how the little prince tamed the fox. And when the time to leave was near:

"Ah!" the fox said. "I shall weep."

"It's your own fault," the little prince said. "I never wanted to do you any harm, but you insisted that I tame you."

"Yes, of course," the fox said.

"But you're going to weep!" said the little prince.

"Yes, of course," the fox said.

"Then you get nothing out of it?"

"I get something," the fox said, "because of the color of the wheat."

Antoine de Saint-Exupéry, *The Little Prince*

What of this second part of my project, my own attempt to achieve a more democratic, dialogical gendered intervention? Did this project bring about more good than harm? While the publication of this book testifies to the rewards and benefits I derived from our collaboration, what did the Zhenskii Svet women get out of it? Who, after all was domesticating, or taming, whom, and with what consequences?

To address this, I return to the metaphor and the relationship that I started with in chapter 1—the notion of taming, and the relationship between the fox and the prince. Taming offers a valuable metaphor for thinking about relationships in the field. First, as Valentina put it when we discussed it, *The Little Prince* is a story of a relationship between two very different creatures, two creatures who ultimately come to understand and accept each other's difference. Second, the metaphor insists upon the mutuality of relationships. The questions I pose above imply a fixity of roles and a rigidity of power relations that both this ethnography and the story of the little prince belie. There is significant give and take between them. The fox undertakes to educate the prince, who to me at times appears like an anthropologist—clueless, naïve, demanding. He comes down from his planet and wants connection and answers. He learns that it's not so simple. The lessons he learns from the fox are matters of the heart. The fox pushes the little prince to reflect on his home, the small planet that he came from, and the relationship with the flower that he fled. Taming also speaks of the tug of responsibility that participants experience toward each other. Finally, as the relationship between the fox and the little prince reveals, taming involves accepting the necessity of letting go and the inevitability of departure. The fox and the little prince ultimately had to part. One might ask—what did the fox gain? But the fox, in the context of his education of the little prince, insists that he did gain. Although his new friend is gone, he is left with the warmth and recollections of their relationship. The memory of their friendship is suffused in the wheat fields around him—when he sees them, he is reminded of the color of the little prince's hair. Here, the environment is imbued with new meaning because of the relationship, the ties of affection between them.

Participatory Action Research accepts the risk of engagement, throwing out the old-style anthropological ethical guideline of "do no harm" to accept risk and the possibility of betrayal (Fals-Borda and Rahman 1991:23).[7] Despite the sometimes evangelical claims of its proponents, PAR cannot resolve social inequities, particularly the global inequities that formed the backdrop of my interactions with Zhenskii Svet. The contradictions of this project remain. Once granted temporary insider status as a member of Zhenskii Svet, I remain privileged by my British citizenship, my immigration status in the United States, and the employment opportunities this affords me. The benefits I have derived through engagement in this project are more substantial, more secure, and altogether greater than those experienced by my friends. This contradiction has at times been most painfully apparent, as when I left Tver' to write up my research just days before the bubble burst and the Russian economy collapsed in 1998, leaving Oktiabrina and her colleagues struggling with the rocky transition to NGO professionalism; as when Oktiabrina found herself temporarily homeless in the early stages of the crisis center project. However, participatory action research offers a way to deal with these contradictions insofar as it acknowledges the power-laden nature of a research relationship and accepts the ethical responsibilities that go with it.

Our research was not truly collaborative from the start, as my story has shown. Indeed, it took me ten months before I was able to gain trust. However, participatory action research, sometimes described as a "method," as a "style," or as a "philosophy" (Fals-Borda and Rahman 1991:16), provided the basis for a creative dialogue across power. Thinking about collaboration helped me formulate my goals and plans. Talking about participatory research methods with Valentina led her to invite me to join the group; it helped me to negotiate a role for myself and to embark on a kind of apprenticeship. It put me in a place from which I could learn and interact. As we have seen, I happened along at an interesting moment, when the group was facing a crossroads, unsure of which way to turn. Over time, as relationships and trust developed, I was able to join the women in their discussions and plans. Gradually around this personal intimacy and trust a new "partial but shared externally related identity" formed (Gibson-Graham 1994:218). This became the basis for a collaborative research project.

What I call "PAR" and what my friends call "our seminars" enabled us to undertake a mutual learning process, a project of "self-education" (*samoobra-zovanie*), as Valentina and Oktiabrina describe it. It has proven to be transformative for all of us. Together we traveled (united briefly in this temporary, contingent alliance) from a critical stance as outsiders, to enter into the partnerships and collaborations with international agencies that we had held back from. We made the decision to work in this contradictory environment, by engaging these discourses in the pursuit of collectivist goals and projects and in an attempt to make gender matter. Was it a good move? Did we succeed? I cannot tell you the answer. I am denied the "complacency of closure" that predominates in social science analysis (Mertz 2002:362), since this is an ongoing story that has no end. This is an "ethnography of uncertainty" (Greenhouse, Mertz, and Warren 2002); ours is a story of subtle and ambivalent gains—as subtle perhaps as the fox's appreciation of the "color of the wheat." We are all now ambivalent insiders, reaping differential rewards and costs. Equal parts fox and prince, Valentina, Oktiabrina, and I—we continue to devise projects across different fields.

Returns

> And he went back to the fox.
> "Good-bye," he said.
> "Good-bye," said the fox. "Here is my secret. It's quite simple: One sees clearly only with the heart. Anything essential is invisible to the eyes."
>
> Antoine de Saint-Exupery, *The Little Prince*

I returned to Tver' in June 2004 after a long interval of three years, briefly leaving the new ties that now root me in Massachusetts to contemplate new forms of connection and collaboration with the members of Zhenskii Svet. From my new position of security, I was coming to propose a new collaborative project between our two universities, to explore and promote the use and potential of community-based learning in Russia.

Once again, Valentina was my first guide. She met me at the station and took me on a walking tour around the city, pointing out the new construction that had taken place—a couple of glitzy malls, some casinos and night clubs, and the newly converted shell of the Tver' Universal Bank, finally renovated to house a large, luxurious supermarket and rows of small boutiques and stores. "It's Las Vegas, on the outskirts of Moscow," she sighed. She told me that in distinct contrast with this glut of commercial activity, the noncommercial sphere (or third sector) had sharply contracted. The political climate had become progressively more hostile towards societal activism and the new governor, a recent Putin appointee, was not sympathetic to nongovernmental groups. The crisis center was not the only casualty; the Humanitarian Institute had closed due to rent payments the city demanded, and the regional (*oblast'*) Human Rights Committee (which Valentina had co-founded and which Zhenskii Svet member Natalia had directed for years) had been shut down. Although nervous at the impending end of the grant cycle, her Center for Women's History and Gender Studies stood out as an oasis of success. She proudly showed me the resources she had been able to secure—the three rooms she had been granted by the university since founding the Center, and the books, Xerox machine, and computers that foundation support had supplied.

As ever, Valentina was buzzing with new projects, both foundation-enabled and voluntary, all of which continued to embody her commitment to bridging theory and practice: "There's no point if it doesn't have a community (*obshchest-vennaia*) basis," she told me. Under the auspices of the Center for Women's History and Gender Studies, she encourages her students to engage in community-based research projects, putting questions to the town administration. She was busy devising a seminar series for journalists and teachers on gender stereotypes. Via the Feminist Press–Russia, she put out affordable, accessible texts on women's studies and gender issues, including conference proceedings, teaching materials, and a local history project commemorating the end of the Second World War entitled "Victory Day through Women's Eyes," for which she had secured the sponsorship of local women entrepreneurs, women she had gotten to know through the Women's Assembly.[8] She told me that her goal was to make her publications affordable and accessible to local people: "In reality, you can print things very cheaply." She had collaborated with a local woman publisher, who kept costs low, sometimes doing projects for cost alone. Indeed, I witnessed her distributing these texts, not only as political gestures to potential allies, but to the people she chanced to meet. On our way to the offices of the local newspaper where we had been invited to give an interview, we stumbled upon a new boutique in one of the side streets. It turned out to a second-hand store, full of imported Danish clothing. Delighted, Valentina congratulated the saleswoman—a retired teacher—for making such good quality and accessibly priced clothes available. On our way out, she pressed a copy of one of their recent publications into her hand.

Over the next few days, we met regularly in her apartment to discuss these new developments and in order that I could share my book manuscript with her. As we sat in her kitchen as before, drinking tea, I saw that despite her transmogrification to NGO professionalism, the apartment had little changed. She and her neighbors were still awaiting the long-promised renovation and, with it, hot water and new plumbing. As she read my characterization of her trajectory over the last decade, she nodded, pausing to correct me at times. She told me that yes, she had become a professional, but she was still interested in what she called, using the English term, "goodwill" work. Indeed, although Zhenskii Svet no longer met, eclipsed by the other projects she and the other women were engaged in, she continued to engage in voluntary societal work through other projects such as the evening school in gender studies, using agency funding to support her. "Foundations pay professional wages, which allows us to keep going with our evening school," which is half professional, half voluntary—"It's like a bridge, she explained, "a bridge between professional work and voluntary societal (*obshchestvennaia*) work."

She expressed no regret or sense of loss about Zhenskii Svet. "It wouldn't make any sense now," she told me, "people wouldn't come if we tried to meet once or twice a week like we used to, they are too busy. Besides, now there are all kinds of different avenues for communication and expression—it's completely different from only five years ago. Now there are lots of TV shows, journalists interview people on the street all the time—I may not like them, but they exist. And information is available in ways it wasn't available then." She smiled, and repeated something she had told me formerly: "It's important that an organization is flexible and changes with the times, otherwise it won't work—like the CPSU (Communist Party of the Soviet Union)."

While previously swamped and overwhelmed, she was now able to focus on a narrower range of activities and undertake the projects that interested her most—her own teaching and scholarship, and nurturing a new generation of women scholar-activists who would take over. She was grooming the next generation, passing opportunities on to them whenever she could—invitations to seminars or to deliver papers in Moscow or other cities. She told me that she dreamed of setting up her own foundation that could support young scientists. "In this sense, I've become a professional, but the idea of Zhenskii Svet lives on. The spirit lives on in our current project, and the enlightenment aspect remains."

Our new project seeks to explore these community-based ventures that the university/nongovernmental/foundation partnership enables. We are embarking on a new collaborative research project that interrogates the new fashion to promote voluntarism and "service" among youth and its relationship to cutbacks in social welfare structures, involving our students in community-based projects. From our different positions, we are once again engaged in similar projects, trying to overcome the gulf between teaching and research, theory and practice.

Oktiabrina and I were reunited too that summer. I told her about my new project and the book, and she filled me in on the dramatic course of events that had caused the crisis center to shut down.

While she prepared the fish she had bought in the local store for our dinner and her daughter chopped salad, I flicked through the stack of photo albums she had piled in front of me, albums she had lovingly compiled in the weeks after the crisis center had closed. I smiled as I looked at the pictures of our 1998 preparatory project—our first trip to Pskov, a summer seminar at Valentina's dacha—and of her subsequent trips abroad (to London, Rome, Mongolia). I found Oktiabrina philosophical; she expressed a surprising lack of bitterness at the events that had at least temporarily cut off her dreams and pushed her back to where she had been five years previously. Indeed, she expressed some relief to be free of the strain. As then, she now supported herself by leech healing in a rented cubicle at the local hospital, drawing a meager salary that left me perplexed as to how she could survive. She and her husband still lived in the communal apartment but now occupied two rooms; after renting it for some time, they had managed to buy the second room from the young man who was registered there. This enabled them to spread out, to unpack their belongings and claim the space in a different way. They had decorated the communal spaces—the kitchen and bathroom—with a lick of new paint. There were plants on the wide sills and the place looked brighter, cleaner, and altogether more homey. Although they had still not received recompense from her husband's stint in Chechnya, she told me that they hoped to be able to buy the third room one day.

Despite this uncertainty, she spoke not of her regrets, but of her accomplishments and how far they had come. As she fleshed out her version of events, she told me that they had been on the cusp of something really great. The mayor had been committed to expanding the work of the center. When the *duma* (city legislature) began to demand rental payments, he had worked with her to formulate an alternative solution, temporarily moving them to a day care center while he tried to find something more suitable and permanent. She had gotten to know him as a person during that time and he had gotten to know her not as a supplicant, but as a healer. She had treated him with leeches for his heart condition during the last months of his life, and a kind of deep respect had grown between them. Once he had died, however, the crisis center lost local support. She told me that she had struggled to the end with an alternative vision that was not shared by her local sponsors, who urged her to charge fees for consultations (one local official even proposed that she offer a commercial sex line to support the hotline for victims of sexual and domestic violence!). She told me that she had not given up hope of reestablishing the center—indeed, she and Valentina were discussing the temporary solution of reestablishing the hotline in the Center for Women's History and Gender Studies—but she insisted that she would do it differently next time, making it a "multi-functional center" that could deal with broader issues of women's health and psychology.

Over the course of the next week, I accompanied Oktiabrina to a number of events. We attended a couple of meetings of the Open World group, an informal club formed by graduates of a U.S. NGO-led program that brought Russian civil servants and professionals to the United States. Her fellow graduates included a member of the city parliament, a journalist, and the former director of the Soros Open Society Institute. They gathered once a week in the computer room at the university, sharing sweets and cognac and planning future projects. The day before I left Tver', she took me to visit a former crisis center colleague, Lena, who had volunteered at the center while she was a law student. I think she proposed the trip partly to reassure me that our work had not been in vain, and partly to give me a leg up with the new collaborative project I was proposing. The two women spoke eloquently about the value of the work they had done through the crisis center and their experience of the "women's collective"—"It helped us find our way and our place and work towards self-sufficiency and a sense of esteem. It was a project of self-education."

Notes

Introduction

1. Perestroika (literally, rebuilding) was a period of reform that was instigated by General Secretary Gorbachev in 1986 and lasted until the demise of the USSR in 1991.

2. They included ecological groups, women's groups (including a handful of groups that identified as feminist), and human rights based groups. M. Steven Fish notes that 1989 was a key year. Popular involvement in independent politics increased dramatically prior to the 1989 ballot for the USSR Congress of Peoples' Deputies, the first even partially democratic national election in the history of the USSR (1995:35).

3. While I recognize its problematic homogenizing quality, I use the term "West" in this text on occasion for the following reasons. In the immediate post–Cold War era, the term was used widely in development literature (for example, exchanges between the newly independent states of Eastern Europe and the former USSR and the United States and Western Europe were characterized as "East-West" exchanges). Here, West signifies capitalism and liberal democracy and East signifies state socialism. Secondly, "West" (*zapad*) was frequently asserted as an emic category by my Russian interlocutors. For example, I was frequently referred to as a "Western person" (*zapadnyi chelovek*). My usage of the term is intended to reflect this reality and the persistence of Cold War ideologies in structuring experience in the immediate post–Cold War period.

4. Wendy Goldman's analysis of debates around the 1926 Code on Marriage, the Family, and Guardianship shows the extent to which working-class women were divided on these issues and the new problems this "emancipation" gave rise to: male irresponsibility, abandoned families (Goldman 1991:125–143). Natalia Kozlova examines the complicated path of women's "emancipation" as revealed through analysis of documents in Tver' *oblast'* (region). Her analysis reveals a good deal of resistance to the project, not only among rural men, but also within Communist Party committees (Kozlova 2000:86–93).

5. Soviet-era women's organizations were official, Communist Party–mandated structures. *Zhensovety* (women's councils) were top-down, centrally orchestrated organizations; their mandate was to "unite all Soviet women in the interests of building Communism" (Racioppi and See 1997:6).

6. The combined body of policies that guided international financial institutions in their dealings with Russia in the early post-socialist period came to be known as the Washington Consensus. Harvard economist Jeffrey Sachs was one of the main architects of these policies; however, in recent articles

he has distanced himself from them and has criticized international agencies such as the IMF for their failure to do enough for Russia in the early reform years (Sachs 1994).

7. Valerie Sperling documents this process, explaining how loans from international financial lending institutions were made contingent on the separation of the industrial and social welfare spheres. According to this logic, if a factory received international loans, it had to turn over its social services (including day care) to the city. Since city budgets were simultaneously experiencing dramatic cuts in funding, this meant the majority of such facilities closed down altogether (Sperling 2000:227)

8. Some of these Russian scholars include Svetlana Aivazova (1998); Olga Khasbulatova (1994); and Valentina herself (Uspenskaia 2000, 2003). In addition to introducing new historical analysis, part of their project has been to make forgotten feminist texts of the prerevolutionary period available in Russia. Aivazova's book, *Russian Women in the Labyrinth of Equality,* includes several such texts: the text of the first Russian Women's Congress of 1908, articles from prerevolutionary women's journals, and the foreword to the Russian edition of John Stuart Mill's book, *The Subjection of Women,* originally published in Russian in 1869.

9. Valentina Uspenskaia writes that *ravnopraviki* was the more common term; however, the term *feminizm* was used in Russia in the late nineteenth and early twentieth centuries to refer to the "independent organizational attempts of women from educated (usually bourgeois) strata of society to obtain recognition of their social rights" (2000:141).

10. This is manifest in the statute agreed upon by the Union of Equal Rights for Women, a coalition that formed in 1905 and united a wide range of radical women. It declared that the fight for women's rights was "indissolubly linked with the political struggle for the liberation of Russia" (cited in Edmondson 1984:39). For more thorough accounts of the complex relationships between socialism and feminism, see Edmondson (1984) and Stites (1978).

11. Fraser uses the term to refer to the prevailing political climate in the post–Cold War era, which is characterized by a shift in "the grammar of political claims making," especially in the terms in which justice is imagined. She shows how, in the context of the resurgence of economic liberalism in the 1990s, the logic of recognition (and the "cultural") wins out at the expense of the logic of redistribution (and concern about social and economic justice) (1997:2)

12. Political scientist Jacqueline Berman examines some of the new post–Cold War humanitarian campaigns in the name of women's rights. In her analysis, she shows how global discourses of trafficking that emphasize East European women's vulnerability to sexual exploitation actually work to shore up exclusionary and racist political positions.

13. In the context of a discussion of the particular ethical challenges of conducting research in formerly socialist states, Hermine De Soto revives feminist scholar Sandra Harding's call for a "politics of solidarity" with our informants (2000:93). In her recent book, Michele Rivkin-Fish explores the chal-

lenges of bringing anthropological insights to public health interventions for women's empowerment and democracy (2005). See also Hemment (2004b).

14. Because of the interventions of the '90s, many anthropologists working in post-socialist states have been drawn into "applied" forms of work—as consultants, evaluators, or translators. Indeed, some have made the case that this convergence between cultural and applied work is true for the discipline as a whole (Hackenberg and Hackenberg 2004; Lamphere 2004).

15. By the '90s, "participation," like gender, had been mainstreamed into international agency agendas. As many critics have pointed out, in the majority of cases, the participation offered local groups by international agencies is constrained and linked to a neoliberal agenda. See Jordan (2003); Paley (2001).

16. Hermine De Soto and Nora Dudwick's edited volume is a notable exception to this trend. Contributors explore the particular challenges of undertaking fieldwork in context of post-socialist states and make a strong case for reflexivity. Contributors discuss complications of negotiating fieldwork relationships and stress the ways fieldworkers must continually position themselves both personally and professionally during fieldwork (2000).

17. Anthropologist Ruth Behar, who has written extensively about the ethical and moral dilemmas of ethnographic fieldwork, writes that methods are often a defense that "reduce anxiety and enable us to function efficiently" when we may be in situations "in which we feel complicitous with structures of power, or helpless to release another from suffering, or at a loss as to whether to act or observe" (1996:6). Against what she describes as the "displacement" that is at the heart of professional anthropology, she advocates writing vulnerably, in a way that includes the author herself (Behar 1996:1–33).

1. Muddying the Waters

1. The talk was titled "Action research and Russian women's community activism: perspectives on the politics of East-West exchange," February 1, 1999. Valentina's visit to the United States was made possible by the Ford Foundation. In 1998 she received an individual grant, which enabled her to visit several Women's Studies programs in the United States as part of a preparatory project to set up her own Center for Women's History and Gender Studies at Tver' State University.

2. The same was true of the project to restructure and reconfigure institutions of higher education and social science disciplines in formerly socialist states. A special edition of the English- and Hungarian-language journal *Replika* is devoted to the topic of Western restructuring of higher education and the social sciences, and poses the question "colonization, or liberation?" I picked up a lot of contentious discussion over this project to reformulate knowledge on online discussions during the mid-to-late 1990s.

3. Some of the early critiques that made their way into print include Drakulic (1987) and Havelkova (1993). Croatian journalist Slavenka Drakulic issued particularly pithy and withering critiques. Her short essays, published in English in the United States (first in *Ms.* magazine, then as books) pointed to

the objectifying gaze of Western feminists and their blindness to their own privilege.

4. In an intellectual division of labor that has much to do with the Cold War (Wolfe 1982:3–23), anthropologists traditionally studied third-world and indigenous peoples, while the so-called second world of the Eastern Bloc was the preserve of the "harder" social sciences—sociology and political science. Beyond this, until the reforms of the mid-to-late 1980s, it was extremely difficult to gain access to do ethnographic work in socialist states. There were a few pioneering exceptions—in the Soviet Union, these included Marjorie Mandelstam Balzer (1992), Caroline Humphrey (1983), Christel Lane (1981).

5. Anthropologists have tended to regard themselves as champions of non-Western peoples. The principle of cultural relativism, which has centrally defined the discipline, has been a flag under which anthropologists have asserted the value of non-Western values and cultural practices.

6. There is nothing new here. Over the last decades, there have been persistent (if marginal) calls from within cultural anthropology to achieve a more socially engaged practice—from Dell Hymes's call to "reinvent" anthropology (Hymes, 1972) to Faye Harrison's call to "decolonize" it (Harrison 1991). However, the discipline of anthropology remains largely split between those who do "theoretical" and those who do "applied" work (Sanday 2003). More recently, this call for collaboration has been advanced by proponents of a "public" (Borofsky 2000), "public interest" (Sanday 2003), "engaged" (Lamphere 2003), or "activist" (Lyon-Callo and Hyatt 2003) anthropology.

7. There are many similar sounding configurations of this methodological approach (practitioners speak of participatory action research, action research, action science, participatory evaluation). These designations signal diverse ideological commitments and points of origin. In discussions of action research, a common distinction is made between "Southern" and "Northern" PAR. Briefly, Southern approaches sprang from sociopolitical critiques of oppression in the global South and are rooted in Marxist theory and the adult critical literacy work of Paolo Freire (1970). They aim to achieve both individual development and (more often) radical social change (Fals-Borda and Rahman 1991). Northern approaches emerged in the industrial North and are associated with organizational change contexts.

8. Anthropologist Davydd Greenwood's action research in the industrial labor-managed cooperatives of Mondragon is an example of PAR's use to achieve democratic change within organizations (Greenwood et al. 1992). Anthropologist Julia Paley learned Freirian-inspired techniques of popular education from her colleagues in the shantytown-based Chilean women's health group *Llareta*. This group has used critical education as a tool to empower participants and to challenge systems of oppression. At their prompting, Paley learns these techniques to run a history workshop (Paley 2001). Some feminist scholars have also seen PAR's promise and reworked it in order to achieve their own distinct objectives. Patricia Maguire is an early pioneer of this feminist appropriation, retooling PAR methodologies as "feminist PAR" in her work with former battered women and in subsequent community-based work in Gallup, New Mexico. J. K. Gibson-Graham worked among Australian mine

workers' wives, synthesizing a "feminist poststructuralist participatory action research" (Gibson-Graham 1994). Working against a model of liberation that assumes essential identities, a unified oppression, and already existing goals, Gibson-Graham's PAR was a project of "discursive destabilization." In the course of their collaborative project, the women participated in a series of political conversations wherein they forged alternative subjectivities and sites of power. For another example of feminist PAR, see McIntyre (2000).

9. See for example Buckley (1992), Posadskaia (1994).

10. NEWW offered a different kind of participation to women's groups that were on the periphery of grants and funding by offering small grants to enable them to buy computers. Various U.S.-based agencies, including the MacArthur and Ford Foundations funded the NEWW On-Line project, which connected thirty-five locales throughout Eastern Europe and the NIS. The project aimed to improve communication and facilitate collaborative projects between women's organizations. NEWW received one of the first two Ford Foundation grants to the region in 1994.

11. Some of these connotations were familiar to me as a Western feminist—man hating, possibly lesbianism (for which there was no public tolerance). But this antifeminism carried other connotations that were unique to the legacy of state socialism. Discredited by Bolshevik and Soviet leaders, feminism was considered a Western bourgeois preoccupation. Ironically, at the same time, feminism and the notion of a women's movement recalled Soviet-era Party-mandated women's activism.

12. We discussed the debates about Western feminist scholars' "colonizing" practices, and the new phase of scholarship that took this as a point of departure—I particularly remember discussing Funk and Mueller's edited volume that brings together critical voices from women scholars from the United States, Western Europe, and former socialist states (1993).

13. Being marked as "international" or "cosmopolitan" had been extremely compromising in Soviet era and was still utilized as a powerful disciplining trope in the 1990s.

14. Travel to the West was still tightly controlled at this time. Valentina told me that her first invitation was nixed by the local administration; her German acquaintances told her that they had put her on the list of persons to be included in the next delegation from Tver', but her name was mysteriously taken off the list. Only after her acquaintances sent her a separate, individual invitation from the city mayor was she able to travel.

15. The first Dubna forum was attended by around two hundred women, representing forty-eight organizations all over Russia. It brought women into contact with each other and stimulated interest in the emergent women's movement. The main topic of the meeting was women's worsening socio-political position in Russia and its slogan—"Democracy minus women is no democracy."

16. This was in preparation for the 1995 parliamentary elections, when the first women's party, "Women of Russia," ran candidates. For accounts of this and women's electoral blocs that formed during the '90s, see Sperling (2000).

17. I include this dialogue because it illustrates the ways local cultural constructions of labor and commerce and morality inform and inflect peoples' responses to post-socialist change. The new models associated with NGO professionalism introduce market logic to activities she previously undertook on a voluntary basis. For extended discussion of these topics, see Humphrey and Mandel (2002); Rivkin-Fish (2005).

18. Valentina often gave lectures on women's history and invited university colleagues to do the same. On a couple of occasions, she organized informal book launches to honor women colleagues whose work pertained to women's history or feminism.

19. In my experience, despite their proclamations to the contrary, few nongovernmental groups in Russia were truly open. Most were clusters of friends or relatives and only advertised their activities to the NGO community, Moscow-based foundations, and their own acquaintances. Other research confirms this (Ishkanian 2003; Kay 2000; Richter 1999; Sperling 2000).

20. As the new and profitable market in post-socialist women has opened up, thousands of international marriage bureaus and dating agencies have been set up. This has caused much consternation among international and regional feminist groups and scholars, who perceive this to be at worst a form of trafficking in women (Global Survival Network 1997). Most people I spoke to in Tver' regarded the phenomenon with resigned pragmatism; while regrettable, it perhaps offered these women their best chance of a good life. Occasionally I heard people voice concern for the poor naïve American men, who perhaps sincerely believed that their Russian fiancées actually loved them. Valentina and some other members of the group had a more feminist construction of this service, and were much more concerned about the welfare of the women and the caliber of the men accordingly.

21. Drawing this comparison is not too far-fetched. At least one of the young women attendees had followed precisely that trajectory.

22. Valentina was one of the first in the city to have Internet access (granted to her by the Washington-based NGO the Network of East-West Women). She was thus able to put local women in touch with opportunities she had learned about online—such as the Open Society Institute programs that specifically sought to provide higher educational opportunities to youth in the former Soviet Union and other formerly socialist states.

23. In 1997 a university head of department earned the ruble equivalent of less than $50 a month. Nonacademic staff earned much less. The value of salaries plunged during successive economic crises. People were forced to supplement their income by undertaking other jobs (sometimes buying and selling at markets, tutoring, journalism) or engaging in informal systems of exchange.

24. I first lived in the university hostel for international students and then rented a one-room apartment in the city.

25. In her ethnography of German reunification, Daphne Berdahl writes eloquently about the strong sense of cultural devaluation East Germans felt in the immediate post-socialist period. As ideologies, values, and past decisions

were discredited, women experienced this cultural devaluation in particularly intimate ways (Berdahl 1999).

26. Participant observation necessitates immersion in "daily life" (those banal and taken-for-granted practices that neither local people nor most social scientists deem worthy of commentary). The ideal typical participant observer deliberately opens herself to experience and interactions that are locally determined. According to the interpretivist tradition (which remains the compass by which most anthropologists navigate), the task is then to make sense of and to represent the "native's point of view" (Geertz 1983).

27. While conventional social science assumes that the right and expertise to design and conduct research reside with the expert researcher, PAR recasts research as a collaborative endeavor between outside researcher and community group and involves community members in research design. In an ideal typical PAR project, the community group invites a researcher to work with them on a project that meets local needs (Greenwood and Levin 1998).

2. Querying Democratization

1. I found that by 1997, the initial enchantment at imported produce had worn off. Many people were wary of foreign foods, particularly of meat products, which were known to contain additives and were regarded as significantly inferior to domestically produced goods. They were often compelled to buy imported goods, however, since local retailers regularly inflated the price of domestic produce. Melissa Caldwell discusses related phenomena in her article (Caldwell 2002).

2. During the Soviet period, health care and child care were provided by the socialist state. While these services were under-resourced and unsatisfactory, they were a crucial part of the social contract (Cook 1993).

3. In the book Alekseeva explains that she has spent considerable time in the United Kingdom and claims to have worked for ten years as a volunteer in various "charitable" projects in Russia. I take Alekseeva to be both a propagandist of the third sector and one of its believers. However, her opinions clearly shifted over time. Although here she lauds the third sector, in a later article published in *Surviving Together* she sounds a more cautionary tale, discussing the differences between U.S. and Russian notions of charity and social responsibility (Alekseeva 1996).

4. *Chainik* literally means teapot. As Alekseeva explains, it is an endearing colloquialism for someone who is a little clumsy, or off-kilter. Here, it serves as a translation of the popular English-language "For Dummies" series.

5. "Third sector" or "voluntary sector" research only emerged in the early1980s, but as a vision of development, it has already achieved a kind of hegemony among international agencies active in post-socialist contexts (Foley and Edwards 1997). Some of the key centers engaged in third-sector research are the International Society for Third Sector Research (http://www.jhu.edu/~istr/), the Yale Program on Nonprofit Organizations (PONPO), the Johns Hopkins Comparative Nonprofit Sector Project, the International Society for Third-Sec-

tor Research at Johns Hopkins, and ARNOVA (The Association of Research on Nonprofit Organizations and Voluntary Action).

6. Following Garton-Ash, I refer here to the work of Vaclav Havel, Adam Michnik, and Georgy Konrad to typify the civil society debates. While it would be problematic to homogenize their work, it can be seen to share a great deal, and these authors were in dialogue with each other. See discussions by Garton-Ash (1990); Gellner (1994); Ost (1990).

7. As Garton-Ash puts it, this position is characterized by the conviction "that moral changes can have a seemingly disproportionate political effect, that consciousness ultimately determines being, and that the key to the future lies not in the external, objective condition of states—political, military, economic, technological—but in the internal, subjective condition of individuals" (1990:193).

8. For commentary on this phenomenon, see Foley and Edwards (1996, 1998). A special edition of the U.S. *Journal of Democracy,* a journal that analyzes and documents the progress of democratization and civil society development, was devoted to the discussion of de Toqueville's work and its continued relevance. The editors conclude their introduction with this statement: "As we enter the new millennium, one might say with little exaggeration, we are all Tocquevillians now!" (2000:9).

9. The question recalls the title of Nikolai Chernyshevskii's nineteenth-century novel, which inspired later generations of Russian revolutionaries. Lenin also published under this title.

10. This call was answered by a rush of empirical research, mostly with survey data (Foley and Edwards 1997). Richard Rose at the University of Strathclyde is one of the foremost social capital theorists in the Russian context.

11. Notice that in both Putnam's model and the "New Policy Agenda," the state is exogenized. In this way, the '90s formulation of civil society is strangely compatible with the '80s oppositionist idea of civil society, which also wrote out and denied the importance of the state. However, as we shall see, the state is more entangled than these models allow.

12. While in the early 1990s the Bank was not interested in NGOs and development, by the late nineties it had an entire division devoted to it (James 1997). In the mid-to-late 1990s, the World Bank became a key supporter of studies that explore the relationship between economic liberalism and democracy (Blair 1997).

13. Sarah Henderson's recent study of Western civil society aid to Russia maps these funding trajectories: in 2000 George Soros's Open Society Institute–Russia channeled over $56 million to NGOs, universities, and other civic organizations; between 1993 and 2001 the Eurasia Foundation allocated almost $38 million to the nonprofit sector; between 1991 and 1998 the MacArthur Foundation approved over $17 million in grants to support civic initiatives in the former Soviet Union (Henderson 2003:7).

14. Recent research confirms that women predominate in nongovernmental politics, rather than formal, electoral politics. See for example Ishkanian (2003); Phillips (2000); Sperling (2000); Zelikova (1996).

15. Putnam himself excluded nonprofit organizations of the third sector from his discussion of associations generative of social capital (1995). However, my point is that his work has been invoked by those who promote the third sector.

16. An article by Saratov ecological activist Ol'ga Pitsunova provides a strikingly similar account. In an interview about the state of the contemporary ecological movement in Russia, she is scathing about the third sector and what it represents. She draws a sharp distinction between the emergent third sector and the "social movement" (*obshchestvennoe dvizhenie*). She describes the third sector thus: "These groups are not societal in essence: these 'revolutionaries' are made up of too narrow circles and are too far from the people" (Pitsunova 1998:24).

17. As one propagandist put it in the *Journal of Democracy*, "Creating a civil society is like cultivating a garden. It is not a project to be achieved overnight by planting institutions in an alien soil, by grafting institutions from abroad, or by drawing up a host of paper organizations that are no more real than plastic plants. It is a process that can be brought to fruition only by the patient cultivation of institutions in soil that Communism for generations sowed with distrust" (Rose 1994:29). This is a strikingly Putnam-esque vision. In his writings, associational activity generates social capital and habits of cooperation, trust, and participation. While social capital adheres in individuals, it and the trust it entails can be extrapolated to government. This is because all forms of social capital are correlated; "Members of associations are much more likely than non-members to participate in politics, to spend time with neighbors, to express social trust, and so on" (Putnam 1995:73).

18. Michele Rivkin-Fish explores this dynamic in her recent book. In her research in Russian hospitals during the mid-'90s, she found that liberal discourses had deep subjective resonance with doctors and patients alike. In the context of an acute public health crisis and deep sense of societal collapse, doctors embraced individualizing kinds of moral change rather than focusing on structural issues and saw their role to be to morally educate men and women to develop their sense of self (2005).

19. Much ink has been spilled on the intelligentsia, which remains a very contested category in the Soviet period. I do not mean to assert the existence of intelligentsia as a unified, homogenized group; rather, I use it as an emic term. In this context, it is used to refer to those who identify with old cultural elites, in opposition to Soviet elites (*nomenklatura*). Although rarely used self-descriptively in the 1990s, I found that the term was often elicited by conversations such as these, where highly educated people reflected on their personal losses and the changes of the last decade.

20. Speaking in the name of the *narod* or moralizing on its behalf is a familiar trope of Russian and East European cultural elites.

21. As I won my first grants in support of my field research (the first six months were unfunded), I was able to offer modest payment to those who assisted me in my research by undertaking technical activities—for example, transcription of interviews, collection of articles. While of interest to us both, this was primarily for my benefit.

22. It is worth noting that the word *imidzh* is a calque, an expression introduced into Russian by translating it from English and supplanting the Russian term *obraz*. Since the '90s, the term has been in wide circulation—for example, in the new job description *"imidzh meiker"* (image maker).

23. The *nomenklatura* system, set in motion after the Bolshevik Revolution, enabled Communist Party bodies to control the appointment and promotion of all leading personnel in social institutions (McAuley 1992:29). The *nomenklatura* were widely regarded as a bureaucratic elite that enjoyed special privileges. The system was officially abolished in 1990 with the collapse of the socialist state; however, the majority of the *nomenklatura* preserved their privilege—either by retaining their positions or by using their influence to secure lucrative new ones in the post-Soviet period (as this example reveals). Comparative research shows that the system proved more durable in Russia than other post-socialist states.

24. The term *blat* refers to the system of informal contacts and personal networks used to obtain goods and services in Soviet Russia. In her comprehensive study of this social practice, Alena Ledeneva describes *blat* as an exchange of access in times of shortage (Ledeneva 1998:37); it was intimately related to the Soviet state, since the state was complicit. *Blat* shifted in form and meaning during the post-Soviet period, when it was partially displaced by market relations. It continues to be used by both by elites, to gain access to lucrative opportunities, and by those who have few resources, where it is a survival mechanism (Ledeneva 1998:175–214). Michele Rivkin-Fish traces the ways informal networks persisted, yet were transformed, in her analysis of transactions between patients and providers in St. Petersburg hospitals (Rivkin-Fish 2005:152–178).

25. Mikhail Khodorkovsky, president of the giant oil company Yukos and the founder of one of the first Russian foundations, was arrested in 2003 for tax evasion. His arrest is widely thought to have been politically motivated—to end his sponsorship of undesirable NGOs.

26. The unpublished report, "Recommendation for Grant Action," was written by Colette Shulman, September 1994, New York. It noted that the women's movement was "highly personalized and politicized" and recommended that resources should be spread out rather than concentrated.

27. The question of the extent to which individuals working within such structures have agency or can "make a difference" has been explored in the burgeoning literature on democracy assistance. Some analysts, adopting a Foucauldian approach, have shown how development projects in post-socialist states, as well as in the so-called developing world, are constrained by the logic of governmentality. This logic deflects attention from structural issues (poverty, the role of the state) to emphasize technical issues (Escobar 1995; Ferguson 1990; Rivkin-Fish 2005). Here, the logic within which these interventions are nested greatly constrains the possibility for reshaping them.

28. The terms of the Humanitarian Institute's grant required them to have formal "partner organizations," with whom they would collaborate and whom they would support.

29.   When I shared this analysis with her in June 2004, she agreed and added interestingly that it was not that she idealized the West, or was straightforwardly "pro-capitalist," but that she had met such good people through her encounters with foundations and agencies. She knew them to be sincere and genuinely interested in fostering her work. Furthermore, she told me that most of the agency representatives she met were deeply critical of the political economy they worked within and had an anticapitalist orientation.

30.   In 1992 George Soros set up the International Science Foundation. The Foundation had a total disbursement of $140 million, which was distributed in the form of small one-year grants and travel grants to individual scientists in the former Soviet Union, to encourage them to stay in Russia and continue with their academic work (Soros 2000:10–16). Indeed, Soros's money also kept many research establishments afloat. Tver' State University is one of thirty-two provincial universities that have received funding from Soros's foundation to set up computer centers. In Tver', the grant paid for a server and hundreds of computers, providing email access to all students.

3. Gender Mainstreaming and the Third-Sectorization of Russian Women's Activism

1.   These authors give an upbeat account of the possibilities for political activism post-1989. They describe the international women's movement as one of the more successful players in a new field of transnational social movements, or "TANs" (transnational advocacy networks). Activists of TANs are "moral" or "social entrepreneurs," who mediate skillfully between international and local actors (Keck and Sikkink 1998:165–198).

2.   In the course of my work, I was made aware of several "scare" moments, when activists feared that the foundations that supported their work might withdraw imminently. The first was in spring 1998 when a new draft tax law passed its first reading, and included provisions to tax all nonprofit organizations as profitable ones (this would have involved NGOs paying tax on free services rendered). The second followed the economic crisis of August 1998, when the collapse of Russian banks meant that accounts were frozen. While many foreign businesses left Russia in the fall of 1998, most foundations remained. The real cutbacks took place later, in 2001.

3.   The Almanac was translated into English and published as *Woman and Russia: First Feminist Samizdat* by Sheba Feminist Publishers, London (Mamonova 1980).

4.   In a critical and self-reflexive account of her participation in these early years, Belorussian feminist scholar Elena Gapova elaborates on this "privileged" designation. She argues that to gain access to feminist texts during the '80s, one had to reside in Moscow or Leningrad, have graduated from a prestigious social science department, work at an elite think tank, and more often than not be a member of the Communist Party, "for only devoted Communists could be entrusted with facing the poisonous effects that bourgeois theorizing could produce" (Gapova 2003:5).

5.   Several of them later published on this topic; see for example Kulik (1997); Uspenskaia (1997).

6. Interestingly, Russian feminist scholar Svetlana Aivazova makes a similar point in her characterization of the prerevolutionary Russian women's movement. She argues that feminism in Russia was never an expression of the "war of the sexes." Rather it "was in the first place like a movement for the freeing of the individual, woman or man" (1998:49). Here, she argues that both men and women were oppressed by the culture of patriarchy, which prevented adult men from achieving independence and self-determination.

7. Steinem's commentary reads thus: "For far too long, Russian women and American women have been kept apart by our respective patriarchs; communist or capitalist, secular or religious. Now, Tatyana Mamonova has built a bridge of understanding for all of us to cross. Thanks to her, we may find that each of us has more in common with each other than with the rulers of our countries."

8. During the reforms of the '80s, members of the intelligentsia who had spearheaded critiques of state socialism (in the form of dissidence and oppositional activity) were invited into a new relationship with the state. In what former Gorbachev aide Pavel Palazchenko termed a "marriage of convenience" (Palazchenko 1999), members of the radical intelligentsia in Moscow and Leningrad were invited to join reformist elements of the Communist Party *nomenklatura* as consultants on economic and social policy issues.

9. This consisted of a number of committees and commissions whose fortunes rose and fell, depending on the broader political environment. In the 1990s, key institutions were the Presidential Commission on Issues of Women, the Family, and Demography, founded 1992, and the Department of Family, Women, and Children's Issues of the Ministry of Social Protection, founded 1992 (Sperling 2000).

10. The mainstreaming of gender did not originate with the end of the Cold War, but the '90s marked the crest of a wave that was already in motion. WID (Women in Development) emerged in the 1970s as a corrective to the Cold War paradigm of development that excluded and marginalized women. An initiative spearheaded by women's activists (Boserup 1970), it sought to make women more central to considerations of development. Devised in such a way as to be persuasive to economists (it asserted that improving women's status made good economic sense) it was highly successful. In the seventies WID was brought to agencies by feminist-oriented "policy entrepreneurs" (Kardam 1991), and by the '80s it had achieved a kind of hegemony in development circles. At the same time, it began to permeate the UN system. WID activities started to increase within the UN system in the early seventies, leading to the 1975 World Conference on Women in Nairobi and launching the UN Decade for Women (1975–1985). By 1985, "an international women's movement had been consolidated and WID was established" (Buvinic 1996).

11. IREX received U.S. government funding to run the Regional Empowerment Initiative for Women program, which addresses the issue of trafficking of women. The Westminster Foundation (funded by the British government) has a program devoted to women and women's political participation; CIDA (the Canadian International Development Agency) has a gender equality port-

folio in their Russia program; the German government has also been active (Henderson 2003).

12. The Open Society Institute created a Women's Program in 1997 to work on various women's issues, including violence against women. Until it shut down in 2001, it was staffed by two long-term Russian women's activists.

13. Ford has focused on four main areas in its support to women's groups: information, communication, and networking; the development of gender studies curricula; domestic violence; and provision of broad-based social support. The bulk of these funds ($1 million during 1994–1999) were devoted to organizations that fostered the exchange of information, communication, and networking among women's groups (Henderson 2003:121).

14. The gulf between Muscovite and provincial salaries was quite startling during the '90s. In the year before the economic crisis of August 1998, an average monthly salary in Moscow was around $400, compared to $50 in Tver'. Foundations typically pay their full-time staff a higher than average wage. What is more (and of equal significance) is that foundation-paid wages are stable. As I have explained in earlier chapters, most women and men in the provinces I spoke to had highly erratic salaries, which were frequently unpaid or paid late.

15. The school was awarded grants under Ford's program to support the development of gender studies curricula in Russia. A large grant was awarded to Moscow Center for Gender Studies to administrate it.

4. Global Civil Society and the Local Costs of Belonging

1. Here I draw on Keck and Sikkink's influential account of the development of "transnational advocacy networks" (TANs), networks of activists that coalesce and operate across national frontiers. They show how the campaigns to combat violence against women marked a significant shift in the evolution of these networks. Prior to this moment, women's activists of North and South had been deeply divided and unable to achieve a common agenda. While Northern (or "first world") feminists had been preoccupied with issues of gender discrimination and equality, Southern (or "third world") women were more concerned with issues of social justice and development, which affected both men and women, albeit in different ways.

2. The UN Convention on the Elimination of All Forms of Discrimination against Women (CEDAW), which was adopted in 1979 and entered into force in 1981, makes no mention of violence, rape, abuse, or battery. However, by mid-1995 violence against women had become a "common advocacy position" of the women's movement and the human rights movement (Keck and Sikkink 1998). Feminist activists first pushed the issue to international prominence at the 1993 Vienna UN Human Rights Conference. Their strategizing coincided with international concern about the systemic use of rape in war in Bosnia, and it was effective. In 1994, the UN High Commission on Human Rights appointed the first special rapporteur on violence against women, and rape in warfare was recognized as a crime against humanity by the Hague Tribunal.

3. The U.S. Congress allocated $1 million to support programs combating violence against women in Russia. The Ford Foundation provided substantial funding for the campaigns, as I have explained. The American Bar Association provided technical and financial support to individual crisis centers. During the late nineties it ran regular seminars in its Moscow office on legal issues pertaining to violence, to which it invited Moscow-based and regional groups. The U.S.-based NGO Women, Law, and Development has a Moscow office, which conducts legal support and trains lawyers to deal with the problem. Several of the embassies provided financial support to individual crisis centers.

4. The bulletin presented the results of an extensive "social analysis" (*obshchest-vennaia ekspertiza*) of the draft legislation. A wide range of individuals, including crisis center staff, women victims, medical professionals, and students were interviewed to collect their input and opinions on the extent of the issue and the effectiveness of existing provisions to combat it (Liborakina and Sidorenkova 1997).

5. A Human Rights Watch report provides the following statistics from the Russian Ministry of Internal Affairs: there were 14,073 registered or reported rapes in 1991; 12,515 in 1995; and 10,888 in 1996 (1997:7).

6. ANNA was the first Russian center to deal with domestic violence. The first center for victims of rape and sexual assault ("Sisters") was set up in Moscow in 1994. Both centers had significant support from the educational institutions where feminist scholars clustered, as I have described. ANNA had offices in the same building as the Moscow Center for Gender Studies (which was established by Pisklakova's mother-in-law, the academic Nataliia Rimashev-skaia), while "Sisters" was supported by the Center for Women, Family, and Gender Studies at the Moscow Youth Institute.

7. The edited volume *Nasilie i sotsial'nye izmeneniia* (Rape and Social Change), published by ANNA with support from the TACIS program of the European Council and CARITAS, an Austrian foundation, presented both theoretical discussions of the social causes of domestic violence and the practical findings of crisis center staff and workers.

8. In 1994 a group of crisis centers came together to form the first Association of Russian Crisis Centers (Zabelina 1996:181). Its aim was to better coordinate crisis center activities and to spread the campaigns nationwide prior to Beijing. Activists from eleven crisis centers came together to undertake research on the scope and nature of violence against women in Russia and produced a report that was submitted to the NGO forum. Russian Association of Crisis Centers for Women: Research, Education and Advocacy Project, *Report for the Non-Governmental Forum of the United Nation's Fourth World Conference on the Status of Women* (1995).

9. In 1996, in response to the recommendations of the 1995 Beijing conference, a Russian presidential decree called for local authorities to make provisions for women victims of sexual and domestic violence. During my research, crisis center activists had input into presidential and parliamentary committees and commissions, and worked on a new draft law on domestic violence.

These initiatives had only limited success, however. After approximately forty draft versions had been drawn up, the bill was rejected by the State Duma in 1998.

10.   This analysis mostly pertains to the mid-to-late '90s. Like other social workers (of state and non-state structures), crisis center workers found themselves on the front line at a time of massive societal upheaval, and they dealt with all the social problems people brought to them. Over time, as different structures set up (NGOs and state), as state power asserted itself, and as people began to feel more stable, crisis centers were able to focus and specialize more narrowly—on domestic and sexual violence. My sense is that this happened most swiftly in Moscow.

11.   Other anthropologists of post-socialism have noted the rhetorical persistence of terms relating to breakdown and crisis in Russian talk. See for example Ries (1997:42–51). Michele Rivkin-Fish documents how the public health crisis of the '90s was also viewed as a spiritual crisis of the nation (Rivkin-Fish 2005).

12.   The name Oktiabrina is taken from the word oktiabr' (October), signifying the Bolshevik revolution of 1917, which took place in October under the Julian calendar. Oktiabrina explained to me that her parents had chosen to name her thus, since she was born on November 7 (the day the revolution took place).

13.   Michele Rivkin-Fish discusses the complexities of power and authority in the post-Soviet medical profession in elegant detail. Doctors were both economically disenfranchised and deprofessionalized, as their class status was undermined by the Soviet state (2005:25). Despite this disenfranchisement, they were irrevocably identified as agents of the discredited socialist state; in her evocative formulation, their state licenses constituted "certificates without charisma" (2005:141).

14.   Leech healing is making a come back not only in Russia, but in Western Europe and the United States. A recent article in the *New Yorker* details its resurgence and association with breakthrough medical techniques in plastic and reconstructive surgery (Colapinto 2005:72).

15.   Although her organization, the Women's Assembly, had no budget or administrative power, she had significant clout. Further, she needed us. As Valentina had explained to me, Shvedova had begun to dabble in the women's movement in order to generate support for herself in the city. Her position, though influential, was insecure and was threatened by the forthcoming presidential elections. The Women's Assembly was an attempt to carve out a power base for herself in the nongovernmental sphere. She was receptive to nongovernmental initiatives, as she wished to be perceived as a supporter of community concerns.

16.   Here, I refer to the ABA-CEELI project—the Central and East European Legal Initiative of the American Bar Association and its Gender Issues program. Under this project, American specialists helped to train Russian lawyers to work with crisis centers.

5. A Tale of Two Projects

1.   One Open Society grant provided support for a conference, the other provided funds to buy books to build up libraries in women's and gender studies.
The latter application was successful.

2.   The three of us sat down and crafted a narrative that laid out the history of
our work so far, requesting $10,000. This attempt was unsuccessful.

3.   Unlike Oktiabrina, their newness was offset by their status and location
within Soviet systems of patronage. Although new to the town, both had
previously worked within party-state structures and hence were recognized
as "ours" (*svoi*) by local members of the administration.

4.   Oktiabrina and I had several audiences with Liudmila Pavlovna in July 1998
as we negotiated the early stages of municipal support. She counseled us on
our approach, and she helped us by advancing the money pledged to us by
the Women's Assembly to enable our study trip to the crisis center in Pskov.
She arranged for the local branch of the Soldiers' Mothers Committee to
lend us the money while the budget was cleared. Olga Mikhailovna organized
all our meetings with the mayor and briefed us as we prepared for our meetings with him; and she gave us insight into the workings of the city administration.

5.   This was very much in the logic of the Ford Foundation, which occupied a
unique status and had a self-consciously different approach to funding. However, it also had to do with the relationship of respect between Mary McAuley
(a well-respected British scholar of Russian politics) and Valentina. They became acquainted during the first Summer School in Gender Studies, which
Ford sponsored and Valentina co-organized in Tver' in 1996.

6.   The acknowledged failures of the early-mid '90s had led to a period of soul-
searching in the donor community, and by 1998 thoughtful foundation representatives were only too aware of the problems of donor support.

7.   There was a sharp narrative switch in the immediate aftermath of the crisis
and in the subsequent years. Liberal triumphalism was displaced by talk
of how Russia is "lost" and is a "failed project." For a particularly striking
example of this tendency, see Tayler (2001).

8.   Cell phones only began to appear in the Russian provinces a little later; by
2004 they were nearly ubiquitous.

9.   When the mayor decided to support the project, he issued an order to the
municipal department for the social protection of the population, requiring
them to assist us. In turn, they authorized the municipal Center for Social
Protection to provide us with salaried positions.

10. The majority of funds went to the Moscow-based crisis center ANNA, which
doled out resources and held training sessions in turn. In 1999, ANNA received Ford Foundation support to run a small grants program to support a
small network of crisis centers in Siberia (Henderson 2003: 126). ANNA ran
a series of competitions to which individual crisis centers were invited to
apply—for example, a seminar series titled "Working with the Police," funded

by TASIS (European Union) and the Austrian organization CARITAS. It also ran trainings for other professionals—for example, a seminar series designed for medical personnel in 2002.

11. Housing was allocated by the Soviet state and still is by its successor. The system allocates living space according to the so-called "sanitary norm," providing nine square meters per person. However, this theoretical entitlement was hard won, and families often waited for a generation or more before the state gave them apartments. Allocations were made through the workplace. Oktiabrina and her family had long been promised housing through her husband's workplace (indeed, this was one of the reasons he decided to work for the *GAI* (traffic police) when they arrived in the city; formerly he had worked as an engineer), but the waiting list was long.

12. The *propiska* (residence permit) was a device by which the Soviet state exercised demographic control. Originally established by Stalin in 1932 in order to restrict mass immigration to the cities, it remains in place today. The *propiska* is the precondition for most civil rights and social benefits, such as formal employment; medical insurance; unemployment benefits; the right to vote and to stand for election (Hojdestrand 2003:2). It is also impossible to be allocated state housing without being registered, a fact which clearly compounded Oktiabrina's problems. Oktiabrina was unregistered for a period of 1½ years, until she managed to resolve the issue.

13. Ledeneva describes a range of responses to *blat*, from the figure of the "blatmeister"—the consummate *blat* practitioner who acts as broker or fixer within social networks—to those who adopt a moral stance towards *blat* and refuse to use it. While I do not see Oktiabrina as a "truth teller"—the most extreme example of *blat*-resister Ledeneva presents us with—this account helps us interpret Oktiabrina's stance, which was not uncommon amongst the women I came to know through my research. As Ledeneva suggests, opposition to *blat* also implies a struggle against the socialist distribution system and the state (1998:117).

14. She was able to access these funds from a Moscow-based expatriate organization, the International Women's Club, which had an emergency fund for crisis centers. She also pledged to invite Oktiabrina on trainings and to assist with further grant applications to IREX.

15. Valentina offered classes in gender studies at the city administration.

16. She had started taking classes with Lena, our Zhenskii Svet friend who was an English language teacher and who was coaching some of the women activists for free.

17. "CWHGS was registered in June 1999 as a not-for-profit, non-governmental women's organization. In December 1999, it was also established as a part of the Tver' State University with educational and research functions in the field of women's and gender issues" (http://www.tvergenderstudies.ru/ab00000e.htm).

18. At this time foundations calculated provincial salaries at approximately $400 a month. Although secure and stable and much more than official university salaries (the equivalent of $100 a month), this was not a fortune by local standards.

19. The Center for Gender Studies was a cell within her department. The resources it received nurtured the department. Books on gender studies received from grants were available to students and faculty, conferences organized could be attended by all, funds that supported her manager also funded the department.

20. British activists visited Tver' in the spring of 2000, holding workshops on domestic violence that were attended by crisis center staff and volunteers and by social workers and psychologists in the city (including some employed by the municipal administration). Oktiabrina, Lena, and one other crisis center volunteer traveled to London in November 2000 to meet with British women's activists. They visited a number of crisis centers and women's groups and were taken on a whirlwind tour of the British criminal justice system, including the Old Bailey.

21. She was selected by the staff of the Crisis Center Association, which by this time was acting as a kind of clearinghouse organization, channeling funds and study trips in the logic I described in chapter 2. Oktiabrina was the only representative from Tver'.

22. The program was titled "Working with law enforcement agencies." Project Harmony was founded in Vermont in 1985 and organized some of the first youth exchanges between the United States and USSR. It grew in the '90s, reaping the benefits of the new funding programs under the U.S. Freedom Support Act, and ran a series of civic education, democracy-promoting programs, of which their Domestic Violence Community Partnership was one.

23. According to the crisis center accounts, between August 1999 and October 2000, twenty-four articles were written about the crisis center and the issue of domestic violence. In addition, members of the staff worked with local TV stations and were featured in four separate programs.

24. She spent about six weeks at Kent State University, where she had been sent by the rector of her university as a kind of special envoy to initiate a new institutional exchange program between the two universities. I invited her to visit me at the University of Massachusetts and arranged for her to give two presentations—to the Five College Slavic Studies faculty seminar, and to my department (the department where I had been hired as an activist anthropologist).

25. The university administration gave the center one salaried position in 2001, which Valentina split between herself (as director) and her office manager. In 2000 she won an Open Society grant to support a conference on integrating gender and women's studies into the curriculum and to conduct a gender revision of social science and humanities textbooks. The Open Society Institute also supported the publication of *Zhenshchiny Istoriia Obshchestvo* (Women, History, Society), a two-volume collection of articles in gender studies by Russian scholars (2002). At the same time, the Russian Ministry of Education had awarded them a small grant in support of the same gender revisions of textbooks—their revision and dissemination through seminars.

26. This expansionist plan was clearly drawn up to meet the requirements of the

funders. She told me that she would much have preferred to be able to consolidate their existing activities, rather than stretch out more.

27. This reveals the ironies of living space allocation.

28. Oktiabrina's husband had signed on to serve in Chechnya for a constellation of reasons. He was at least partly motivated by a strong sense of duty; he told me that if he had not volunteered, the next candidate in line was a young boy. He was partially motivated also by their desire to accelerate the process of living space allocation. If his workplace allocated them a room in the city, they would be able to exchange it for a second room in their current communal flat, or somehow upgrade to a flat. As of 2005, they have still not received this entitlement.

29. She told me she received the equivalent of $60 a month from IREX for the duration of the nine-month project, and that her husband's salary was about $90 a month.

30. Several other scholars who have written on the Russian campaigns against violence against women note this shift in donor priorities also—see Ishkanian (2003) and Johnson (2004:234).

31. In 2004, the center won a third grant of $74,000 to "integrate a gender studies perspective into the core university curriculum and establish the Feminist Press–Russia" (http://www.fordfound.org/grants_db/view_grant_detail .cfm?grant_id=220694, accessed August 19, 2005). I should add that the press is an official filial of the original Feminist Press at the City University of New York. Valentina met with the press's founder, Florence Howe, during one of her visits to the United States and negotiated for this arrangement. Feminist Press–Russia is the only such filial to exist.

32. The conference, held in September 2004, was titled *Gender po-russki* (Gender in Russian).

33. Ford is an unusual donor and has a distinctive way of dealing with the organizations it supports. As a private foundation, it is "in it for the long haul," as Mary McAuley put it to me; it sets long-term goals and prefers to work in long-term partnerships, allowing its recipients considerable autonomy and providing substantial support. Certainly Valentina had a high degree of autonomy in her decisions about the content of her work; she was able to pitch ideas to the Ford Foundation, rather than the other way around. Further, she was granted considerable latitude in her accounting, which allowed her to be creative in making things work.

34. When we met to discuss my manuscript in June 2004, Valentina explained that her students participate on a voluntary basis and the school was still free and open to the public, but that she paid the teachers when she could. She told me that she and some of her colleagues would keep going even without funding, "but I'd be ashamed to ask that of the others [the younger women]."

Conclusion

1. The so-called Orange Revolution was a series of protests and demonstrations that took place in Ukraine during 2004–2005 in response to allegations of cor-

ruption and voter intimidation during the presidential elections. These mostly youth-run demonstrations led to a run-off vote in which opposition candidate, Viktor Yushchenko, defeated the incumbent, Viktor Yanukovych. U.S. governmental support of NGOs associated with the Orange Revolution was highly controversial in Russia, where political leaders have taken steps to guarantee that similar processes do not take place at home. In a meeting with human rights activists on July 20, 2005, President Putin announced that he would not tolerate foreign money being used to finance the political activities of NGOs. In the fall of 2005, the Russian State Duma began considering a bill that will force all NGOs to reregister ahead of upcoming national elections.

2. One example is NGO Watch, a collaborative project initiated in 2003 by the American Enterprise Institute and the Federalist Society. NGO Watch particularly targets NGOs that undertake advocacy work on behalf of "liberal" causes. For discussion of this, see The Public Eye.

3. Here I locate the work of Steven Sampson, Michele Rivkin-Fish, and David Abramson among others.

4. Arundhati Roy acknowledges this point in her otherwise scathing condemnation of NGOization (2004).

5. Professional qualifications automatically increase with service within state structures. Additionally, state employers will sponsor employees to take higher education courses and additional exams. Workers of the nongovernmental sphere doing similar work are denied such support.

6. Susan Brin Hyatt also grapples with this dilemma and poses questions about the implications of the critique of neoliberalism for our scholarship and scholarly practice. At the same time that she critiques the new fashion for community service learning (CSL) on American campuses, she offers CSL as a framework for simultaneous engagement and critique. See also Lyon-Callo and Hyatt (2003).

7. In their edited volume *Action and Knowledge: Breaking the Monopoly with Participatory Action Research,* Fals-Borda and Rahman state that "PAR has the best chance of surviving the test of time only if it tells the people that it can betray them, and that only an aware and ever-vigilant people is not betrayed" (1991:23).

8. This book comprised a collection of letters, photographs, and interviews with local women veterans and witnesses.

References

Abramson, David. 1999. A Critical Look at NGOs and Civil Society as Means to an End in Uzbekistan. *Human Organization* 58 (3): 240–250.

Abu-Lughod, Lila. 1991. Writing against Culture. In *Recapturing Anthropology: Working in the Present,* ed. R. G. Fox, 154–163. Sante Fe: American School of Research Press.

Aivazova, Svetlana. 1998. *Russkie zhenshchiny v labirinte ravnopraviia.* Moscow: RIK Rusanova.

Alcoff, Linda. 1994. The Problem of Speaking for Others. In *Feminist Nightmares: Women At Odds,* ed. S. Weisser and J. Fleischner, 285–309. New York: New York University Press.

Alekseeva, Ol'ga. 1996. Sharing Salt Strengthens Society. *Surviving Together* (Winter 1996): 3–4.

———. 1996. *Tretii sektor: blagotvoritel'nost' dlia chainikov.* Moscow: Charities Aid Foundation.

Alvarez, Sonia E. 1998. Latin American Feminisms "Go Global": Trends of the 1990s and Challenges for the New Millennium. In Alvarez, Dagnino, and Escobar 1998, 293–324.

Alvarez, Sonia E., Evelina Dagnino, and Arturo Escobar, eds. 1998. *Cultures of Politics, Politics of Cultures: Re-visioning Latin American Social Movements.* Boulder, Colo.: Westview Press.

———. 1998. Introduction: The Cultural and the Political in Latin American Social Movements. In Alvarez, Dagnino, and Escobar 1998, 1–25.

Anheier, Helmut, Marlies Glasius, and Mary Kaldor. 2001. Introducing Global Civil Society. In *Global Civil Society 2001,* ed. H. Anheier, M. Glasius, and M. Kaldor, 3–22. Oxford: Oxford University Press.

Asad, Talal. 1973. *Anthropology and the Colonial Encounter.* London: Ithaca Press.

Attwood, Lynne. 1997. "She Was Asking for It": Rape and Domestic Violence against Women. In *Post-Soviet Women: From the Baltic to Central Asia,* ed. M. Buckley. Cambridge and New York: Cambridge University Press.

Balzer, Marjorie Mandelstam, ed. 1992. *Russian Traditional Culture: Religion, Gender and Customary Law.* Armonk, N.Y.: M.E. Sharpe.

Behar, Ruth. 1993. *Translated Woman: Crossing the Border with Esperanza's Story.* Boston: Beacon Press.

———. 1996. *The Vulnerable Observer.* Boston: Beacon Press.

Berdahl, Daphne. 1999. *Where the World Ended: Reunification and Identity in the German Borderland.* Berkeley: University of California Press.

———. 2000a. Introduction: An Anthropology of Postsocialism. In *Altering States: Ethnographies of Transition in Eastern Europe and the Former Soviet Union,* ed. D. Berdahl, M. Bunzl, and M. Lampland, 1–13. Ann Arbor: University of Michigan Press.

———. 2000b. Mixed Devotions: Religion, Friendship, and Fieldwork in Postsocialist Eastern Germany. In Dudwick and De Soto 2000b, 172–194.

Berman, Jacqueline. 2003. (Un)Popular Strangers and Crises (Un)Bounded: Discourses of Sex-Trafficking, European Immigration, and National Security under Global Duress. *European Journal of International Relations* 9 (1): 37–86.

Blair, Harry. 1997. Donors, Democratisation and Civil Society: Relating Theory to Practice. In Hulme and Edwards 1997, 23–43.

Borofsky, Robert. 2000. Public Anthropology: Where To? What Next? *Anthropology News* 45 (5): 9–10.

Boserup, Ester. 1970. *Women's Role in Economic Development.* London: Allen and Unwin.

Bridger, Susan, Rebecca Kay, and Kathryn Pinnick. 1996. *No More Heroines? Russia, Women and the Market.* London: Routledge.

Bruno, Marta. 1997. Playing the Co-operation Game. In *Surviving Post-Socialism: Local Strategies and Regional Responses in Eastern Europe,* ed. S. Bridger and F. Pine, 170–187. London: Routledge.

Buckley, Mary, ed. 1992. *Perestroika and Soviet Women.* Cambridge: Cambridge University Press.

Bunch, Charlotte. 1990. Women's Rights as Human Rights: Toward a Re-vision of Human Rights. *Human Rights Quarterly* 12: 486–498.

Burawoy, Michael, and Katherine Verdery. 1999. Introduction. In *Uncertain Transition: Ethnographies of Change in the Postsocialist World,* ed. M. Burawoy and K. Verdery, 1–17. Lanham, Md.: Rowman & Littlefield.

Buvinic, Mayra. 1996. *Investing in Women: Progress and Prospects for the World Bank.* Washington, D.C.: Overseas Development Council and International Center for Research on Women.

Cabana, Steven, Fred Emery, and Merrelyn Emery. 1995. The Search for Effective Strategic Planning Is Over. *Journal for Quality and Participation* (July/August): 10–19.

Caldwell, Melissa. 2002. The Taste of Nationalism: Food Politics in Postsocialist Moscow. *Ethnos* 67 (3): 295–319.

Chambers, Robert. 1997. *Whose Reality Counts? Putting the First Last.* London, U.K.: Intermediate Technology Publications.

Chuikina, Sonya. 1996. The Role of Women Dissidents in Creating the Milieu. In Rotkirch and Haavio-Mannila 1996, 189–204.

Clifford, James. 1988. On Ethnographic Authority. In *The Predicament of Culture,* ed. J. Clifford, 21–54. Cambridge, Mass.: Harvard University Press.

Clifford, James, and George Marcus. 1986. *Writing Culture: The Poetics and Politics of Ethnography.* Berkeley: University of California Press.

Colapinto, John. 2005. Bloodsuckers: How the Leech Made a Comeback. *The New Yorker,* July 25, 72.

Comaroff, Jean, and John Comaroff. 2001. Millennial Capitalism: First Thoughts on a Second Coming. In *Millennial Capitalism and the Culture of Neoliberalism,* ed. J. Comaroff and J. Comaroff, 1–56. Durham, N.C., and London: Duke University Press.

Cook, Linda. 1993. *The Soviet Social Contract and Why It Failed: Welfare Policy and Workers' Politics from Brezhnev to Yeltsin.* Cambridge, Mass: Harvard University Press.

Cooke, Bill, and Uma Kothari. 2001. *Participation: The New Tyranny?* London, New York: Zed Books.

Crapanzano, Vincent. 1980. *Tuhami: Portrait of a Moroccan.* Chicago, London: University of Chicago Press.

Creed, Gerald. 1995. An Old Song in a New Voice: Decollectivization in Bulgaria. In *East European Communities: The Struggle for Balance in Turbulent Times*, ed. D. Kideckelpp, 25–45. Boulder, Colo.: Westview Press.

Crombie, Alistair. 1987. The Nature and Types of Search Conference. *International Journal of Lifelong Education* 4 (1): 3–33.

Cruikshank, Barbara. 1999. *The Will to Empower: Democratic Citizens and Other Subjects.* Ithaca, N.Y.: Cornell University Press.

De Soto, Hermine G. 2000. Crossing Western Boundaries: How East Berlin Women Observed Women Researchers from the West after Socialism, 1991–1992. In Dudwick and De Soto 2000, 73–99.

Dorsey, Ellen. 1997. The Global Women's Movement: Articulating a New Vision of Global Governance. In *The Politics of Global Governance: International Organizations in an Interdependent World*, ed. P. F. Diehl, 335–358. Boulder, Colo.: Lynne Rienner Publishers.

Drakulic, Slavenka. 1987. *How We Survived Communism and Even Laughed.* London: Vintage.

Dudwick, Nora, and Hermine G. De Soto. 2000. *Fieldwork Dilemmas: Anthropologists in Postsocialist States.* Madison: University of Wisconsin Press.

Dudwick, Nora, and Hermine G. De Soto. 2000. Introduction. In Dudwick and De Soto 2000, 3–8.

Edmondson, Linda. 1984. *Feminism in Russia, 1900–17.* Stanford, Calif.: Stanford University Press.

Einhorn, Barbara. 1993. *Cinderella Goes to Market: Citizenship, Gender and Women's Movements in East Central Europe.* London: Verso.

Enslin, Elizabeth. 1994. Beyond Writing: Feminist Practice and the Limitations of Ethnography. *Current Anthropology* 9 (4): 537–568.

Escobar, Arturo. 1995. *Encountering Development: The Making and Unmaking of the Third World.* Princeton, N.J.: Princeton University Press.

Evans, Peter, and Helen Evans. 2003. NGOs: The New World Order. Article dated June 20, 2003, http://www.americandaily.com/article/2094 (accessed April 28, 2006).

Fals-Borda, O., and Muhammad Anisur Rahman, eds. 1991. *Action and Knowledge: Breaking the Monopoly with Participatory Action Research.* New York: Apex.

Farmer, Paul. 2003. *Pathologies of Power.* Berkeley: University of California Press.

Feldman, Shelley. 1997. NGOs and Civil Society: (Un)stated Contradictions. *ANNALS, AAPSS* 554 (November): 46–65.

Ferguson, James. 1990. *The Anti-Politics Machine: "Development", Depoliticization and Bureaucratic Power in Lesotho.* Cambridge: Cambridge University Press.

Fernandes, Walter, and Rajesh Tandon, eds. 1981. *Participatory Research and Evaluation: Experiments in Research as a Process of Liberation.* New Delhi: Indian Social Institute.

Fine, Michelle, Lois Weis, Susan Weseen, and Loonmun Wong. 2003. For Whom? Qualitative Research, Representations, and Social Responsibilities. In *The Landscape of Qualitative Research*, ed. N. K. Denzin and Y. Lincoln, 107–131. Thousand Oaks, Calif.: Sage Publications Ltd.

Fish, M. Steven. 1995. *Democracy from Scratch.* Princeton, N.J.: Princeton University Press.

Fisher, William. 1997. "Doing Good?" The Politics and Anti-Politics of NGO Practices. *Annual Reviews in Anthropology* 26: 439–464.

Foley, Michael, and Bob Edwards. 1996. The Paradox of Civil Society. *Journal of Democracy* 7 (3): 38–52.

———, eds. 1997. Social Capital, Civil Society and Contemporary Democracy. Special issue, *American Behavioral Scientist* 40 (5) (March/April 1997).

———. 1998. Social Capital and Civil Society Beyond Putnam. *American Behavioral Scientist* 42 (1): 124–139.

Fraser, Nancy, ed. 1997. *Justice Interruptus: Critical Reflections on the "Post-Socialist" Condition.* New York and London: Routledge.

Freire, Paolo. 1970. *The Pedagogy of the Oppressed.* Trans. M. B. Ramos. New York: Herder.

Fukuyama, Francis. 1992. *The End of History and the Last Man.* New York: Free Press.

Funk, Nanette, and Magda Mueller, eds. 1993. *Gender Politics and Post-Communism: Reflections from Eastern Europe and the Former Soviet Union.* London: Routledge.

Gal, Susan. 1997. Feminism and Civil Society. In Scott, Kaplan, and Keates 1997, 30–45.

Gal, Susan, and Gail Kligman. 2000. *The Politics of Gender after Socialism.* Princeton, N.J.: Princeton University Press.

Gapova, Elena. 2003. Writing Women's and Gender History in Countries in Transition. Toronto: Paper presented at the annual meeting of the American Association for the Advancement of Slavic Studies.

———. 2004. Conceptualizing Gender, Nation and Class in Post-Soviet Belarus. In Kuehnast and Nechemias 2004, 85–102.

Garton-Ash, Timothy. 1990. *The Uses of Adversity: Esssays on the Fate of Central Europe.* New York: Vintage Books.

Geertz, Clifford. 1983. *Local Knowledge.* New York: Basic Books.

Gellner, Ernest. 1994. *Conditions of Liberty: Civil Society and Its Rivals.* New York: Allen Lane/Penguin Press.

Gessen, Masha. 1995. Sex in the Media and the Birth of the Sex Media in Russia. In *Postcommunism and the Body Politic,* ed. E. E. Berry, 197–228. New York and London: New York University Press.

———. 1997. *Dead Again: The Russian Intelligentsia after Communism.* London: Verso.

Gibson-Graham, J. K. 1994. "Stuffed If I Know!": Reflections on Post-Modern Feminist Social Research. *Gender, Place and Culture* 1 (2): 205–223.

Goldman, Wendy. 1991. Working-Class Women and the "Withering Away'" of the Family: Popular Responses to Family Policy. In *Russia in the Era of NEP,* ed. S. Fitzpatrick, A. Rabinowitch, and R. Stites, 125–143. Bloomington: Indiana University Press.

Goode, Judith, and Jeff Maskovsky. 2001. *New Poverty Studies: The Ethnography of Power, Politics, and Impoverished People in the United States.* New York: New York University Press.

Grant, Bruce. 1999. Return of the Repressed: Conversations with Three Russian Entrepreneurs. In *Paranoia within Reason,* ed. G. Marcus, 241–268. Chicago: Chicago University Press.

Gray, Francine du Plessix. 1989. *Soviet Women Walking the Tightrope.* New York: Doubleday.

Greenhouse, Carol, Elizabeth Mertz, and Kay Warren. 2002. *Ethnography in Unstable Places: Everyday Lives in Contexts of Dramatic Political Change.* Durham, N.C., and London: Duke University Press.

Greenwood, Davydd, and Jose Luis Gonzalez Santos et al. 1992. *Industrial Democracy as Process: Participatory Action Research in the Fagor Cooperative Group of Mondragon.* Assen: Van Gorcum.

Greenwood, Davydd, and Morten Levin. 1998. *Introduction to Action Research.* London: Sage Publications Ltd.

Grewal, Inderpal, and Caren Kaplan, eds. 1994. *Scattered Hegemonies: Postmodernity and Transnational Feminist Practice.* Minneapolis: University of Minnesota Press.

Habermas, Jurgen. 1989. *The Structural Transformation of the Public Sphere.* Cambridge, Mass.: MIT Press.

———. 1990. What Does Socialism Mean Today? The Rectifying Revolution and the Need for New Thinking on the Left. *New Left Review* 183: 3–21.

Hackenberg, Robert A., and Beverly H. Hackenberg. 2004. Notes Toward a New Future: Applied Anthropology in Century XXI. *Human Organization* 63 (4): 385–399.

Hann, Chris, ed. 2002. *Postsocialism: Ideas, Ideologies and Local Practices in Eurasia.* London: Routledge.

Hann, Chris, and Elizabeth Dunn, eds. 1996. *Civil Society: Challenging Western Models.* London and New York: Routledge.

Haraway, Donna. 1991. *Simians, Cyborgs and Women: The Reinvention of Nature.* New York and London: Routledge.

Hardt, Michael, and Antonio Negri. 2000. *Empire.* Cambridge, Mass.: Harvard University Press.

Harrison, Faye. 1991. *Decolonizing Anthropology: Moving Further Toward an Anthropology for Liberation.* Washington, D.C.: Association of Black Anthropologists.

Havelkova, Hana. 1993. "Patriarchy" in Czech Society. *Hypatia* 8 (4): 90–96.

Hemment, Julie. 2000. Gender, NGOs and the Third Sector in Russia: An Ethnography of Russian Civil Society. Ph.D. dissertation, Department of Anthropology, Cornell University, Ithaca, N.Y.

———. 2004a. Global Civil Society and the Local Costs of Belonging: Defining "Violence Against Women" in Russia. *Signs: Journal of Women in Culture and Society* 29 (3): 815–840.

———. 2004b. Strategizing Gender and Development: Action Research and Ethnographic Responsibility in the Russian Provinces. In *Post-Soviet Women Encountering Transition: Nation Building, Economic Survival, and Civic Activism,* ed. K. Kuehnast and C. Nechemias. Washington, D.C.: Woodrow Wilson Center Press.

Henderson, Sarah L. 2003. *Building Democracy in Contemporary Russia: Western Support for Grassroots Organizations.* Ithaca, N.Y., and London: Cornell University Press.

hooks, bell. 1981. *Ain't I a Woman: Black Women and Feminism.* Boston: South End Press.

Hulme, D., and M. Edwards, eds. 1997. *NGOs, States and Donors: Too Close for Comfort?* New York: St. Martin's Press, in association with Save the Children.

Human Rights Watch Report. Russia. Too Little, Too Late: State Responses to Violence Against Women 1997. New York: Human Rights Watch.

Humphrey, Caroline. 1983. *Karl Marx Collective: Economy, Society and Religion on a Siberian Collective Farm.* Cambridge: Cambridge University Press.

Humphrey, Caroline, and Ruth Mandel. 2002. The Market in Everyday Life: Ethnographies of Postsocialism. In *Markets and Moralities: Ethnographies of Postsocialism,* ed. C. Humphrey and R. Mandel, 1–16. Oxford: Berg.

Hyatt, Susan Brin. 2001a. From Citizen to Volunteer: Neoliberal Goverance and the Erasure of Poverty. In *New Poverty Studies: The Ethnography of Power, Politics, and Impoverished People in the United States,* ed. J. Maskovsky and J. Goode. New York: New York University Press.

———. 2001b. "Service Learning," Applied Anthropology and the Production of Neo-liberal Citizens. *Anthropology in Action* 8 (1): 6–13.

Hyatt, Susan Brin, and Vincent Lyon-Callo. 2003. Introduction: Anthropology and Political Engagement. *Urban Anthropology* 32 (2): 133–146.

Hymes, Dell. 1972. *Reinventing Anthropology*. New York: Pantheon Books.

Ishkanian, Armine. 2003. Importing Civil Society? The Emergence of Armenia's NGO Sector and the Impact of Western Aid on Its Development. *Armenian Forum* 3 (1): 7–36.

James, Estelle. 1997. Whither the Third Sector? Yesterday, Today and Tomorrow. *Voluntas* 8 (1): 1–10.

Johnson, Janet Elise. 2004. Sisterhood versus the "Moral" Russian State: The Postcommunist Politics of Rape. In Kuehnast and Nechemias 2004, 217–238. Washington, D.C.: Woodrow Wilson Center Press.

Jordan, Steven. 2003. Who Stole my Methodology? Co-opting PAR. *Globalisation, Societies and Education* 1 (2): 185–200.

Kalb, Don. 2002. Afterward: Globalism and Postsocialist Prospects. In Hann 2002, 317–334.

Kardam, Nuket. 1991. *Bringing Women In: Women's Issues in International Development Programs*. Boulder, Colo.: Lynne Rienner Publishers.

Kamat, Sangeeta. 2001. The Privatization of Public Interest: NGO Discourse in a Neo-liberal Context. Paper presented at 100th Annual Meeting of the American Anthropological Association, November 28–December 2, in Washington, D.C.

Kay, Rebecca. 2000. *Russian Women and Their Organizations: Gender, Discrimination and Grassroots Organizations, 1991–96*. Basingstoke: Macmillan.

Keck, Margaret E., and Kathryn Sikkink. 1998. *Activists beyond Borders: Advocacy Networks in International Politics*. Ithaca, N.Y.: Cornell University Press.

Khasbulatova, Ol'ga. 1994. *Opyt i traditsii zhenskogo dvizheniia v Rossii, 1860–1917*. Ivanovo: Ivanovskii GosUniversitet.

Khodyreva, Natalia. 1996. Sexism and Sexual Abuse in Russia. In *Women in a Violent World: Feminist Analyses and Resistance across "Europe,"* ed. C. Corrin. Edinburgh: Edinburgh University Press.

Klimenkova, Tat'iana. 1996. *Zhenshchina kak fenomen kul'tury*. Moscow: Preobrazhenie.

Kozlova, Natalia. 2000. Zhenotdely v kontekste emansipatorskogo proekta Bol'shevikov. In Uspenskaia 2000, 86–92.

Kuehnast, K., and C. Nechemias, eds. 2004. *Post-Soviet Women Encountering Transition: Nation Building, Economic Survival, and Civic Activism*, Washington, D.C.: Woodrow Wilson Center Press.

Kulik, V. 1997. Zhenshchiny i revolutsionnye sobytia 1917 goda. In Uspenskaia 1997, 23–27.

Kurti, Lazlo. 1997. Globalization and the Discourse of Otherness in the "New" Eastern and Central Europe. In *The Politics of Multiculturalism in the New Europe: Racism, Identity and Community*, ed. T. Modood and P. Werbner, 29–53. London, New York: Zed Books.

Lamphere, Louise. 2003. The Perils and Prospects for an Engaged Anthropology. A View from the United States. *Social Anthropology* 11 (2): 153–168.

———. 2004. The Convergence of Applied, Practicing, and Public Anthropology in the 21st Century. *Human Organization* 63 (4): 431–443.

Lane, Christel. 1981. *The Rites of Rulers: Ritual in Industrial Society—the Soviet Case*. Cambridge: Cambridge University Press.

Lang, Sabine. 1997. The NGOization of Feminism. In Scott, Kaplan, and Keates 1997, 101–120.

Ledeneva, Alena V. 1998. *Russia's Economy of Favours.* Cambridge: Cambridge University Press.

Liborakina, M. I., and T. A. Sidorenkova. 1997. Net nasiliiu v sem'e. Moscow: Informatsionnyi Tsentr Nezavisimogo Zhenskogo Foruma.

Lyon-Callo, Vincent, and Susan Brin Hyatt. 2003. The Neoliberal State and the Depoliticization of Poverty: Activist Anthropology and "Ethnography from Below." *Urban Anthropology* 32 (2): 175–204.

Mamonova, Tatyana. 1980. *Women and Russia: First Feminist Samizdat.* London: Sheba Feminist Publishers.

———. 1988. *Russian Women's Studies: Essays on Sexism in Soviet Culture.* Oxford, New York: Pergamon Press.

Mandel, Ruth. 2002. Seeding Civil Society. In Hann 2002, 279–296.

Marsh, Rosalind. 1996. Anastasiia Posadskaia, the Dubna Forum and the Independent Women's Movement in Russia. In *Women in Russia and Ukraine,* ed. R. Marsh, 286–297. Cambridge: Cambridge University Press.

Mascia-Lees, Frances E., Patricia Sharpe, and Colleen Ballerino Cohen. 1989. The Postmodernist Turn in Anthropology: Cautions from a Feminist Perspective. *Signs* 15 (1): 7–33.

McAuley, Mary. 1992. *Soviet Politics 1917–1991.* New York: Oxford University Press.

———. 2001. *The Big Chill: Civil Society in Russia in a New Political Season.* Ford Foundation Report, Winter 2001, 1–3. http://www.civilsoc.org/resource/ffw2001.htm (accessed April 28, 2006).

McIntyre, Alice. 2000. *Inner City Kids: Adolescents Confront Life and Violence in an Urban Community.* New York: New York University Press.

Mertz, Elizabeth. 2002. The Perfidy of Gaze and the Pain of Uncertainty: Anthropological Theory and the Search for Closure. In Greenhouse, Mertz, and Warren 2002, 355–378.

Messer-Davidow, Ellen. 2002. *Disciplining Feminism: From Social Activism to Academic Discourse.* Durham, N.C., and London: Duke University Press.

Mohanty, Chandra. 1991. Under Western Eyes. In *Third World Women and the Politics of Feminism,* ed. C. Mohanty, A. Russo, and L. Torres, 51–80. Bloomington: Indiana University Press.

———. 2003. *Feminists Without Borders: Decolonizing Theory, Practicing Solidarity.* Durham, N.C., and London: Duke University Press.

Moore, Henrietta. 1988. *Feminism and Anthropology.* Minneapolis: University of Minnesota Press.

Moraga, Cherrie, and Gloria Anzaldua. 1983. *This Bridge Called My Back: Writings by Radical Women of Color.* New York: Kitchen Table, Women of Color Press.

Obeyesekere, Gananath. 1992. *The Apotheosis of Captain Cook: European Mythmaking in the Pacific.* Princeton, N.J.: Princeton University Press.

Ost, David. 1990. *Solidarity and the Politics of Anti-politics: Opposition and Reform in Poland since 1968.* Philadelphia: Temple University Press.

Ottaway, Marina, and Thomas Carothers. 2000. *Funding Virtue: Civil Society Aid and Democracy Promotion.* Washington, D.C.: Carnegie Endowment for International Peace.

Palazchenko, Pavel. 1999. US and USSR: What Went Wrong and What is Right? Presentation to the Cornell Peace Studies Program, October 14, 1999.

Paley, Julia. 2001. *Marketing Democracy: Power and Social Movements in Post-Dictatorship Chile.* Berkeley and Los Angeles: University of California Press.

Phillips, Sarah Drue. 2000. NGOs in Ukraine: The Making of a "Women's Sphere." *Anthropology of East Europe Review* 18 (2): 23–29.

Pilkington, Hilary. 1992. Whose Space Is It Anyway? Youth, Gender and Civil Society in the Soviet Union. In *Women in the Face of Change,* ed. S. Rai, H. Pilkington, and A. Phizacklea, 105–129. London: Routledge.

Pisklakova, Marina, and Andrei Sinel'nikov. 2000. *Nasilie i sotsial'nye izmeneniia.* Moscow: TG Iupiter.

Pitsunova, Ol'ga. 1998. Obshchestvennoe Ddvizhenie ili tretii sektor? *Biulleten' Moskovskogo ISAR,* 24–25.

Posadskaia, Anastasiia, ed. 1994. *Women in Russia: A New Era in Russia's Feminisms.* London: Verso.

Putnam, Robert. 1993. *Making Democracy Work: Civic Conditions in Modern Italy.* Princeton, N.J.: Princeton University Press.

———. 1995. Bowling Alone: America's Declining Social Capital. *Journal of Democracy* 6 (1): 65–78.

Racioppi, Linda, and Katherine O'Sullivan See. 1997. *Women's Activism in Contemporary Russia.* Philadelphia: Temple University Press.

Regentova, Marina, and Nataliia Abubikirova. 1995. No title. Moscow: Unpublished manuscript.

Richter, James. 2000. *Power, Principles and the Russian Campaign Against Domestic Violence, or How Taking Agency Seriously Changes the Constructivist Picture.* Unpublished manuscript.

———. 2004. Governmentality, Foreign Aid, and Russian NGOs. Unpublished manuscript.

———. 2002. Evaluating Western Assistance to Russian Women's Organizations. In *The Power and Limits of NGOs: A Critical Look at Building Democracy in Eastern Europe and Eurasia,* ed. Sarah E. Mendelson and John K. Glenn, 54–90. New York: Columbia University Press.

Ries, Nancy. 1997. *Russian Talk: Culture and Conversation during Perestroika.* Ithaca, N.Y., and London: Cornell University Press.

Rifkin, Jeremy. 1997. The Information Age and Civil Society. *Surviving Together* (Summer 1997): 7–10.

Riles, Annelise. 2001. *The Network Inside Out.* Ann Arbor: University of Michigan Press.

Rivkin-Fish, Michele. 2004. Gender and Democracy: Strategies for Engagement and Dialogue on Women's Issues after Socialism in St. Petersburg. In Kuehnast and Nechemias 2004, 288–312.

———. 2005. *Women's Health in Post-Soviet Russia: The Politics of Intervention.* Bloomington: Indiana University Press.

Robinson, M. 1993. Governance, Democracy and Conditionality: NGOs and the New Policy Agenda. In *Governance, Democracy and Conditionality: What Role for NGOs?,* ed. A. Clayton, 35–52. Oxford: INTRAC.

Rosaldo, Renato. 1989. *Culture and Truth: The Remaking of Social Analysis.* Boston: Beacon Press.

Rotkirch, A., and E. Haavio-Mannila, eds. 1996. *Women's Voices in Russia Today.* Aldershot: Dartmouth.

Roy, Arundhati. 2004. Public Power in the Age of Empire. Presentation made in San

Francisco on August 10, 2004. http://www.democracynow.org/static/Arundhati_Trans.shtml (accessed April 28, 2006).

Sachs, Jeffrey. 1994. Toward Glasnost in the IMF. *Challenge* 47 (3): 4–11.

Saint-Exupéry, Antoine de. 1943. *The Little Prince.* London: Harcourt.

Salamon, Lester, and Helmut Anheier. 1997. *Defining the Nonprofit Sector: A Cross-national analysis.* Manchester: Manchester University Press.

Salmenniemi, Suvi. 2005. Civic Activity—Feminine Activity? Gender, Civil Society and Citizenship in Post-Soviet Russia. *Sociology* 39 (4): 735–753.

Sampson, Steven. 1996. The Social Life of Projects: Importing Civil Society to Albania. In Hann and Dunn 1996, 121–142.

———. 2001. Supporting Civil Society through the Strengthening of Local NGOs. Baku, Azerbaijan: Conference on the Role of NGOs: From Refuge to Durable Solutions in the Caucasus.

———. 2002. Beyond Transition: Rethinking Elite Configurations in the Balkans. In Hann 2002, 297–316.

Sanday, Peggy Reeves. 2003. Public Interest Anthropology: A Model for Engaged Social Science. Paper presented at the SAR Workshop, Chicago. University of Pennsylvania, http://www.sas.upenn.edu/~psanday/SARdiscussion%20paper.65.html (accessed May 9, 2006).

Sassen, Saskia. 2002. *Globalization and the Illegal Trafficking in Women.* Paper presented at the University of Massachusetts, Amherst.

Scheper-Hughes, Nancy. 1995. The Primacy of the Ethical: Propositions for a Militant Anthropology. *Current Anthropology* 36 (3): 409–420.

Scott, J., C. Kaplan, and D. Keates, eds. 1997. *Transitions, Environments, Translations.* New York: Routledge

Seligman, Adam. 1998. Between Public and Private: Towards a Sociology of Civil Society. In *Democratic Civility: The History and Cross-Cultural Possibility of a Modern Political Ideal,* ed. R. Hefner, 79–111. New Brunswick, N.J.: Transaction Publishers.

Shostak, Marjorie. 1983. *Nisa, the Life and Words of a !Kung Woman.* New York: Vintage Books.

Silverman, Carol. 2000. Researcher, Advocate, Friend: An American Fieldworker among Balkan Roma, 1980–1996. In Dudwick and De Soto 2000, 195–217.

Snitow, Ann. 1999. Cautionary Tales. *Proceedings of the 93rd Annual Meetings of the American Society of International Law.* Washington, D.C., 35–42.

Soros, George. 2000. Who Lost Russia? *New York Review of Books,* April 13, 10–16.

Sperling, Valerie. 2000. *Organizing Women in Contemporary Russia: Engendering Transition.* Cambridge: Cambridge University Press.

Spivak, Gayatri Chakravorty. 1988. Can the Subaltern Speak? In *Marxism and the Interpretation of Culture,* ed. C. Nelson and L. Grossberg, 271–316. Urbana and Chicago: University of Illinois Press.

Stacey, Judith. 1988. Can There Be a Feminist Ethnography? *Women's Studies International Forum* 11 (1): 21–27.

Stites, Richard. 1978. *The Women's Liberation Movement in Russia: Feminism, Nihilism and Bolshevism 1860–1930.* Princeton, N.J.: Princeton University Press.

Susser, Ida. 1996. The Construction of Poverty and Homelessness in U.S. Cities. *Annual Review of Anthropology* 25: 411–435.

Tayler, Jeffrey. 2001. Russia Is Finished. *The Atlantic Monthly* 287 (5): 35–52.

Trondman, Mats, and Paul Willis. 2000. Manifesto for Ethnography. *Ethnography* 1 (1): 5–16.

Uspenskaia, Valentina (V.I.). 1997. *Zhenshchiny v sotsialnoi istorii Rossii.* Tver': Tverskoi Gosudarstvennyi Universitet.

———. 2000. Sufrazhizm v Kontse XIX–Nachale XX Veka. In Uspenskaia 2000.

Uspenskaia, Valentina (V.I.), ed. 2000. *Zhenskie i gendernye issledovaniia v Tverskom Gosudarstvennom Universitete.* Tver: Tverskoi Gosudarstvennyi Universitet.

Uspenskaia, Valentina, ed. 2003. *Aleksandra Kollontai: Teoriia zhenskoi emansipatsii v kontekste rossiiskoi gendernoi politiki.* Tver': Feminist Press–Russia.

Verdery, Katherine. 1996. *What Was Socialism, and What Comes Next?* Princeton, N.J.: Princeton University Press.

Voronina, Olga. 1993. Soviet Patriarchy: Past and Present. *Hypatia* 8 (4): 97–111.

Watson, Peggy. 1993. Eastern Europe's Silent Revolution: Gender. *Sociology* 27 (3): 471–487.

———. 1997. Civil Society and the Politics of Difference in Eastern Europe. In Scott, Kaplan, and Keates 1997, 21–29.

Wedel, Janine. 1998. *Collision and Collusion: The Strange Case of Western Aid to Eastern Europe 1989–1998.* New York: St. Martin's Press.

Whyte, W. F., and K. K. Whyte. 1991. *Making Mondragon: The Growth and Dynamics of the Worker Cooperative Complex.* Ithaca, N.Y.: ILR.

Wolf, Eric. 1982. *Europe and the People Without History.* Berkeley: University of California Press.

World Bank. 2001. *Engendering Development: Through Gender Equality in Rights, Resources and Voice.* New York: Oxford University Press.

Zabelina, Tat'iana. 1996. Sexual Violence Towards Women. In *Gender, Generation and Identity in Contemporary Russia,* ed. H. Pilkington, 169–186. London and New York: Routledge.

Zelikova, Julia. 1996. Women's Participation in Charity. In Rotkirch and Haavio-Mannila 1996, 248–254.

Index

abortion, 5, 8

acquaintance. *See* networks

activism, women's: in Bolshevik era, 8, 28, 76; and civil society discourse, 74; at Cold War's end, 2, 10; collaborations, 2–3, 9, 12, 15, 22–23, 26, 29; in dissident era, 35–37; and Dubna forums, 69, 79–80; effect of international aid, 4–6, 51, 69–70, 81–83, 163n2; as form of elite identification, 5, 76, 163n4; and gender mainstreaming, 2, 140–41; in Germany, 31; history of, 2–3, 7–8, 75–84; independent women's movement, 79–80, 82; and Marxism, 6–7; in Moscow, 28, 69–70, 82; and network politics, 73–74, 142; and perestroika, 2, 5; in post-socialist era, 5, 10–11, 22, 41, 73, 77–84, 143; *ravnopraviki* (equal rights activists), 7, 154n9; and socialist politics, 7–8; and societal movement, 51, 53; in Soviet era, 2, 5, 75–76, 153n5; and third sector, 47, 53–54, 69–70, 72–73; in Tsarist era, 7; and violence against women, 4, 94–95; and voluntarism, 53–54. *See also* feminism; Zhenskii Svet

agency, 12–13, 16, 142, 144–45, 162n27

aid, international: and civil society, 10–11, 50–51, 58; conceptualizations of, 15–16, 21–22, 46–47; development agendas, 2–3, 9–11, 13–14, 21–22, 46–47, 139–40, 155n15; development discourses, 53, 154n12; and gendered interventions, 2–6, 13–14, 51, 80–84, 93, 140, 142, 164n10; and network politics, 142; and New Policy Agenda, 10; and societal movement, 46–47; and third sector, 60–61, 69–70, 72–73, 83; from Western governments, 21–22; and women's activism, 4–6, 51, 69–70, 81–83, 163n2. *See also* foundations

Albright, Madeleine, 95, 118

alcoholism, 14, 59

Al'manakh: Zhenshchinam o Zhenshchinakh, 75

American Association of University Women, 1, 55

American Bar Association (ABA), 109–10, 111, 117, 119, 166n3

ANNA (Association No to Violence), 97, 108, 111, 117, 119, 166n6, 168–69n10

anthropology: applied, 13, 24, 155n14, 156n6; and colonialism, 23; conceptions of power, 19–20, 21, 23–25; critical, 4, 13, 140; critiques of, 13, 23–24, 142; and cultural relativism, 156n5; feminist, 4, 17; fieldwork, 4, 17, 23, 25, 155n16; methodology, 4, 13–14, 17–20, 24–26, 34–35, 39, 155n17, 156n7; participatory (*see* PAR; participant observation); and political projects, 4, 13; of postsocialism, 13, 23, 154–55nn13–14, 155n16, 156n4, 158–59n25; and reflexivity, 17–18, 24–25, 142; and representation, 17–18, 24, 112; and responsibility, 17–18, 20, 25, 42–43, 135; and social engagement, 13, 156n6. *See also* ethnography

ANZhI (Association of Independent Women's Initiatives), 33

blat (informal networks), 60, 104, 122, 162n24, 169n13

Bolshevik era: and feminism, 8, 28, 76; and women's rights, 5, 8

British Charities Aid Foundation (CAF), 47, 55

British Council, 81, 127–28

CEDAW, 78, 165n2

Center for Women and Families, 57

Center for Women's History and Gender Studies (Tver'), 127–28, 137–38, 149, 170n19; planning of, 42, 93; funding, 114–15, 127, 155n1

child care. *See* day care

civil society, 10–13, 49–54, 139, 140; and anti-politics, 49, 52, 160n6; and capitalism, 49, 139; and Cold War's end, 50–51; and democratic revolutions, 50, 161n17; discourse, 11, 49–50, 73, 74, 111; and gender, 51, 74–75, 80–81; and international aid, 10–11, 50–51, 58; origins of, 49; and post-socialism, 11, 50–53, 74; as signifier, 49–50; and third sector, 48, 113; and voluntarism, 52–53; Western support for, 10–11, 50, 51–58; women's participation, 51, 80–81

Clinton, Hillary Rodham, 95

Cold War, end of, 9–10, 21–23, 80–84; and civil society, 50–51; and development agen-

gender education, 22, 97, 108, 127, 128
gender mainstreaming, 2–4, 10–13, 80–84, 98, 140–42, 164n10
gendered interventions: 2–6, 13–14, 51, 80–84, 93, 140–41, 164n10
glasnost', 96–97
globalization, 11, 16
Gorbachev, Mikhail, 30, 78, 96, 153n1, 164n8
Gortensia. See Zhenskii Svet crisis center
grassroots and grassroots organizations, 5, 56, 73, 94, 140, 141

Havel, Vaclav, 49, 160n6
health care, 46, 99, 159n2, 161n18, 167n11
Humanitarian Institute ('Tver'), 58–65, 130, 148

IMF (International Monetary Fund), 46, 139
Independent Social Women's Center (Pskov), 102
Independent Women's Forums (Dubna), 32, 69, 72, 79–80, 157n15
information center (Moscow NGO), 69–74
intelligentsia, 2, 37, 56–57, 63, 161n19, 164n8; view of the West, 2–3
international aid. *See* aid, international
international marriage and dating agencies, 37, 158n20
International Women's Club, 128, 169n14
IREX (International Research and Exchanges Board), 40, 128, 131, 133

Joint U.S.-Russia Conference on Family Violence (Moscow), 118

Khrushchev, Nikita, 75
Kollontai, Alexandra, 28

labor, gendered division of, 6–8, 52, 61
Ledeneva, Alena, 61, 162n24, 169n13
liberal democratic theory, 50, 139
The Little Prince, 19–21, 34–35, 88, 112, 135, 146, 148. *See also* taming; ties; trust
LOTOS group (Leaugue for Emancipation from Social Stereotypes), 78

MacArthur Foundation, 46, 69, 82
Mamonova, Tatiana, 75, 77
marketization, 2, 11, 16, 22, 37–38, 46, 78, 154n7
marriage bureaus, 158n20
Marxism, 6–7
maternal health care and leaves, 3, 78
McAuley, Mary, 3–4, 114–15, 127, 168n5

medical profession, 104, 105, 161n18, 167nn13–14
methodology, 4, 13–14, 17–20, 24–26, 34–35, 39, 155n17, 156n7. *See also* PAR
Michnik, Adam, 49, 160n6
Moscow, 28, 45, 69–70, 72, 165n14
Moscow Center for Gender Studies (MCGS), 26, 78, 79–80

neoliberalism, 3, 52–53; critiques of, 52–53, 172n6; and development, 4, 48, 139–40, 141; and economics, 50; and state restructuring, 3, 46, 52, 68
networks, 17, 57, 63, 73–74, 86–87, 142; of acquaintance, 113, 121–23, 125, 128; and crisis centers, 95, 103, 107–109, 117, 134–35, 166n8; feminist, 4, 5, 81–82; and foundations, 128; as organizational strategy, 73–74, 86–87; personal, 88. *See also blat*
New Policy Agenda, 10
NEWW (Network of East-West Women), 12, 26, 157n10
NGOs (nongovernmental organizations): and agency, 144–45; and anti-Western sentiment, 12; and civil society, 51, 140; critiques of, 140–43; and democratization, 9–11, 52, 139, 161n17; as elite, 12, 41, 58, 60, 68, 71–72, 92, 140, 143–44; and empowerment, 6–7; and gender, 6–8, 16–17, 52, 61, 143; and gendered divisions of labor, 6–7, 52, 61; government view of, 61; and grassroots, 73–74; and international aid, 46–47, 52, 60–61, 133; in Moscow, 69–70, 72–73; and partnerships, 59–61; professionalization of, 5, 52, 60, 134–35, 143–45, 158n17; Putin's opposition to, 68, 141; resource allocation, 61–63; rhetoric, 71; as service providers, 52; and third sector, 52–53, 70, 72–73
nomenklatura, 60–61, 162n23

obshchestvennaia rabota. See societal work
obshchestvennoe dvizhenie. See societal movement
Oktiabrina (Zhenskii Svet member), 35, 39, 91, *92,* 103–11, 131–33, 150–51; and Zhenskii Svet crisis center, 103–11, 113–26, 132–36, 150
Open Society Institute, 2, 47, 66, 82, 113, 119
Open World group, 151
Orange Revolution (Ukraine), 141, 171–72n1

PAR (participatory action research), 20, 24–26, 156n7, 156–57n8; Cornell University PAR Network, 19; and empowerment, 156–

57n8; feminist, 25–26, 156–57n8; and post-socialist states, 14; and reflexivity, 17–18; and research encounters, 14, 43, 147–48, 159n27; "search conferences," 91; seminars, 106

participant observation, 35, 39, 41, 88–89, 159n26

perestroika, 2, 5, 153n1; and women's activism, 2, 5, 28, 30, 78

Pisklakova, Marina (ANNA director), 97

Posadskaia, Anastasiia (MCGS director), 79–80

post-socialism, 7, 14; anthropology of, 13, 23, 154–55nn13–14, 155n16, 156n4, 158–59n25; anti-Communist backlash, 22, 66; and civil society, 11, 50–53, 74; conceptualizations of, 13; and development projects, 16, 162n27; ands economic inequality, 2–3, 6, 16, 37–38, 54, 78; and ethnography, 7, 11–12, 14, 42–43; and feminism, 8–9, 16, 22–23, 32, 38, 75, 77–80; and New Policy Agenda, 10; and PAR, 14; post-socialist condition, 10, 12–13, 154n11; and reformulation of knowledge, 23, 155n2; and state responsibility, 16; and UN, 9; view of gender, 5, 8–9; and violence against women, 97–98; Washington Consensus, 10, 153–54n6; and women's activism, 5, 10–11, 22, 41, 73, 77–84, 143; and women's political representation, 2, 8, 157n16; women's view of, 9

power, 19–20, 21, 23–25, 147

privatization. See under economy

Pskov crisis center, 102–103, 133

Putin, Vladimir, 12, 68, 141

Putnam, Robert, 50, 63, 111, 136–37, 160n11, 161nn15,17

reflexivity, 17–18, 24–25, 142

representation, 17–18, 24, 112

reproductive rights, 7

responsibility: ethnographic, 17–18, 20, 25, 42–43, 135; individual, 52, 61; social, 46, 71; state, 6–7, 16, 46, 53; third sector constructions of, 47–48, 71

Russian Social Democratic Labor Party, 7–8

Sachs, Jeffrey, 153–54n6

Saint-Exupéry, Antoine de. See The Little Prince

samizdat, 75, 76

self-help, 3, 53, 61

"shock therapy," 6, 139

"Sisters" (center for victims of sexual violence, Moscow), 166n6

social capital, 10, 11, 13, 50, 51, 61, 62–63, 161n17

socialism, state: and civil society, 11, 49; and empowerment, 5, 7, 8; and gender equality, 5–6, 8, 74–75; and family, 5; and feminism, 157n11; and societal movement, 2, 16

societal movement (obshchestvennoe dvizhenie), 2, 16, 51, 53, 110, 143, 161n16; and international aid, 46–47

societal work (obshchestvennaia rabota), 41, 55–57, 137

Soros, George, 66, 163n30. See also Open Society Institute

Soviet era: censorship, 30; collapse of Soviet state, 9, 21; concept of civil society, 49; Communist Party of the Soviet Union, 8, 30, 55–56, 66; and families, 5; feminism, 29–30, 157n11; and foreign visitors, 31; full employment, 8, 46; and gendered division of labor, 8; health care, 6–7, 46; view of the West, 40, 43; and violence against women, 96–97; women's activism, 2, 5, 75–76, 153n5; and women's rights, 5, 8, 30, 31

St. Petersburg crisis center, 101–102

Stalin, Josef, 8, 29

state: and civil society, 49, 52; reconfiguring, 3, 10, 16, 46, 52–53, 68, 110, 139–40; responsibility, 6–7, 16, 46, 53

Summer School in Gender Studies (Tver'), 84

taming, 19–21, 34–35, 39–43, 91, 112, 126, 135, 145, 146–47

third sector, 46–49, 51–54, 55–68, 70–74, 144, 159–60n5; and civil society, 48, 113; critiques of, 63–66, 141; discourse, 52, 56, 61; and donor foundations, 60–62, 66–67, 71–72, 83; as elite, 58, 60–62, 68, 141, 143–44; and gender divisions, 48, 53–54, 61, 68, 83–84; and international aid, 60–61, 69–73; models, 60; and NGOs, 52–53, 70, 72–73; power distribution, 48–49; and social paternalism, 63–64; and societal work, 55–57, 161n16; and women's activism, 72; women's participation in, 53–55, 67–68, 70–74

ties, 19, 42–44, 91, 131, 147, 148

Tocqueville, Alexis de, 50, 160n8

trafficking of women and girls, 4, 12, 72, 134, 136, 154n12, 158n20

transition from socialism, 4; and civil society, 11; and ethnographic research, 7, 11–12, 14, 42–43; and feminism, 22; and Ford Foundation, 2, 46; gendered effects of, 2–4, 5–7, 37–

Yeltsin, Boris, 78

Zhenskii Svet (Women's Light), 15–16, 27–40,
84–87, 144–45, 149; Center for Women's
History and Gender Studies, 42, 93, 112–13,
127–28, 131, 134, 145–46; collaborative
seminars, 42–43, 91–93, 125–26, 127, 148;
and consciousness-raising, 30, 38; crisis
center project (*see* Zhenskii Svet crisis center); feminist identity of, 27, 29, 32; foreign
visitors, 31–32, 39–40; and local involvement, 90–91; local view of, 32, 85–86; members' view of feminism and gender, 32, 38;
members' view of *zapad* (the West), 39–40;
membership, 37–38; and Moscow-based activists, 84; organization of, 33–37, 42, 89–
91; and outreach, 32; as project of enlightenment, 66–67, 93, 137; proposed projects,
27, 28–29, 34–35, 42, 87; publishing house
project, 42, 93; "search conference," 91;

theorization of international aid, 4; and
third-sector/NGO funding, 15–16, 20, 41–
42, 84–85, 89, 93, 110–11; view of social
responsibility, 46; women's center project,
92, 103

Zhenskii Svet crisis center (*Gortensia*), 106–
11, 112–26, 128–29, *132*, 145; and Center
for Women's History and Gender Studies,
134; clients, 119–20, 126, 129, 134; closing of, 138, 145, 151; educational and
outreach activities, 108, 120, 129, 131;
funding, 64, 67–68, 103, 128, 131–33,
135; hotline, 119–20, 123, 129, 145, 151;
and local concerns, 101–102; organizational issues, 121; planning of, 1, 15, 29,
34–35, 42, 94; seminars, 125–26; and Social Protection Agency (Tver'), 120–21,
124; and specialization, 102–103; training, 103, 128–29, 145; and voluntarism,
121–22

JULIE HEMMENT is Assistant Professor of Anthropology at the University of Massachusetts, Amherst.